JOE CINQUE'S
CONSOLATION

HELEN GARNER

JOE CINQUE'S CONSOLATION

PICADOR
Pan Macmillan Australia

First published 2004 in Picador by Pan Macmillan Australia Pty Limited
St Martins Tower, 31 Market Street, Sydney

Reprinted 2004 (four times)

National Library of Australia Cataloguing in Publication Data:

Garner, Helen, 1942– .
Joe Cinque's consolation.

ISBN 0 330 36497 9.

1. Trials (Murder) – Australian Capital Territory.
2. Murder victims – Australian Capital Territory. I. Title.

345.94702523

Typeset in 12/16 pt Bembo by Post Pre-press Group, Brisbane, Queensland
Printed by McPherson's Printing Group, Maryborough, Victoria

Papers used by Pan Macmillan Australia Pty Ltd are natural, recyclable products made from
wood grown in sustainable forests. The manufacturing processes conform to the environmental
regulations of the country of origin.

AUTHOR'S NOTE

I gladly acknowledge the different kinds of help I have been given, by those people who spoke to me about this story, by those who would not, and by those who could not.

I offer special thanks to Richard Refshauge SC; Allison Will; Detective-Sergeant Harry Hains; Jennifer Giles and Hilary Bonney; Judith Lukin-Amundsen; Hilary McPhee; Robin Laurie and Mandy Mitchell-Taverner; Michael Gawenda and James Button; Claire Wood and the staff at Auscript; Manning Clark House; the University of Newcastle.

The loyalty of my family and my friends, over these five years, has meant more to me than I can say.

'. . . to place, consider, deplore and mourn . . .'
GITTA SERENY

'Suffering is not enough.'
THICH NHAT HANH

PART ONE

The first time I saw Joe Cinque among his friends and family, the first time I ever heard his voice, was in the living room of his parents' house in Newcastle, in the winter of 1999.

By then, of course, he had already been dead for nearly two years.

This is the story of how I got to know him.

The house he died in, on Sunday, 26 October 1997, was not far from the Canberra ambulance headquarters. The paramedics would have been able to reach him in a flash, but it took the dispatcher almost twenty minutes to get the right address from the hysterical young woman who placed the 000 call. Like all emergency calls, this one was recorded.

Male Dispatcher: Okay, and the phone number you're ringing from?
Could I get an ambulance please? I have a person potentially overdosed on heroin.
Potentially overdosed?
Well, he's not — he's vomiting everywhere blood stuff.
He's vomiting blood? Right okay, what's the address?
Is that a bad sign?
What's the address?
Can you hang on, please just tell me is that a bad sign?
That's — well it's not good if he's vomiting blood.
Oh, is he going to be okay?
I don't know, I'll send an ambulance for them to check him out.
Fair enough.
What's the address?
30 . . . Antill Street.
Is that a flat or a house?
Oh, it's a flat.

What number in Antill Street?
What's going to happen?
What's the flat number?
Oh shit, shit.
Listen to me.
Oh, hang on, what am I going to do?
Settle down. Settle down.
Okay, what am I going to do?
Well if you tell me the address I'll get an ambulance out to you.
Will he be okay?
I don't know, we'll have to get an ambulance to you to assess him.
What is the number of the flat in Antill . . .
Is — is — oh shit.
What is the number of that flat in Antill Street?
It's um, 79.
Flat 30, 79 . . . Is that correct?
Yeah. No — hang on . . .
Flat 30 . . .
Hang on, where's the ambulance?
The ambulance is at Dickson. Now just calm down. What's your name? What's your name?
Oh shit, he's vomiting blood, what are . . .
What's your name?
Is he going to die?
What is your name?
Tell me, tell me, please.
What is your name?
Oh — oh God — Olivia.
What is your name please?
Olivia, Olivia — oh fuck — hang on, hang on . . .
What's the phone number you're ringing from?

Hang on, his heart's still beating.
Good. Right, now just settle down, for God's sake.
Flat 30, 79 Antill Street.
Flat 30, 79 . . .
No – 79 Antill Street.
What's the flat number?
It's a townhouse.
It's 79 in Antill Street?
Yeah, yeah, get here quickly.
All right, we'll get someone there shortly.

Phone disconnected. Recording resumed:

Male Dispatcher: Ambulance Emergency.
Yeah, 79 Antill Street?
Now listen to me – listen to me.
Sorry.
Just be quiet for a moment and listen to me.
Right, right.
It's no good you carrying on like that if I don't know where to send the ambulance.
Okay, 79 Antill Street, go . . .
What is the problem?
He's OD'd on heroin I think.
Right, okay.
Quick, oh . . .
The ambulance is on its way to you now . . . Is he breathing?
I don't know.
Well – check for me?
No.
Okay, do you know how to do mouth-to-mouth resuscitation?

There's a lot of blood coming out of his mouth.

Right, okay clear that away.

How?

Roll him on his side . . . Put your finger in his mouth, and clear it out.

Right, right, hang on.

. . . Okay, do you know how to do mouth-to-mouth resuscitation?

Oh shit, oh shit.

Do you know how to do mouth-to-mouth resuscitation?

Yes, I do.

Well start doing it now.

What if there's still stuff in his mouth?

Get the stuff out of his mouth, put your finger in his mouth and get it out.

Shit, shit.

You've got to do something about it. You're the one that's going to help him right at this moment. The ambulance is on its way to you . . .

What am I doing?

I don't know what you're doing. Has the patient got a pulse?

Has –

Can you feel the pulse?

Their heart?

Yes.

Yeah. Yeah.

Right, okay, continue mouth-to-mouth resuscitation.

Mouth – I'm clearing that.

Clear the airway and continue mouth-to-mouth resuscitation.

His teeth won't open – he – his mouth's not opening properly.

Well, prise it open.

Yeah.

Pinch off his nose. Pinch off his nose, open his mouth, tilt his head back slightly and blow into his mouth.
Yeah, yeah.
Okay, continue that – do not stop.
Oh don't stop – okay.
Don't stop . . .
Okay, is someone here? Someone's here.
Just continue the resuscitation.
He'll be all right, won't he?
I can't answer – I cannot answer that over the phone. Just continue the resuscitation.
Oh God, I can't – I can't . . .
Well, go outside and get the ambulance officers.
Is he there?
Go outside and get the ambulance officers. Two three, are you on location?
Ambulance Officer: We're approaching.

As the ambulance sped towards the house, the paramedics spotted on the nature strip a young woman with long dark hair, desperately waving. They ran inside and up the stairs and found, lying diagonally across the double bed with the phone lead stretched over his legs, a naked young man. Vomit was coming out of his mouth before they even touched him: they saw that mouth-to-mouth resuscitation had filled his stomach with air. He was not breathing, but when they touched his skin, it was warm. They seized him and laid him on the floor with his feet pointing to the doorway.

'How much has he had?'

'He's had a hundred and fifty,' said the girl.

'You mean three lots?'

'Yes,' she said, 'and he's had some Rohypnol.'

The paramedics got down on the carpet and started to work on the young man's body. The frantic girl asked them if they were going to use Narcan. No, they were not. *Massage his heart!* they shouted at her, and she obeyed, but she didn't pound his chest hard enough: like most people she had no idea of the amount of force it takes. They tried to get a tube into his trachea, to keep his airway clear, but quantities of dark brown vomit kept coming up his throat and out of his mouth. There was so much of it clogging his airway that, try as they might, they could not get the tube past it. The brown muck was everywhere, all down the sides of the bed and on the floor, and it kept coming. At the second attempt they thought they'd got the tube in right, but there was so much vomit in there that they couldn't be sure. They laboured over his body for more than five minutes. When they saw that it was too long since he had taken a breath – when they saw that he was gone – they gave up the attempt and stood back.

The young woman began to shriek: 'It wasn't supposed to happen this way! We were supposed to go together!' The senior ambulance officer tried to cover the dead man with a sheet, but the girl flung herself on the naked body and began to embrace it fiercely, screaming, 'Can't you do anything? This is not happening! I don't believe this! You can't stop! You have to bring him back!' She tried to kiss the dead man; she sat on top of him, moving back and forth; she pulled at his face. They had to drag her out of the room. She kept fighting to get back in; when one of the paramedics blocked the bedroom door with the bulk of his body, she began to dart and rush about the house, moving restlessly from room to room, up and down the stairs, pacing, shaking both hands in front of her chest, rambling incoherently.

The paramedics called the police. The girl asked if she could go out and get some cigarettes. They told her she couldn't go anywhere till the police arrived. They asked her if a suicide note had been written. She said no. She told them the suicide had been planned for two months, and that the dead man had taken the drugs at about three in the morning.

The fire brigade arrived. One of the three fire officers was a woman. She noticed that the distraught girl was wearing a long, pale dress in a light-weight material: its skirt was stained with long streaks of dark fluid. Her lips and the skin around her mouth were smeared with dark stuff. The girl told the woman firefighter that the dead man's name was Joe. 'He had a lot last night,' she said urgently, gripping the fire officer's arm very tight. 'He had a lot this morning. Who's going to tell his parents?'

Into this squalid, hysterical scene walked four police officers: one uniformed woman and three male detectives.

'What happened?' asked one of the men.

The girl replied in a babbling rush. 'The original plan was *I* was going to do it,' she said. 'We were supposed to go together. I gave him four Rohypnol. I'd had some. Then . . . I had some heroin – I just kept pumping it into him to put him to sleep, so he wouldn't –'

The detective cut across her. 'Listen carefully. You are not obliged to say anything unless you wish to do so, and anything you do say will be recorded and may later be used in evidence.'

'Yes – yes,' she said.

'Wouldn't what?'

'Wouldn't be awake when I killed myself.'

They arrested her near the front door of the house, and put

her into the police car. She tried to get out, she fought to get out, so they handcuffed her. Her name was not 'Olivia'; it was Anu Singh. They drove her to the police station, and charged her with murder.

Two days later, the police went to the house of Singh's closest friend, Madhavi Rao, and took her in as well. She too was charged with murder.

The first I heard of this tale was in March 1999. I received a phone call at home in Sydney from a respected senior journalist. He wanted to put me on to a story he had heard around the traps. Two young women, Anu Singh and Madhavi Rao, law students at the Australian National University, were being tried in Canberra for the murder of Singh's boyfriend. The journalist wasn't too clear on the details, but there was a bizarre touch – a special dinner party had been held at the couple's house before he was killed. Had the guests been told that 'the crime of the century' was to be committed in the course of the evening? Anyway, Rohypnol in the young fellow's coffee, heroin in his arm, convulsions, vomiting, death.

A *dinner* party? My imagination supplied, with distaste, a cartoon version of the scene: a candle-lit table of glossy students in their twenties, flashing their brilliant teeth and lashing about with their manes of hair, while in their midst, sitting modestly, smiling to left and right, believing himself loved and among friends, their chosen victim picked up his fork to eat his last meal.

Apparently, said the journalist, the one whose boyfriend had been killed was 'head-turningly beautiful, the daughter of a wealthy family, spoilt rotten'. The other one he hadn't heard much about, but the word seemed to be that she was 'nicer'. He wasn't sure how to pronounce it or what nationality the victim was, but the name, he thought, was something like *Cinque*.

'If it's such a great story,' I said, 'how come *you're* not writing it?'

'Look,' said the journalist patiently. 'I can do history. I can do politics. I can even do economics, at a pinch. But I can't do psychology.'

He didn't spell it out – you're *interested* in women at the end of their tether – but I saw at once why I was the writer he had called. Four years earlier I had published a book of reportage called *The First Stone*, about two young women law students in Melbourne who had brought charges of assault against the head of their university college. By questioning the kind of feminism that had driven the story, and by writing it against the determined silence of the two women and their supporters, I had opened myself to long months of ferocious public attack. The parallels between that story and this one were like a bad joke. No way was I going back out there.

As it happened, though, I had recently been forced to acknowledge that *I* was a woman at the end of my tether. I was fifty-five. My third marriage had just collapsed in a welter of desolation. I was living alone in Sydney, in a rented flat, on the fifth floor of a building on the top of a hill. I had no job, and lacked the heart to look for one. I knew I had to get out of my own head, to find some work to do. The journalist, whatever his motives, was offering me a story. But what did I care about these students and their trashy adventures?

It was only a feeble sort of politeness, the inability to say a straight no to someone who thought he was doing me a favour, that made me copy down the phone number of the journalist's contact, and call it.

The person who answered the phone was a tentative young woman. She told me she had been acquainted with Anu Singh and Madhavi Rao at university; she was a close friend of one of the guests at the fateful dinner party.

'I've got ethical problems,' she said. 'I don't want to rat on my friends. But the story's in the public domain now, isn't it.'

She sounded less than convinced by her own argument, but offered to meet me in two days' time at the NSW State Library cafe in Macquarie Street. A blue-stocking, I thought; a swot. She'll chicken out for sure; and when she does, I'll be able to fade out too, without giving offence to anybody. But before our date, acting on a trickle of curiosity, I went to the office of a newspaper I often wrote for, and asked to see the cuttings file.

It was already surprisingly bulky. The murdered man's name was Italian: Joe Cinque. He had been killed on 26 October 1997. The two women had gone on trial together in 1998, but a month into those proceedings, a legal problem had arisen. The jury had been dismissed and the joint trial aborted. The women were now to be tried separately, each with her own defence counsel. The trial currently in progress was Anu Singh's.

Anu Singh, I gathered from the phlegmatic daily court reports, was the daughter of two doctors, a rather bright student who had come from Sydney to Canberra to study law at ANU. She was a keen recreational drug user and her student career had been chequered. But by 1997, the final year of her course, she was living in the Canberra suburb of Downer with Joe Cinque, a young civil engineer variously described in the press as her boyfriend, fiancé and de facto husband. He was a stable fellow with a good job and they planned to marry as soon as she graduated.

Singh's closest female friend was Madhavi Rao, by all accounts a quieter and more studious person. Like Joe Cinque, Rao was devoted to the floridly glamorous Singh, and solicitous of her welfare. But looking after Singh seems to have been an ever more onerous task, for she was a drastic dieter and a driven frequenter of gyms, obsessed with her physical imperfections both real and imagined: she had worked hard for her six-pack; she declared that she would 'rather be dead than fat'.

During 1997 Singh got into her head the idea that she was suffering from an incurable and fatal muscle-wasting ailment. She consulted dozens of doctors. None of them would confirm her diagnosis but her conviction was unshakeable. She traced her condition to the fact that, in her endless quest for thinness, she had swallowed large doses of a vomit-inducing syrup called ipecac. This, like many things that were wrong in her life, she blamed on Joe Cinque: she claimed he had told her that models used ipecac to control their weight. She resented, too, the fact that while living with him she felt as if she had effectively 'become a housewife'.

A month before she killed Joe Cinque, Singh had apparently approached a university counsellor, and alleged that Joe had hit her several times and abused her verbally. She claimed that Joe blamed her for the abuse, saying he had 'never been violent to a woman before'. But she could not leave him, she told the counsellor, because she was rendered financially and emotionally dependent on him by her 'medical condition'.

In the terse style of the press clippings, the story grew more and more bizarre. Singh's fantasies were far-fetched and fluctuating. She used the words 'vendetta' and 'rampage'. She bragged to companions that she had studied psychiatric texts and knew the law, that it would be easy to convince people you were insane. To her friends she spoke often and dramatically of killing herself – and as for Joe, she told some friends she would drug him so he would be asleep while she committed suicide, and others that she would go the whole hog and take him with her.

Madhavi Rao, whose counsel had described her as 'a doormat' with a tendency to 'become involved in flights of fancy', had apparently been privy from the start to these plans. Together the two women were said to have researched suicide methods at the university library. Singh tried to get hold of a gun. When this failed they turned their attention to drugs. Fellow-students were happy to give Singh and Rao injecting lessons, to score heroin for them and even to explain what dosage would bring about instantaneous death. Guests were summoned to a dinner party. After they had gone home, Singh laced Joe Cinque's coffee with the sedative Rohypnol, then, while he was unconscious, gave him a lethal hit of heroin.

But the young man did not die the prompt and quiet death that she had been advised would follow such a dose. He lingered. For hours. Right through the night and into the following morning.

Towards noon, according to the cuttings, Singh started to get cold feet. She phoned the friend who had got hold of the Rohypnol for her, a girl called Bronwyn Cammack, and told her what she had done to Joe. His lips, she said, were 'a tiny bit blue, and he was taking a breath every ten seconds or so'. She begged Cammack to come over and revive him. Cammack, a sometime heroin user, insisted Singh dial emergency at once. Singh threw an hysterical fit: Joe didn't know she'd given him the drugs – if the paramedics brought him round with Narcan, he would find out what she'd done and would be furious. Cammack stood firm. So Singh dialled 000, but by the time the ambulance reached the house, it was too late.

While she was in custody after Joe Cinque died, Singh wrote a series of letters to her family and others. These were seized from her locker at the Belconnen Remand Centre, and admitted into evidence at her trial. *I watched him die*, she wrote. *Didn't save him. Then I thought, fuck, I don't want to die . . . The prosecution has a very strong case against me. I could be looking at 20 years . . . What a mess I have made out of a potentially perfect life. How much I wish this didn't happen so my life could be normal now – married to Joe, couple of kids, luxury, the works. I had the perfect life. Attractive, money, law career, everything. Now nothing because of my utter, utter stupidity . . . I could have had the most wonderful man in the world . . . Now everyone else is better off than me, when I had it all . . . I bet everyone is laughing at me now. People would have envied me before. Now no one would want to be in my shoes.*

The letter got under my skin, with its panicky tone, its angry, shallow clichés. *I had it all. Luxury, the works, the perfect life.* It was a very *adolescent* voice. She seemed to lack a language deep enough for the trouble she was in, a language fit for despair. With dread I recognised her. She was the figure of what a woman most fears in herself – the damaged infant, vain, frantic, destructive, out of control.

In the fluorescent glare of the newspaper office I studied the pictures, smudged and blackened by the photocopier.

The first was an indistinct close-up, perhaps from a family album, of a young man with his peaked cap on backwards. He grinned frankly, straight into the lens, but the flash had bleached out his forehead, nose and mouth; the contrast gave his eyes a dark, warm glisten.

The second photo showed the same man standing against what looked like a kitchen wall. He was holding proudly in his arms a slender young woman in a striped T-shirt and black jacket. Her dark hair was up, her eyebrows were skilfully plucked into wing shapes. The man's bare arm was strong, but the masculinity he radiated looked very youthful: he reminded me of the Italian and Greek high school boys I used to teach. He held his chin up with a shy, almost defensive smile, while the girl in his embrace turned her head to beam into the camera with the ease of someone accustomed to being adored and to looking good in photos.

The third picture was crisply focused, a professional news shot of a different young woman, against a background of asphalt. She paid the camera no attention. Her black hair was bobbed, with a centre part. She wore an open-necked striped shirt, rimless spectacles and no make-up. She looked serious, round-cheeked and strong-browed.

Anu Singh raised my girl-hackles in a bristle. Joe Cinque provoked a blur of warmth. Madhavi Rao filled me with a wary, puzzled curiosity. These were my instinctive responses, and over the ensuing years, as I picked a path through this terrible story, they remained remarkably stable. But that day in the newspaper office, ploughing through the repetitive cuttings, I thought it was all a waste of time. I was way behind the action. I had already missed the entire Crown case against Anu Singh. There was nothing here for me. I might as well go home.

Still, I kept my rendezvous at the State Library. The contact turned up, right on time: a straight-backed young woman with well-brushed brown hair and an intelligent, watchful face. We sat down and ordered coffee. I knew her name but she begged me, with an anxious grimace, for anonymity.

'I'm angry,' she said. 'I never even met Joe Cinque, but I'm *angry*. People close to this have been miserable ever since – even the ambitious ones. It stuffed *me* around, and I'm peripheral. It's the waste – the waste of someone's life.'

She described the two women in fast, vivid strokes: 'Anu's tall. She's thin. She came across as a very sexual person. She *talked* about sex a lot. She always had lots of men after her. She's got the hair to the knees, the tailored suit – whereas Madhavi's more the independent rock, Triple-J type of woman, with a pierced nose – warm, and a bit vague, with strong beliefs about stuff like environmentalism. Madhavi won't cope in gaol. Anu will, but not Madhavi. She'll be manipulated.'

Most of all, she wanted me to understand *about drugs*. This story might strike me as weird, she said, but in Canberra as it was in 1996, 1997, 1998, when hard drugs had cut a huge swathe through the city, it wasn't weird at all. Small-time dealers hung out at all the university colleges. There were a lot of bored rich kids. The ANU Bar was where people would go to buy dope. Plenty of drugs were exchanged there for sex: fresher girls, she said, were 'prepared to fuck guys in the toilet in exchange for a couple of tabs of ecstasy'.

I tried to register this gross fact without blinking, but she flashed me a wry look. 'Here,' she said. 'I brought you something.' She took out of her bag a folded sheet of newsprint and passed it across the cafe table. We shook hands and said goodbye.

On the train home I opened the paper she had given me. It was a double-page tabloid spread from the *Daily Telegraph*'s report of the committal proceedings: the transcript of the emergency call that Anu Singh had made to the paramedics while Joe Cinque lay dying on their bed.

It was the shrill blast of this dialogue that broke through my indifference and galvanised me: the killer's voice pleading, dodging, feinting; the dispatcher's desperate striving for command; and the jolting visual flashes of Joe Cinque's death throes – the close presence, behind the screaming, of a young man's body *in extremis* – his limbs, his mouth, his teeth, his heart.

PART TWO

PART TWO

I understand now that I went to Canberra because the break-up of my marriage had left me humiliated and angry. I wanted to look at women who were accused of murder. I wanted to gaze at them and hear their voices, to see the shape of their bodies and how they moved and gestured, to watch the expressions on their faces. I needed to find out if anything made them different from me: whether I could trust myself to keep the lid on the vengeful, punitive force that was in me, as it is in everyone – the wildness that one keeps in its cage, releasing it only in dreams and fantasy.

That day, though, as I went straight home, called the airline and packed a bag, I was still thinking of myself as a writer at a loose end who had stumbled on something interesting. I thought I would be able to slip quietly into the court with my notebook for a shield. I could watch and listen for a while, satisfy my curiosity, and wander out again at will, unscathed and free of obligation. But I was about to learn a hard lesson. A story lies in wait for a writer. It flashes out silent signals.

Without knowing she is doing it, the writer receives the message, drops everything, and turns to follow.

⚬⚬

When I got to the ACT Supreme Court on 6 April 1999, Anu Singh's defence was already in progress. It took me a moment to get my bearings. The courtroom was so palely timbered and greenly curtained, so shallow and wide and muffled by carpet, that it could have been a suburban lounge room.

Two women were stationed side by side on padded chrome chairs, out in the middle of the space. One was a tall, blonde, scraggly-haired security guard. The other was Anu Singh. Her hair, dark and reddish-tinted and very long, was pulled back and firmly bound into a thick club that bulged on the nape of her neck. She was wearing street clothes: a long skirt and a dark-blue jacket laced criss-cross in the small of her back. Her bare feet were slipped into high wedge-heeled sandals. She sat very still, very erect, with her right leg crossed over her left. Beside her slouching escort she looked dainty, almost prim. A sliver of profile was all I could see of her face.

The witness on the stand could only be her father. Heavy-shouldered, with a close-clipped beard, Dr Singh leaned back in the chair with his hands folded on his belly. He was a man of substance, unfazed by the formality of his surroundings; but the version of his daughter's life that the barrister was drawing from him, as I slid into the back row of the gallery, was a sorry one.

Anu, he was saying, had been barely a year old when the family migrated from the Punjab and settled in Newcastle. She was a clever little girl, but very clingy. She slept in her parents' bedroom till she was four or five. Puberty hit early – by thirteen she was 'fully developed'.

As a teenager she became a real headache, slacking off on schoolwork, wearing revealing clothes, refusing to help her mother, always sneaking out to see boys. Then, from year eleven, the dieting started. Somehow she stayed near the top of her class, and in year ten she was dux. Her HSC score was high, but not first rank. In 1991 she went to Canberra to study economics and law at the Australian National University.

She coped poorly away from home, he thought – always on the phone to her mother – until in late 1993 she took up with a fellow student, Simon Walsh. Dr Singh was annoyed with her for becoming a vegetarian and overdoing the aerobics classes, but for a while she seemed to become more stable.

In 1995, the doctor went on, the Singh family left Newcastle and moved to a middle-class suburb of Sydney. That year Anu came home from uni at the September break in an odd state. She wouldn't go out or dress up, but sat about in casual clothes, crying for no apparent reason. Whenever her father saw her she was coming out of the shower. She paced the floor all night.

Any woman who has left home for university could fill in the gaps here, I thought. Drugs. Booze. Stupid, risky sex. 'Love' affairs. Casual wounding. Pregnancy. Abortion. What do parents know? What can a girl afford to tell them about her stampede towards danger and self-damage?

Another set of parents sat in the middle of the front row of the public gallery. They looked like Italians. They sat shoulder to shoulder, quiet and still, rarely speaking or turning to each other, but it was obvious who they were. Around their attentive heads glowed an aura of anguish.

That summer of '95–'96, Dr Singh told the court, his daughter became frighteningly thin – no more than forty kilos. She ate nothing but Coke and TimTams. He could see her bones. She would pull up her shirt (here his voice choked, he wept, he wiped his eyes; his daughter, listening on her chair, did the same) and show him hanging skin. 'Look,' she would say, pinching it. 'It's fat.'

Dr Singh told her she had an eating disorder and must see a psychologist. She flatly refused, and begged and pestered till he made an appointment for her to have liposuction. Such was the power of his daughter's will that he even paid a deposit of several hundred dollars to the cosmetic surgeon. At the eleventh hour she cancelled.

In September 1996 she brought home a new boyfriend, a young man from Newcastle called Joe Cinque. His daughter was happy, said Dr Singh. He could see it in her face. But that summer her litany of complaints began again: aching legs, hot flushes and pains, things crawling on her skin. She became withdrawn and tearful. She refused to see a psychiatrist.

By May 1997 she was convinced that her muscles were gone. Life wasn't worth living, she said. In August, she started to sell her clothes and give away her CDs. When she went back to university, her parents twice rang the Mental Health Crisis Team in Canberra; but each time they came to Anu's house, she sent them away.

'On 26 October 1997,' said the barrister, 'you saw your daughter?'

'In the Canberra lock-up,' said Dr Singh. 'She was agitated, crying, pinching and pulling at her arms. She asked me "Where am I?" We could only stay ten minutes, because of her state of mind.'

Cross-examined by the Crown, Dr Singh said his daughter missed Joe now, that she was deeply saddened he was no longer with her – I glanced at the couple in the front row, and saw Mrs Cinque's shoulders stiffen – but she had never told her father she regretted killing Joe, for Dr Singh had never asked her anything about how Joe had died.

'She has never told you she injected him with heroin?'

'I didn't raise that question,' said Dr Singh. 'She's too disturbed. It's a very sad thing. I don't want to bring it up. I only tell her all the time, "What you did, you were sick. You were *sick*." We have general chitchat. I want to relax her. I talk about family. I talk about religion. I talk about peace of mind.'

'What religion are you?' asked the prosecutor.

'I believe in humanity.'

'And *her* beliefs about humanity?'

'She is too young,' said her father, 'to have any beliefs.'

What I needed was a journalist. At the break I looked around the lobby for one of those shockingly young reporters who are sent to cover Supreme Court trials. The squalor and misery they are exposed to every day can make them seem thick-skinned, even coarse: I like them. They are always good company, full of 'facts' and keen to gossip and speculate. I spotted two of them, smartly-dressed and friendly-looking women in their twenties, hanging about near the glassed-in atrium with its struggling plants. I sidled up and introduced myself. They were a classic pair: one a thin, quiet, thoughtful blonde, the other dark, irreverent and bouncily talkative. Yes, they'd been there for everything I'd missed – the whole Crown case against Anu Singh. What the hell, I asked them, was this story about a dinner party? And where was the jury?

With gusto and a fair amount of eye-rolling, they filled me in. There had been more than one dinner party at the couple's town-house, in the week before the murder. Singh would send out her friend Madhavi Rao at the last minute to round up a random crew of guests from neighbouring student households. Some who'd been called to give evidence had heard gossip about a suicide plan, others had been told about a possible murder, but with a single notable exception they all claimed not to have taken it seriously. One girl, though, told the court she had actually dropped in to Rao's house the morning after one of the dinners and asked, 'Did anything happen? Did anyone die?'

Anyway, Anu Singh had been in Belconnen Remand Centre for eighteen months. She now admitted having given Joe Cinque the lethal dose, but she was going for diminished responsibility. For this defence to work, the journalists said, you had to prove that at the time you did the crime you were suffering from 'an abnormality of mind'. And this meant a lot of psychiatric evidence. Singh's counsel – the sharp-voiced little guy with dark red cheeks – was Jack Pappas. The Crown Prosecutor, taller and rangier and less aggro in style, was Terry Golding.

As for the jury – there wasn't one. Singh had chosen to be tried by judge alone. The journalists laughed at the look on my face. Yes, you could do that in the ACT. He was Justice Ken Crispin, the same judge who had presided over the earlier jury trial that had been aborted. He was a Christian, they said, 'a lay preacher' in the Uniting Church. As a barrister he had acted for Lindy Chamberlain. He wrote a book about her case. He had also appeared for the victims in the Chelmsford Deep Sleep Therapy trial. He was well thought of in Canberra. People liked him.

And the other girl? The 'doormat' friend?

Madhavi Rao, said the journalists, was out on $100,000 bail, on condition that she live at home in Sydney with her parents: her father, a high school teacher, had put up the family house as surety. She would have her own separate trial, later in the year.

The young journalists spoke of Anu Singh with a complete lack of sympathy, indeed with a rough contempt. 'And you should have seen some of her *friends* who gave evidence,' said the dark one, with a short, scornful laugh. 'Talk about flaky!' She stretched her neck, lowered her eyelids, and moved her head about in a parody of swan-like hauteur.

'What sort of clothes?' I asked, dismayed at how much I had missed.

'Oh – Country Road,' she said, pulling a face. 'Daddy will pay. *Daddy will pay.*'

In her cynicism I heard an echo of the primitive female hostility that had made the back of my neck prickle at the sight of Anu Singh's photo in the *Canberra Times*. It occurred to me that if I had been Singh's defence counsel, I too would have seized any opportunity to get rid of the jury, particularly if it had contained women.

When the court rose that day I carried my backpack along Northbourne Avenue and took a room in the first hotel I could stand the sight of. It was a warm afternoon. I lay on the bed for a while thinking about Anu Singh and her distracted visits home from university. I wondered if *my* parents had guessed what was the matter with *me*, in 1964, when I took the train home to Geelong after I had had an abortion. I thought about money. I tried to figure out a way to follow this trial without having to commit myself to a publisher. Then I walked back to Civic and bought myself two new notebooks and a bunch of pens.

Next morning in the courtroom, just before the judge made his entrance between the grey-green velvet curtains, I heard someone at the bar table humming. It was only a worker absent-mindedly settling down to a long day's slog, but how awful it seemed, this light, tuneful sound.

⚘

A video of Anu Singh's charging was to be shown.

The monitor on the bar table sprang to life.

On the bright rectangle a figure dressed from neck to ankle in glaring synthetic white is jerking to and fro in front of a high bench or counter, behind which a man in uniform stands. Her hair is clumped on top of her head in a knob, and her arms are swaddled against her torso as if by a straitjacket – no, it's only the peculiar white jumpsuit she's wearing, and her doll-like stance. Voices urge her to stand still, but she can't, she won't.

Do you wanna do me a favour, says a man's voice, *and stand back on the yellow line? Just step back on to the line, just so the camera can film you properly.*

Yep, says the white figure. But she keeps sighing, raising her hands to her hair, turning and pacing and moving about.

You are charged, the voice announces, *that in the Australian*

Capital Territory on the 26th of October 1997 you did murder Joe – he stumbles over the name, and bungles it – *Joe Ching-koo. Do you understand that?*

❧

In the public gallery Mrs Cinque put one hand over her eyes, then, holding her head high, folded and refolded her hanky.

❧

The tiny white-clad puppet on the screen rocks and jerks. Her answers to the laborious utterances of the police sergeant are more like sighs and murmurs than speech: she can't seem to get her breath. The voice cautions her formally, asks her if she understands, cautions her again. It charges her with murder, then with *administering to another person, namely Joe Ching-koo, a stupefying drug namely heroin, likely to endanger a human life.*

Just stand back a little bit, the voice keeps telling her. *Just stand on the yellow line.*

Has anyone called? gasps the figure in white. *Ah – ah – ah – did you speak to my parents?*

They're coming down to Canberra.

Are they? Energy surges into her voice.

They know where you are.

What'd you tell them?

That you're on a murder charge, that Joe had died . . .

Okay, says the figure in white, rocking, pacing, shifting in and out of shot. *Okay – when do I leave here?*

'Never!' shouted Joe Cinque's mother from her seat in the gallery. She too rocked and rocked, folding her arms across her belly. Her husband sat hunched and motionless beside her.

The video, with its fixed camera, garish colours and muffled dialogue, was packed with more meaning than the most professional production. It was raw with pain. The Cinques and Dr Singh were sitting as far away from each other as they could get in a gallery that had only four rows of seats, but their faces in profile wore the same expression: heavy, the mouths low, the skin and flesh sagging off the bone.

The video machine had developed a glitch, and the court adjourned briefly while it was repaired. Anu Singh left with her escort. She passed her father at the end of his row. They did not look at each other. Everyone else filed out into the carpeted hall. People vanished into the toilets, or drank water at the cooler from tiny waxed-paper cups. A group of whispering law students went into a huddle round their tutor. Sun came flooding through the glass walls of the atrium.

Outside the building it was a late summer morning, grass-scented, brilliant. Joe Cinque's father walked to the very edge of the lawn. He was a solitary figure under the high, pure Canberra sky. He dragged fiercely on a cigarette, clenching his jaw and staring across the dark green grass at the traffic.

The first expert witness called by Anu Singh's defence was Dr Kenneth Byrne, a clinical and forensic psychologist who practised in Melbourne. He was a New Yorker in his forties with pale hair and eyelashes, tasselled loafers, and a neatly packed little overnight bag that rested against the leg of his chair.

It was immediately plain that Dr Byrne was in his element: he spoke with the relaxed and smiling assurance of a pro. His thing today was measurement, and in particular something called the Minnesota Multiphasic Personality Inventory. He declared the MMPI the most widely researched psychological test in the world. It was designed to measure pathology. A computer could score it. The person being tested was presented with 556 propositions, to which the possible responses were *agree/don't agree*. It was sensitive enough to pick up faking – a subject's attempt to make herself look healthier, or sicker, than she really was.

Byrne rode the buffetings of Golding's cross-examination in a breezy, high-handed style. Something about him got up my nose. Was it his debonair and stagy demeanour, his habit of addressing the judge man-to-man, his didactic listing and numbering of points as if to a roomful of freshers? Or was it the famous MMPI itself, with its bombastic title and claims to omniscience? In my irritation I was tempted to think of the MMPI as an enjoyably wanky life-style quiz of the sort one fills out to kill time in a doctor's waiting room. Maliciously I even permitted myself to imagine Anu Singh whiling away several idle hours, smoking cigarettes and doodling in the margins and ticking the little boxes, in her cell.

The Anu Singh that Dr Byrne described to the court, however, was a disturbed and suicidal young woman, lost in a deluded belief that she would soon die from a degenerative disease. She suffered, he said, from a severe borderline personality disorder, which he dated to her mid-adolescence, and a severe depression, which she had had well before she came into custody. He worked his way down a list of the features that signalled the existence of a borderline personality disorder: of a possible nine, Anu Singh exhibited the high score of six.

In the lobby at lunchtime I stood about with the two journalists. They giggled and glanced this way and that, comparing notes in whispers on how many of Dr Byrne's categories and symptoms seemed to apply to *them*. A problem in establishing a solid sense of *Who am I?* Definitely. Mood swings? Absolutely. Significant impulsivity? Of course. Fear of abandonment? *Totally.* Easily angered? I mean, *hellooow?*

Our laughter was slightly shrill. No one said it but we were all thinking, *Call that mental illness? She's exactly like me.*

As the break was ending, I came out of a toilet cubicle and saw Joe Cinque's mother standing with her back to me, combing her hair at the mirror. She moved aside to let me at the basin. We glanced at each other's reflections and smiled. She was a solid, broad-faced woman of fifty or so, rather handsome, with straight brows, tilted eyes of a striking clear green, and thick hair cut short and tinted fair.

'I see you writing in court,' she said in a friendly tone. 'Are you journalist?'

I blushed. The blunt truth would have been, 'Right now, in spite of my notebook, I'm still only perving.' But I said, 'Sort of. I'm a freelance writer.'

She nodded, zipped up her capacious bag and stepped past me to the door. She moved carefully, as if some part of her body hurt her. In repose her face held the shape of courtesy, but her brow was frozen, her expression severe: she radiated such iron fatigue and reined-in sorrow that when she stopped smiling, the world around her darkened. Something inside me, something I had forgotten was there, gave a lurch. I did not want her to get away. I leaned after her and touched her sleeve.

'Excuse me, Mrs Cinque. If I wanted to write something about this trial, would you be prepared to speak to me?'

She turned and examined me with dry attention, up and down. 'Yes.'

I told her my name.

'Maria Cinque,' she said, with a slow, formal nod. Then, limping slightly, she hurried back into the court and took up her position beside her husband in the front row of the gallery.

When the police searched Madhavi Rao's house, the day after Joe Cinque died, they found in her bedroom rubbish bin a torn-up diary. The detectives took it away and glued it back together. It was a journal that Anu Singh had kept during her last two years of high school. How it had got into Rao's wastepaper basket, or when it had been torn to pieces and by whom, did not concern Mr Pappas. He asked Dr Byrne to tell the court what its contents showed about the sort of teenager Anu Singh had been.

The diary was passed hand to hand along the bar table: a bundle of pasted-together pages in a clear plastic bag. I was aware of holding my breath. The pathos of one's girlish fancies and romances, the idea that they might one day be laid out before strangers in open court – it was enough to make a woman faint with shame. I glanced at Anu Singh. She sat quite still on her chair, one leg folded over the other, her hands clasped in her lap, her hair bound thickly and firmly on her neck.

Four words, said Dr Byrne, summed up the preoccupations of the girl who had kept this diary: *Will boys like me?* If a boy did like her, she was an attractive person. Nothing much else seemed to supply her with that reassurance, and to get it she was prepared to engage in a very risky degree of sexual activity. He listed the developmental stages that a girl in years eleven and twelve should pass through, and the qualities we would expect to see in her. Evidence for any of these qualities, he said, was completely absent from Anu Singh's diary.

What *was* in it, then? Surely, I thought, remembering with a shudder the reams of self-obsessed ravings that had flamed in the backyard bonfires of my life, a diary is the one place where a girl can indulge her unacceptable narcissism with impunity?

But the diary showed, said Byrne, that he had been right about Singh's serious and very long-standing depression. On the day she killed Joe Cinque she was mentally ill, even psychotic. Yes, a borderline personality disorder *was* an 'abnormality of mind'.

Her plan was 'a homicide/suicide arrangement –'

Mrs Cinque in the gallery let out a sceptical grunt.

Dr Byrne did not pause in his flow. On a continuum that ranged from clear and rational at one end to completely psychotic and insane at the other, he said, Anu Singh was well down towards the dark end. She would also have been highly *suggestible*. Her friends and associates, he said, had either implicitly encouraged her along the fatal pathway, or failed to restrain her from it.

Her reasoning in the moments before Joe Cinque's death was 'bizarre' and 'grossly impaired'. Before she rang the ambulance, she had made a hysterical phone call to the young woman who had helped her get the Rohypnol. One minute Singh was screaming to her to come and help; the next she was shouting, 'It's too late! There's black stuff coming out of his nose!'

Mrs Cinque flinched. Her upper body bowed forward over her folded arms. Her husband sat staring straight ahead.

On Thursday the court was adjourned till the following Monday. At dusk my flight was called. I stepped out of the terminal for the short walk across the tarmac, and took a gasp of fresh, cool air. Several big, grey-blue arrowheads of cloud lay parallel with the low hills, in whose gathering darkness points of light winked. Later, remembering the beauty of those clouds, I would pick up the significance of 'arrowheads'. But as I took the few steps between building and plane, grateful after a day spent indoors to be inhaling the perfume of dry grass, I suddenly understood that Anu Singh would be *incarcerated*. Her life was ruined. Her youth was lost. For whatever reason, she had thrown it all away.

Back in Sydney, my hilltop flat was just a set of rooms. What little homeliness I had managed to imbue it with before I left for Canberra had already leaked away. I could not get interested in my new couch. The famous view across the valley to Bondi bored me. I found I missed the trial: the daily intensity of the drama as it unfolded, the rituals of leaping to one's feet and bowing, the silent companionship of the other watchers, the long tracts of intent listening. I could hardly wait for Monday.

I got to the court early, straight from the plane, so I could watch the lawyers.

As the power dynamic between students reveals itself in a classroom before the teacher strides in, so does the pecking order at a bar table. Everything social at this table seemed to revolve around Anu Singh's counsel, Jack Pappas. He was a tough little package of a man with an almost shaven head, a hooked nose, the rosy cheeks of good circulation, and the thick neck of a boxer. You could have drawn a diagram of the lines of attention that centred on him. His voice was the sharpest and most carrying, his enunciation the crispest, his pacing the most leisurely, his gestures the most dramatic. The jokes were his, and others laughed.

A quieter figure was the young man in a dark suit who often took the seat beside Mrs Cinque, or hovered briefly over her with his hand on her shoulder. Thank God they had another son. He looked an appealing person, even at a distance: thick dark hair well cut, a tanned face, a body free in its movements of affection and concern. The couple would turn their stiff faces up to him, and nod, or smile. His presence seemed to lighten something in them. In the complex field of the courtroom's dynamic, he was a site of benevolence and warmth.

When the lawyers were settled at their table, before the judge entered, Anu Singh materialised in her ankle-length skirt and high sandals. She had a springy, tight-bottomed, almost bouncing walk, and she came in fast and silently. The young security guard who was her escort that day sat down beside her, propped his elbows on his knees and turned to chat with her. She sat in her customary neat posture, but with lowered head. The guard had the look of a country boy. He tilted his face, smiling and grinning at her in a flirting manner. He bent his head and shoulders right down to his knees and peeped up at her sideways, as if to get under her resolute ignoring of him. In any other circumstance you would have said he was coming on to her. She remained quite still, with her back to us and her head bowed. Her father, several rows back in the gallery, watched them with a heavy face.

The prosecutor, Terry Golding, took on Dr Byrne about the meaning of Anu Singh's journal. 'There's no research text,' said Dr Byrne, 'to guide us in reading a diary.' Maybe not, but any woman there could have made a pretty fair stab at it.

Golding read out quotes and the two men duelled over them. Isn't *this* rational? Isn't *this* normal? It certainly is not! If *my* daughter had written that I'd be very concerned! They clashed over the teenaged Singh's account of how she suddenly lost interest in one boy she had been sleeping with, dumped him, and went off with another. The discarded one, she wrote, *was really cool about it. He said that he expected it to happen. I am really glad that we can still be friends.*

'Doesn't that show,' said Golding, 'the capacity for developing some intimacy in the relationship with the first boy?'

'No!' said Byrne. 'She's a self-centred, angry girl who's punishing this boy quite unnecessarily. She sees boys as an expendable commodity. You get one, you use him up, you throw him away.'

Memories from my own selfish and carelessly hurtful youth flashed through my head, scenes I did not care to examine. I shifted in my seat. I had joked with the journalists about it, but this stuff was getting too close for comfort.

Dr Byrne was asked to comment on a mysterious list of names that had been found in Anu Singh's locker at the remand centre.

He examined it carefully, then raised his eyes and said, 'She had developed fantasies of revenge against the people on this list. Like a grandiose child, she was resentful that people did not conform to her wishes. I have no way of knowing if they were fantasies or real plans.'

The judge ordered the suppression of the names on the list. Dismissed, the psychologist packed his papers into his bag and zipped it up with a tearing sound.

The two journalists took me across the road to a restaurant called Tosolini's. We sat outside under plane trees still in leaf. Huge buses kept roaring round the corner in low gear. To hear each other we had to lean right in over our plates.

The young women were even more in sympathy than I with Mr Golding's argument that Singh's teenage diary contained 'normal' thoughts and attitudes, even behaviours. We confessed with blushes to our own ghastly adolescent diaries, at least as bad as Anu Singh's, which we had all destroyed on leaving home. None of us could even begin to imagine why Singh had carried hers with her into adult life.

'And whose were the names that the judge suppressed, on that list?' I asked.

'They were on the back of a letter,' said one of them with a shrug.

The women looked at me with raised eyebrows, then picked up their forks and attacked their salads.

On Tuesday morning Anu Singh came in wearing a dark blue tailored jacket in a soft synthetic fabric, fitted to the curve of her waist – that womanly roundness she had fought so hard to eradicate from her body. Her hair was still hanging down her back, and while we all waited for the judge, she put it up. Although her back was turned to us, it was an almost indecently intimate and histrionic display, a series of age-old, deeply feminine gestures. First, the raising of both arms and the gathering of the hair in two hands. Then the twisting and rolling and flicking and doubling back of its dark mass, redder towards the tips, into a thick club; the binding of it with a broad black stretchy band; then the patting, the sensitive roaming of the flattened palms against the smooth round curve of her head; the feeling for loose strands at the temples and the anchoring of them over and behind the ears. All was in order. Satisfied, the small flexible hands flew up, out, and down to her lap, where they would lie, hour after hour, neatly clasped and occasionally twisting, while her inner life (or lack of it), her disturbances, her madnesses and cruelties were stripped bare and paraded before a small, intent cluster of strangers.

Her father, in the back row of the public gallery, watched without expression the dance of hands and hair. His chin was sunk over his knotted tie.

⸎

The second expert called by Anu Singh's defence was an English-
man with soft, tousled white hair, a slight shoulder-stoop and a
gently self-deprecating expression: Paul Mullen, Professor of
Forensic Psychiatry at Monash University and Clinical Director of
the Victorian Institute of Mental Health.

When Mr Pappas, running him through his credentials, asked
him if he was indeed born on 28 September 1944, he replied in a
mild, jesting tone that would not have been out of place at a cocktail party, 'So my mother gives me to understand.' Nobody
laughed. His vague, sweet smile did not falter: it would turn out
to be his characteristic expression, as much a part of his persona as
the humourless didactic mode was of Dr Byrne's. But in an airy
assertion of independence which went unchallenged, he chose not
to take the chair on the witness stand, and gave evidence on his
feet. Later, when declining Mr Golding's invitation to be seated
for cross-examination, he explained with his charming smile that
he had been trained in the customs of British courts, 'where only
the elderly, the frail and the totally disabled sit'. He reminded me
of a certain minor character in a D. H. Lawrence novel: the upper-
middle-class educated man who disconcerts the unsophisticated
farmers with his 'courtly, naïve manner, so suave, so merry, so
innocent'.

Like Dr Byrne, Professor Mullen had visited Anu Singh at
Belconnen Remand Centre. He had interviewed her for over five
hours. He was confident in declaring that she had been suffering
from a 'significant depressive illness' throughout 1997. Indeed, it
was *necessary* to postulate a depressive illness in order to explain her
actions on the day of 'the tragic killing of Mr Cinque'.

At Mullen's use of the word 'tragic', the tone of the proceedings subtly altered. He was about to haul them up out of
pathology and into the realms of archetypal drama. The clunky

American jargon of testing and measurement was not his style. He spoke with a relaxed eloquence, in flowing sentences of interesting syntax and vocabulary.

He talked about the brief periods of elation, even of positive happiness, that witnesses had noticed in Anu Singh shortly before she committed the crime. To explain these he introduced the concept of *masked* depression. She had certainly not had *manic* depression, the most severe sort; but she did have *affective instability* – and some of the best descriptions of this, said Mullen with his amiable smile, are to be found not in psychological texts but in literature – books written by people of high intelligence and creative ability who have also suffered from depression – Virginia Woolf, for example, in her novel *Mrs Dalloway*.

Professor Mullen struck me as so plausible that I was surprised when his written report was fiercely challenged by the Crown. In a fury of correction Mr Golding now filleted the document of unsubstantiated material straight from the mouth of Anu Singh – specially things she had told Mullen about the character of the man she had killed. 'Would you go then to the paragraph *Relationship with Mr Cinque*? Would you delete *fairly straight*? And *materialistic but protective*? Would you delete *when inflamed by jealousy* down to *with another man*?' So ruthless was Golding's attack that the professor made a comical protest. 'You want me to strike that out too?' he said with a rueful laugh. 'All my best lines are going!'

At lunchtime, to clear my head, I went for a walk in the autumn sunshine across Garema Place, the broad pedestrian precinct in the centre of Canberra. Men and women who work in government departments stride across this square with identity cards swinging on long chains round their necks. Junkies slouch whining in phone booths. Magpies perch, warbling their absent-minded melodies, on the chair-backs of outdoor cafes. As I walked I brooded crankily on the business of the defence psychiatrists. How can an expert witness hired by the family of the accused possibly be considered disinterested? This couldn't be right. I must have misunderstood. Why didn't the court itself appoint and pay the experts? Or was this a dumb question?

As I returned across the thick, dark-green grass to the Supreme Court, I saw Mr and Mrs Cinque seated quietly together on a bench under a leafy tree. They seemed composed and civilised, sitting outdoors to take the air and to eat slowly a picnic lunch they had brought with them, while everyone else rushed into the cafeteria and bolted down bags of take-away, or blew ridiculous sums in restaurants.

Anu Singh entered the court, shoulders high and cramped, her club of hair half-loosed from its moorings. She got into position on her seat and, with obsessive niceness, arranged her long skirt over her crossed leg and ankle. She had a remarkable ability to sit still in one unchanging position, hour after hour, occasionally flexing and relaxing her shoulder muscles. The padded, steel-framed chairs that she and her escort occupied stood on a section of floor where several metal loops were recessed into the carpet. I couldn't help thinking, with a slightly sick feeling, of the trapdoor of a gallows. In another country or a different era, she would have been hanged for this.

Who would want to cross-examine Professor Mullen? In the face of his highly evolved manner, his light, nonchalant laugh and his nimble footwork, it was the most unenviable job imaginable. Mr Golding battered away at him about *rational*. Wasn't it *rational* that Anu Singh had delayed calling the ambulance because she didn't want Joe Cinque to find out she had injected him with heroin?

'To the extent that she was utterly terrified of this man,' said Mullen, 'it doesn't seem rational – no.'

Utterly terrified? Where was *that* coming from? He slid the phrase in so silkily that it made hardly a ripple.

'*I watched him die and I didn't save him*,' quoted Golding. 'Why is that a psychiatric illness? Wasn't she just a very selfish young woman?'

The professor turned on the prosecutor a gaze of shocked reproach. 'Your notions of selfishness,' he said, 'extend way beyond mine. This isn't a selfish act. It's an *extraordinary* act. To try and reduce it to the mundane notion of selfishness does such harm to the awfulness of these events.'

'And the fact that after all her elaborate planning she didn't kill *herself*? Does that suggest she wasn't all that depressed?'

'I'll tell you what *she* said,' said Mullen. 'It made sense to *me*. She said, "*Up to that time it was like executing some power plan. Seeing him lying there gasping for breath brought me back for a moment to reality.*" '

Mrs Cinque lurched forward and clutched her arms to her

belly, as if she had been stabbed. The young man in the dark jacket put his arm round her shoulders. She went pale, a bad yellow colour. She unfolded a tissue and held it to her mouth. She struggled to compose herself. I wanted to cry out with horror, and pity.

When the court rose at the end of the day, Anu Singh turned to Professor Mullen as she passed him with her guard, and flashed him a bright smile. She gave him a little wave. She mouthed to him, 'Thank you!' The ordinariness of her demeanour knocked the breath out of me.

Why wasn't she down on her knees, grovelling for forgiveness? From the Cinques? From the whole human race? Begging for pardon, and with no sense that she was entitled to it, no expectation of ever receiving it?

Mullen had fought hard for her. He had gone to the wire. 'Utterly terrified', this phrase he had plucked from the ether and tossed down so casually before the judge, could only have been an artful way of hinting at what Golding had forced him to excise from his report. On a dumb gut level I did not believe Anu Singh had been 'utterly terrified' of Joe Cinque. It was unthinkable that the cause of 'utter terror', if it had existed, wouldn't have emerged much earlier in the story, and been heavily leaned on by her defence.

On my way across Garema Place I noticed an internet shop. I sat down at a computer, went to google.com, and keyed in the name of Professor Mullen. The entries scrolled down and down and down forever.

I stumped back along the broad eucalypt avenues to the hotel. My room had an ugly floral bedspread and purple net curtains. I couldn't sit still. I went downstairs to the bar and drank some whisky. I tried to examine rationally my response to Byrne and Mullen. Were they really as glib as they seemed? Psychiatry is very hard to gainsay, I thought. If you aren't satisfied by a category from the *Diagnostic and Statistical Manual of Mental Disorders* which claims to explain a person's dreadful actions, you are thrown back on simple, quotidian concepts of moral disapproval such as Mr Golding's *selfish*, that shallow, old-fashioned, tinny little word that rang so cheap and caused the cultivated professor to throw up his hands. At the other end of the scale you may wind up having to endorse terms like *wicked* or *evil* – words that people these days (unless they are discussing Islamic terrorists) find repugnant, because they sound religious, or primitive, or naïve – or, more convincingly, because they mark the point at which we are overcome by fear and revulsion – the point where we stop thinking and start shouting. But does psychological sophistication over-ride a sense that some actions are just plain *bad*? How much of human behaviour, in the end, *can* one understand?

Tout comprendre, c'est tout pardonner. When I came upon this maxim, as a young student of literature in the '60s, I extravagantly admired it and took it as a guide. Only a few years later, though, I read Thomas Mann's *Death in Venice*, and found that his character Aschenbach scorns what he calls the 'flabby humanitarianism' of the saying. I hated seeing my treasure of wisdom scorched by his off-hand contempt.

Now, though, I wondered if one ought to be wary of allowing oneself to 'understand' so readily – to skate all the way through to forgiveness. Doesn't a killer have to carry any responsibility for her actions? Doesn't she have to make some sort of *reparation*? Because when all is said and done, one brutal fact remains.

Joe Cinque is dead.

On Wednesday I learnt something that amazed me: the two Crown psychiatrists had not been permitted to interview Anu Singh. They had to base their reports on documents: the results of the MMPI and a Rorschach test, Singh's medical reports, the police statements of various witnesses, and some of the letters Singh had written from custody.

'How can this be?' I asked the journalists. 'When her whole defence rests on psychiatric assessment?'

It was her legal right to remain silent, they said. Once you chose not to give evidence – and Singh had made this choice at the start – you didn't have to say anything to anybody. Pappas, they told me, had even tried to argue that the Crown shouldn't be allowed to call psychiatric evidence in reply to Byrne and Mullen. Crispin had ruled against him on this. But the defence had offered the Crown shrinks access to Singh only if they first agreed to support the defence of diminished responsibility. This floored me. It seemed so madly unjust, so meaningless and perfunctory, that I didn't even know how to phrase a question about it, or to whom I should direct it.

First the Crown called Dr Susan Hayes, Associate Professor of Behavioural Sciences from the University of Sydney. Hayes was a small, motherly-looking woman of fifty or so in a cream jacket and shiny ear-rings. Her manner was modest and her voice so quiet that one had to strain to hear it, in the muffling acoustic of the carpeted courtroom.

She came at the matter from a fresh angle: the eating disorder. The sort of depression that comes over a woman when she can't achieve the body image she desires, she said, is different from clinical depression. At such times a woman can experience an ultimate dislike of the body that can tip over into ideas of suicide.

Dislike of the body. I imagined every woman in the court thinking, with an ironic twist of the mouth, *Tell me about it!* Suddenly, after all the lofty conceits bandied about by Byrne and Mullen, this was starting to feel real. Maybe only another woman could intuitively grasp the extent to which Singh, like the rest of us, was ruled by her body, imprisoned in it and condemned to struggle against it. But, oddly, this insight did not melt the hearts of the women who sat listening in court. On the contrary, the more like an ordinary woman Singh came to appear, the less sympathy she had to draw on, and the more the psychiatrists' explanations of her behaviour sounded like excuses which would not stand up in the harshly sceptical forum where women face the judgement of their sisters.

Hayes took a tremendous pounding from Mr Pappas for her view that many of Singh's fancied complaints – rotting flesh, ants crawling under her skin, a different head on her body – might be interpreted not as signs of psychosis but as side-effects of the recreational drugs she was taking.

He roared, he sneered.

Her voice trembled with anger, it sank at times to a thread. She dug her heels in. She became quietly mulish.

He had to push her every inch of the way to the desperate

phone call Singh made to Bronwyn Cammack while Joe Cinque lay dying. Didn't this show, Dr Hayes, that her thinking was grossly disordered?

'There was *conflict* in her mind,' said Hayes stubbornly. 'She was *in two minds* about calling the ambulance. She wanted to *appear* to be saving him, but not to actually save him.'

The court rose. I chanced to bump elbows with Dr Hayes in the crowded lobby. I must have flashed her a sympathetic look, for she grinned at me and pulled a self-mocking face. 'It's so frustrating!' she muttered. 'They want you to make absolute statements! I can't! I work in probabilities. And when it comes to *intent*! Most of the people I see say that forming a conscious intent was the *furthest* thing from their minds.'

She hurried away. My two young journalists emerged from their neighbouring courtrooms.

'There's a couple of junkies in there,' said the fair-haired one, putting her notebook away, 'about to be sentenced. Their five-week-old baby had every bone in its body broken. The mother's still hitting up. She was nodding off in court. But she's still got custody. And she's pregnant again.'

'How's your thing going?' asked the dark one, jerking her thumb at Justice Crispin's court.

'Still the shrinks,' I said.

She breathed out hard through her nose. 'Anu Singh puts on acts!' she said. 'Let *me* up there! *I'll* tell them she puts on acts for Daddy!'

They trudged off to file their copy from the so-called Media

Room, a narrow windowless cupboard full of computers and phones.

I walked into the toilets and found Mrs Cinque there again, at the mirrors, skilfully outlining her lips with pencil. We greeted each other. She seemed open to conversation. I asked for her phone number and she gave it to me. She watched me copy it into my notebook, and said tentatively, 'In couple months I got to go overseas. I had a very bad operation on my foot, I have to get it fix. But after that, in a few months . . .'

Again the formal nod, the sustained eye contact, the sombre smile. She snapped shut her large leather bag and went out the door with her slow, stiffened gait.

When the court rose that day, while I was still crouched on my chair scribbling notes, Dr Singh stepped down from the gallery and into the well of the court where his daughter was speaking with her lawyers. Seeing him approach, she turned slightly towards him, smiled, and said, 'Okay, Dad.' At the same time she made a spontaneous fence in front of her waist, with her two hands bent sharply back at the wrist and her palms towards him: *Back off.* As both a daughter and a parent I felt the stinging whack of that gesture.

I caught up with Dr Singh on the shallow stairs, just inside the big doors. I introduced myself as 'a writer' who 'might want to write something about this trial'. I offered my hand and he took it: his was very dense, warm and dry. I told him who I wrote for and his face brightened. 'Come outside,' he said.

Out there in the lobby I was awkwardly aware of the Cinque

family, three metres away at the water cooler. I hoped Mrs Cinque wouldn't change her mind about me if she saw me speaking to Dr Singh. He was a big, blustery man and he spoke with energy and eagerness, leaning down to me: a great rush of words surged out of him. I could see his thick dark lashes, the glistening pale skin at the corners of his eyes: was it moistening with tears?

'We want people to *know* about this story!' he said. 'We want it to be a *warning*! You see that poor girl over there –' (it took me a couple of beats to realise he meant Mrs Cinque) '– sometimes she's angry. I don't blame her. *I'm* not angry. I know my daughter will go to gaol. When we heard Joe was dead we were *devastated*. He would come to our house! She was going to *marry* him! We will give you an interview. As long as you like. We will *all* speak to you.' He patted his pockets for a card. 'It would have to be in Sydney.'

'I live in Sydney. Give me your card tomorrow.'

But he did not want to let me go. He began vehemently to criticise Dr Hayes. 'She was trying to please the prosecutor! She does not concede that eating disorder and depression are linked! This has been scientifically proved but she does not concede it! She's a psych*ologist*. We don't think much of psychologists. We prefer psych*iatrists*. You must hear both sides! If you only hear the injured party's side – this mother here – she is angry because her boy is dead. But our daughter –'

He got himself under control, and stepped back with a tense smile and a nod.

I picked up my bag and headed for the street. Hearing a woman's voice as I passed the water cooler where Mr and Mrs Cinque were standing, I glanced back and saw the good-looking young fellow, with well-cut dark hair and a wedding ring, lean back from their tight group in a burst of laughter. What a strong family they must be.

The April evening was warm. Drifting through Civic, I climbed a flight of stairs to a Japanese restaurant, took a table and ordered something clean and delicate to eat. While I waited, tired out from a day of writing at speed, of trying to follow the battling arguments, my thoughts slid vaguely to Anu Singh, this young woman whose horrible deed had seized my imagination in such a troubling way. What was she doing now? Out at Belconnen Remand Centre. With slop for food. Under harsh fluorescent strips.

And Joe Cinque is dead.

The next morning I was standing in the sun outside the court building when the dark young man who often sat next to Mrs Cinque rocked up to me with his hand out. 'Hullo,' he said. 'We haven't met, but I've heard you're taking an interest. My name's Harry Hains.'

'Oh! I thought you were the Cinques' other son!'

He laughed. 'No! I'm the police officer in the case.'

Close up I could see the Australian Federal Police logo on the tip of his tie, but it took me a moment to shift my preconceptions. 'I saw you being so nice to Mrs Cinque – I thought –'

He shrugged. 'They've had a very hard time. I've got quite a close relationship with them. Been up and down to Newcastle.' He was smoking, but politely, holding the cigarette down low behind him, out of sight. He looked young, maybe in his late thirties, and his face was smiling and mobile, with warm brown eyes and a lively expression. I didn't know there were detectives like this: I lived near Kings Cross, where they had a different reputation.

'There's definitely something wrong with the girl,' he went on, 'but there's something wrong with all of us. None of us have got a perfect personality. None of us would say we'd never hated anyone. But . . .'

He took a furtive drag on his cigarette. When he breathed out, the skin around his eyes contracted into fine wrinkles.

'What about the other woman,' I said, 'Madhavi Rao? How does she fit into the story?'

He looked around. People were stirring themselves and walking into the building. 'Wait for her trial,' he said, dashing out his smoke. 'You'll see.'

That morning the last of the four psychiatric expert witnesses was called to the stand. When I had first spotted this tough-looking man, with his designer stubble and short greying hair, louring against a wall outside the courtroom, I had idly cast him as Greek or Lebanese, and probably a detective, he was so dark and hulking and self-contained, so perfectly at ease in the outer chamber of a criminal court. But his name turned out to be Dr Michael Diamond, and the minute he opened his mouth, his nipped-off consonants and fastidious vowels placed him as a South African. He was a graduate in medicine from the University of Cape Town who practised as a psychiatrist in North Sydney. He settled his considerable bulk into the chair, dropped his chin on to his chest, and studied his interlocutor from under his brow.

Diamond shifted seamlessly between technical vocabulary and ordinary moral language. It was startling to hear him throw round terms like 'immature and dramatic display' or 'superficial, glib attention-seeking'. He didn't accept that Anu Singh thought she was dying. He didn't agree with Professor Mullen's emphasis on 'masked depression'. And he was not convinced that when she killed Joe Cinque she was suffering from a significant abnormality of mind.

He was more interested in her borderline personality disorder, her eating disorder, and her body image disturbance. She could think all right, he said, and she could reason. Where her real impairment lay was in *the process of maturing*. She couldn't handle complex emotions. She couldn't withstand a less than perfect body image. She couldn't resolve conflict in her life in a mature way. She couldn't maintain composure, or control her moods.

And he took a very tough view of the frantic phone call to Bronwyn Cammack when Joe Cinque lay dying. He quoted Singh's response to Cammack's enraged command: '*I can't call the paramedics. I gave him the drugs. He doesn't know. He'll be furious.*' The reasoning behind this was not disordered, he said. It was focused and purposeful. Her fantasy was that she could be *rescued*. She was trying to get her friend to reverse what she had done, so as to keep it away from the authorities. It was clear and callous reasoning, he said, at an intensely distressing time.

Of all the four expert witnesses, Diamond was the one whose demeanour was least affected by the change in tone between examination and cross-examination. Nothing piqued or rattled him. There was something immovable, almost sphinx-like about him in the witness chair, a massive, stable repose. He sat there unperturbed while Pappas strafed him from left and right.

'Is borderline personality,' said Pappas, 'an abnormality of mind?'

'I don't accept that,' said Diamond. 'It's a disorder of psychological development that occurs very early in life. There are people with borderline personality disorder who have no problem with their *mind*. But they can *exhibit* abnormality of mind, particularly when they're threatened with abandonment. They lack a secure and developed sense of self to rely on in times of difficulty. They feel susceptible to annihilation – that they might fail to exist.'

'Borderline personality disorder,' said Pappas, 'is not a transient condition, I take it?'

'Personality *per se*,' said Diamond bluntly, 'is not transient. We are who we are.'

Diamond tackled the conundrum at the heart of the story: the fact that Singh had talked so obsessively about killing herself and yet had ended up killing someone else. The whole scheme, he said, with its support roles and large cast of extras, had been a tremendous drama she was staging – part of her narcissistic need to be taken seriously and helped. She derived so much gratification from being at the centre of this drama that the point was *not* to commit suicide.

'The purpose is not death,' said Diamond. 'Death here is almost ignored. The purpose is to keep the drama going for as long as possible. Look at the business of arranging the dinner party – assembling the gathering, putting energy into it. But when the support and feedback is suddenly no longer available – and when the moment comes for her to inject *herself* – the whole thing evaporates.'

Steady and calm, sunk in his chair with his hands clasped easily in his lap, Diamond argued Pappas back against the wall about the depressive illness that the defence psychiatrists had diagnosed in Anu Singh. 'Depression,' he said, 'is fairly responsive to medication. According to her medical records, she took four months of Prozac with no response. She was a narcissistic person in terrible distress –'

Mrs Cinque cut across him in a low, bitter voice: '*Bullshit.*'

'– who tenaciously sought help, but never pursued it or undertook any form of treatment. What she did was, she *consulted*. She had her beliefs challenged and she moved on. This is *not* the way people with profound depression respond. The subjective experience of depression is unbearable. It's very difficult *not* to reach out for help.'

Justice Crispin leaned down from the bench and addressed Dr Diamond. 'I just wonder, though, Doctor,' he said, in an oddly dogged tone. 'What if somebody who really believes they're dying goes to a doctor. What if the doctor says to them, "I can't find out what's killing you, but hey – I'll refer you to a psychiatrist who'll make you feel happier while you die"? Would the patient really say, "Okay – I'll have some psychiatric treatment so I'll be cheerier as I cark it"?'

A thought flashed across my mind. I forgot it at once, but years later there it was, scribbled in the margin of my notes. *He's going to send her home.*

The following morning the two barristers summed up. Perhaps it was the absence of a jury to impress with grand, passionate rhetoric that made the final speeches so pedestrian and anti-climactic. The story dwindled to a halt. Justice Crispin promised a judgement 'sometime next week', and adjourned.

I stayed in my seat and watched Anu Singh, with her hair well bound and wearing a long, fluttery skirt, thank Mr Pappas and his solicitor. She shook hands with them, using the two-handed grip that denotes ardent sincerity. She smiled at each man and managed to speak to him a few intense words before her guard led her away. Again I noticed her odd, erect, slightly bouncing walk as she was ushered rapidly up the stairs and out through the double doors into the lobby. Much later, watching the animated movie *Toy Story* with my grand-daughter, I would be reminded of Singh's gait by that of Buzz Lightyear at the moment when he sees on TV a commercial for himself, and realises that he is not a unique and invincible intergalactic superhero but merely a mass-produced plastic doll labelled MADE IN TAIWAN. It was the walk of someone desperately trying, against a total collapse of self-image, to maintain *bella figura*.

I turned to leave the court and saw that the quieter of the two journalists, the fair-haired one, had been sitting behind me, also watching. We looked at each other, but did not speak. We were the last to go.

The driver of my cab to the airport told me that he had spent six and a half years in the police force. He had left because he 'wanted to become a human being again'.

'What made you feel you'd stopped being human?'

'Ooooh,' he said, thinking as he drove, 'if I saw a dead body it'd be . . . well, not exactly a *joke*, but . . .'

'Do you mean you'd become hard?'

'Not hard. More . . . that I'd seen everything. Nothing could surprise me any more. There was no joy left in life. And as soon as I realised that, I said to myself, Right. Time to get out. And I went back into hospitality. Motels – relief managing, for a chain. The wife and I went all over Australia. Never stayed anywhere for more than eight days. We had two suitcases, that was all. We *loved* it. One day we'd be in Dubbo, the next in Armidale. It was *great*.'

He told me he was forty-two, but he looked much younger: a tough, handsome bloke, who laughed and smiled a lot, as if he enjoyed being alive.

What would become of D-C Harry Hains? How could that warmth and openness last?

✂

At home in Sydney, life lost its forward impetus and became limp and pointless. My mind slackened off again into self-obsession and regret. My family was far away, my friends busily absorbed in their own affairs. The only thing that could drag me out of my own cramped sorrows and shove me into the reality of other people was the story of Joe Cinque's murder.

As the week between the trial and the judgement dragged along, I became restless. I paced, I ate lollies, I scrubbed every surface in the flat, I washed clothes that weren't dirty, I got up at four in the morning and heaved furniture from room to room. I wasn't just worried about getting back to Canberra on time. I was agitated by the prospect of a solemn judgement on the meaning of a woman's life.

Do we identify with a criminal in that we too secretly long to be judged? Popularly, being 'judgemental' is ill thought of and resented. But what if we want our deeds, our natures, our very souls to be summed up and evaluated ? A line to be drawn under our acts to date? A punishment declared, amends made, the slate wiped clean? A born-again Christian, trying to explain his new sense of freedom, once said to me, 'All my debts are paid.' Anu Singh, with her 'promiscuity', her frantic need to be found attractive by men, her 'using up' of men and 'throwing them away'; her perhaps turbulent relationship with her father; her blaming of a man for everything that was wrong in her life; her crazed desire for revenge on him; her lack of empathy with others, her self-absorption, her narcissism: I was hanging out for judgement to be pronounced on *such a woman*.

By mid-week I had taken a punt that Justice Crispin was the sort of bloke who liked his desk to be clear by Friday afternoon: I booked a flight and a hotel. On Thursday afternoon the DPP called me and said they were 'ninety-five per cent sure' that the judgement would be delivered the next day. I threw skin cream and a toothbrush into a bag and took a cab to the airport.

In Canberra the late April air was bright and dry. I checked into my hotel and walked to Garema Place. Even on a pleasant autumn afternoon the enormous plaza, designed at some more innocent era of the city's history, was made squalid by the drifts of anxious junkies, distracted by their searching, who congregated round the phone booths at the top of the rise near the bus termi-nal. At five o'clock the temperature dropped and there was a dark edge to everything. I turned a corner on my way back to the hotel and saw in the west a pure sky with one tiny orange cloud float-ing in it.

Does a person get any sleep at all, on the night before her acts are to be judged?

The next morning was fine and sunny. I walked along North-bourne Avenue towards the court. I didn't feel good. There was something wrong with my stomach. I had a general sensation of bodily disturbance. Was it loneliness, as usual, or was I coming down with something? Could I be gearing up for a heart attack? The first person my eye fell on, in the lobby of the Supreme Court, was Dr Singh. At the sight of him I understood what was wrong with me: I was sick with suspense. I greeted him and he spun round to face me.

'What view will you take?' he cried, almost babbling with tension. 'What view? From what view? You must write it from the point of view that it is not a game! People say, "Oh, he's a doctor. He got the best psychiatrists for her" – but if it was a game, would we have called the Mental Health Crisis Team? Would we? Would *you?*'

I asked him for his phone number. He rattled it off and rushed away.

Inside, the courtroom was transformed. During the fortnight of the trial proper, observers had been few and far between, but today the public gallery was packed. The greater volume of flesh and clothing and shoe leather produced a different acoustic: the ceiling felt lower, the air denser, harder to breathe.

Anu Singh was brought in. Instead of her customary single guard, she had today an escort of two: a wild-eyed, thuggish-looking fellow on one side, and on the other a woman with straw hair. Anu Singh's own hair was shinier, less tightly clumped on the nape of her neck. She was dressed in a dark jacket and trousers, and high backless shoes. She looked smaller. She did not cross her legs, but placed her feet neatly side by side, then lowered her head and fidgeted with her fingers.

The tipstaff behind the velvet curtain rapped a warning on the floor. Justice Crispin entered on a tide of seriousness, not with his habitual hasty sweep, but slowly, almost grandly, looking sombre as always, but also paler, and with his head held higher, giving more eye contact: offering his face. He bowed and sat down. Laying his papers on the bench before him, he raised his eyes to the room, and launched into it without prologue or preamble.

'I find the defendant not guilty of murder,' he said, 'but I find the defendant guilty of murder.'

Mrs Cinque uttered a choked cry.

A stunned, thick silence filled the court. What? *What* did he say? How can she be guilty of murder and yet *not* guilty of murder?

Mr Pappas leapt to his feet. 'Your Honour,' he said. 'I believe your Honour has made an error. You said "Guilty of murder", but with respect, your Honour, you meant "Guilty of *manslaughter*".'

Three beats. No one breathed. The judge had made a colossal, clanging Freudian slip.

Crispin raised his head. His face was blank with shock. With a lawyer's reflex he muttered, 'I withdraw that.' He pulled the document to him and read out the judgement again, correcting himself emphatically: 'I find the defendant not guilty of murder, but I find the defendant guilty of *manslaughter*.'

The dead man's mother burst into wild sobs. D-C Hains, who was sitting right behind her, laid his flat palm against her back and held it there.

Justice Crispin set the date for the sentencing hearing: 21 June. More psychiatric evidence, he said, would be presented on that day.

Mrs Cinque covered her face and wept aloud.

'The judgement,' said Justice Crispin, 'is fifty pages long. You'll need time to read it.'

He got to his feet and so did we. He bowed; we bowed. He strode out.

Mr Pappas turned from the bar table to where Anu Singh was sitting between her guards. This time there were no handshakes. A cluster of men in dark suits and black robes closed round the young woman. I glanced down to scribble in my notebook. When I looked up, Anu Singh's metal-framed chair and those of her escorts were being brusquely moved aside. Two uniformed sheriffs bent over the piece of floor on which the chairs had previously stood, where the little handles were recessed into the carpet. The two men inserted their forefingers into the metal loops, gripped them, and lifted. I saw what they were for: a whole section of the floor reared up on hinges, revealing, at an acute angle, the bare timber planks of a staircase. The two guards guided Anu Singh towards the trapdoor. She stepped into the hole. Down she went, with her head bowed. The last thing to disappear was her hair, bound in its thick club.

Mrs Cinque stood in the front row of the public gallery, barely an arm's reach from the hole in the floor. In a hoarse, wild voice she cried out; she cursed the descending girl. '*This* is where you belong. You stay. For *ever*. Rot in hell, you bitch. *Devil*.' The girl was already too deep to be seen. The floor closed over her and became once more a rectangle of carpet.

People pressed into the aisles and up the shallow stairs to the doors. A sheriff was handing out copies of the judgement. I grabbed one and pushed out into the lobby. The crowd was moving sluggishly away and out towards the open air. I staggered to a chair against the wall. The Singhs – father, mother and a teenage brother I had not seen before – moved past me slow and swimmingly, like figures in a dream. The boy looked devastated and puffy-eyed. The mother, shell-shocked, somehow maintained her dignity, eyes down, dark-faced, inward. Dr Singh caught my eye and made a formal nod to me, almost a bow.

One of the young reporters hurried past me: 'I'm gonna go file.'

Out on the broad front steps of the Supreme Court, in blinding dry sun and chill air, the TV and radio journalists swarmed in a tight gang: the older cameramen in jeans and boots, silently lugging the heavy gear on their shoulders; the jabbering young journos in their power suits and gelled hair and make-up, yelling to each other, tossing their harsh jests back and forth.

'So!' said a sleek girl of twenty, with a shrill, cynical laugh. 'He bought her story!'

'Manslaughter still gets twenty years, though,' murmured a less glamorous young woman, pressing her notebook to her chest. 'She could be in for quite a while.'

Twenty years! Stunned, I got the sum wrong: I thought, She'll be *my* age by the time she gets out. Filled with an obscure shame, I slunk around behind the jostling mob and lurked on the lower steps, pretending to be only a passer-by. I tried to stay near the camera crews; I was comforted by their closed mouths, their stoical detachment. A sheriff came out through the revolving glass door and announced that the Cinques had been taken out of the building by a back door. There was no one to wait for now but the Singh family. I couldn't take any more of this. I turned away, gripping Justice Crispin's judgement under my arm, and jogged across the plaza to a line of saplings in large pots. With my back to the court I crouched against the cold concrete rim of a planter box and howled into my hanky. I didn't even know who I was crying for.

By the time I had pulled myself together and crept out from behind the potted hedge, the journalists had dispersed. I climbed the deserted steps and cut through the Supreme Court lobby. Already the entry to 'our' courtroom was teeming with a fresh cast of characters: the same weird horse-hair wigs and scholarly gowns, but inside them different barristers, ready to prosecute and defend different people, to conjure up a whole new variation on the eternal themes.

How soon even a frightful event like Joe Cinque's murder is swept away into the past! Something in me rose up, indignant for him. What – not even a decent, respectful pause? No breathing space? On, on rushes time, without hesitation, without mercy.

And yet the matter still hung unresolved: two months must pass before his killer would be sentenced, and the trial of Madhavi Rao, the second accused, was not even slated.

PART THREE

As soon as I got home to Sydney I caught one of those convenient stinking colds that hit freelance workers at times when they need to think rather than write. I crawled into bed with the judgement, a hot-water bottle and a stack of clean hankies, and stayed there for a week. Nobody came near me. I slept at odd hours of the day and night. Whenever I woke, I picked up the fifty-four-page document and tackled it again.

A jury, I realised, is not required to give reasons for its verdict, but a judge must account for his. I racked my brains, trying in vain to get a handle on the bizarre tale it told. It wasn't only the cold that made my concentration lurch about and fail to grip: it was the events themselves, flickering and sliding away from my intelligence. Every time I thought I had finally got the hang of their sequence, I would come across a detail that blew my understanding of the thing sky-high. The hardest thing was to believe that people like these were capable of such acts.

And it began to dawn on me that though Joe Cinque died at lunchtime on a Sunday, *it took practically the whole weekend to kill him*.

I called Dr Singh. Yes, he remembered me. I reminded him of our conversation about a possible interview. He became wary.

'What would be the *meaning* of your story? Every story has a meaning.'

I gave a bumbling reply: I didn't know yet; I was still trying to understand what had actually happened, let alone what it meant. There was a brief silence as he absorbed this. Then, in his slurring, rapid, husky voice, hitting the odd high note for emphasis, he began to speak.

'Because Helen, in Anu's case there was *no vendetta*. I tell it to you in a nutshell. Joe was going to become my *son-in-law*. They were going to get *married*. There was no vendetta against Joe. It was all due to her psychotic delusions. This is a girl who went to many, many doctors but none of them could diagnose her! *We* knew. *We* rang bloody Mental Health! My wife knew! She said, "My daughter is moving towards psychosis! This state can become suicidal! Homicidal!" But in this country I can't – I can't schedule her. I can't *schedule* her. You know what schedule is? You know what it is?'

'Commit.'

'Yes! I can't schedule her!'

Like a gospel preacher setting up call-and-response, he spoke in staccato stabs, establishing a strong rhetorical beat and leaving a pause after each sentence for my endorsement. Spontaneously I picked up his rhythm and began to utter brief sounds at appropriate moments.

'That judge,' he said. 'He knows about psychiatry! He was judge for the Chelmsford Deep Sleep Therapy case! I bet that man has studied a lot! I bet he's gone through . . . When this case is over, I may write something myself. I may write a book! Maybe a little movie! So people can *know*! What can *happen*! She was a happy-go-lucky girl! Beautiful girl! Beautifully dressed! Who went to clubs!'

A book? A little movie? Went to clubs? Mesmerised by his way of speaking, I sat there at the high window with the phone to my ear, looking out at the rain, the trees losing their leaves, the tall mist coming in from Bondi to blot out the coast and fill the valley. Dr Singh talked on and on in urgent bursts, as if leaning over me, haranguing me, and all the while, in a sort of half-stunned dream, I kept up my end, playing my supporting role: *Huh, mmm, huh:* wordless sounds that meant no more than *You're speaking, I'm listening.*

He paused for breath and I woke from my trance.

'Perhaps I should send you one of my books?'

He told me his address and made me promise not to give it to anyone. As soon as we had hung up, I crawled along the bottom bookshelf and hunted out copies of *The First Stone* and *True Stories.* While I was wrapping them for the post I thought that I should send them to Mr and Mrs Cinque as well: I had to do the same for both sides, and to make it clear to each family that I was speaking to the other. Everything was starting to get complicated. I took two more copies off the shelf and made a second parcel.

The next day, having to push against a powerful resistance, I called the Newcastle number Mrs Cinque had given me. Her husband answered. I introduced myself and mentioned the trial. A silence fell. I asked to speak to his wife. There was a rapid murmuring of Italian in the background, then Mrs Cinque, very cautious, came to the phone. I told her my name and reminded her of our meeting in the Supreme Court toilets. Her voice lightened a little.

'I remember you now. I see you talking to her father. You know how I feel about him.'

I suppressed an urge to apologise. She paused, then drew a quivering breath, and out of her poured the first gushes of a cataract of pain.

'We are devastated. We are in a mess. We spent thousands and thousand of dollars travelling up and down for what I rudely call this *bullshit* in the courts. We had to have a motel room in Canberra for thirteen weeks. We're nearly broke. If it was me I'd hang her right outside the court. But you can't do that, because we live in a country where – where justice –' Her voice flagged, then rallied. 'We trust the courts to do it – and she gets manslaughter. *Manslaughter!* Manslaughter's when you drive in the street and have an accident. We're so angry with justice – you got no idea.

'The morning after the judgement, my son is on the front page of the paper here in Newcastle. They say he use drugs. But he no use drugs! He's civil engineer, he has successful career, he has nothing to do with drugs.

'I've always got fresh memory – like it happened yesterday. This law student who sold her the drugs – who teach her how to inject – he got his name suppressed. *He sold her the drugs!* While my son was dying he sold her *more* drugs, and my son dies. All these law students, eight, nine – they know what she's doing – for three days they do nothing! And now they're all working as lawyers and my son is dead.

'If you know my son, what sort of man he was! He was not an angel. He had his faults, like everybody. But he appreciate very much what we did for him – Catholic school, university – we pay. He was naïve, that's all. He didn't believe she was going to do it. He must have thought she was just gonna try and get him on drugs, that's all. But she was the devil. My friend was talking about the devil and I said to her, "Don't take the devil lightly. The devil's not ugly. *The devil's not ugly.*"

'She deprive me of everything. He had no children. I will never be grandmother of his children now.' She began to weep. 'He loved children so much. Now people will forget him. They go on, they have their children, *they forget him*. I will fight till my dying day,' she said, but the threat was so vague, and her voice so weakened by tears, that it was no more than a tiny fist being brandished, a very long way away.

With the hanky in my hand, I waited. She composed herself. 'If you write a book,' she said, 'can it make trouble for us?'

'I can't promise to write the book you want, Mrs Cinque,' I said. 'I'd have to listen to both sides. I would never want to do anything that made you suffer more – but I can't promise not to – because whatever *anyone* writes will hurt you.'

She heard me without protest. This is a woman, I thought, who has learnt to ask very little of life.

'We pay his way through uni,' she said, 'but if you do this book – if there is profit – I want maybe a scholarship? To help somebody? I want people to remember him. Something in his name. So – you think – ?'

Her awkward suggestion wrung my heart.

I called Dr Singh at his clinic.

'You understand, Helen,' he said in his rapid, slurring accent, 'that nothing has yet been resolved. You understand that until after the sentencing we can't say anything. But if you wanted to write a book about her, I would be prepared to help pay for the publication of it.'

'Oh, that wouldn't be necessary, Dr Singh,' I said, trying to conceal the sting to my pride. 'I'm sure I wouldn't have any trouble getting it published.'

A book *about her.* A book *about my son.*

That afternoon, as I was rubbing out my underlinings in Justice Crispin's judgement so as to photocopy clean pages for Mrs Cinque who, incredibly, had not been given or sent a copy, my eye fell on a passage Crispin had quoted from a 1996 decision in NSW, *R v Gieselmann*:

> Whilst the behaviour of the accused could legitimately be taken into account in determining whether she had been suffering from an abnormality of mind, abnormal or outrageous acts could be seen as the result of other things such as stupidity or *simple wickedness.*

I sat and stared at the words. What is 'simple wickedness'? Does such a thing exist? Was there ever such a thing, or did it die with the arrival of psychiatry?

On 3 June 1999 I hired a car in Kings Cross and drove up the F3 to Newcastle, where the Cinques lived in the southern suburb of Charlestown. Their house stood at the top of a hill, on a wide, rather bare street. It was a two-storey red brick building with Italian-style arches, a balcony, and a facade that included the roller-doors of a double garage. Outside its front door, on well-trimmed buffalo grass, grew a thick, pointed, dark-foliaged cypress tree.

I rang the bell. A woman's voice called out, 'Hullo?' I stepped back and saw Mrs Cinque leaning over the balustrade above my head. She was smiling.

At the door she shook my hand and invited me in. The raging figure of the courtroom was transformed, on her home ground, into a welcoming housewife pleasantly clad in dark jumper, pants and flat shoes. The front hall was dim, with a terrazzo floor, a mirrored coat-stand, and a staircase elbowing away to the upper storey. Mrs Cinque led me into a living room whose brick walls were hung with family photos and trophies. Here she stopped and faced me, and got straight to the point.

'I got two videos of Joe,' she said. 'You want to see 'em? I'll make some coffee.'

She settled me on a velvet-covered sofa and withdrew through an archway to the kitchen. While I waited for her, I couldn't help looking at a large hand-tinted photo that hung in a frame near the window. It must have been taken around 1970: a head-and-shoulders portrait of Maria and Nino Cinque on their wedding day. They were young, their features were soft, they were smiling. At first glance I saw it as a record of simple, formal happiness; but as I gazed at it, it seemed to me that the face of the bride, a pretty woman with long hair parted in the middle and drawn back under a lace veil, was so bright with energy that she seemed to be leaning forward in the frame, ready to leap out into the world of her future. *Now I am a wife!* said her eager expression. *I will be a mother!*

Mrs Cinque soon returned, carrying on a tray two tiny cups of espresso. The VCR was loaded and primed to go. She handed me my coffee, sat down and aimed the remote. The first video was in blurry black-and-white. It showed a rock & roll band crammed on to a proscenium stage in what looked like a school hall.

'That's him,' said Mrs Cinque. 'The singer.'

A thin, shy, cheerful-looking teenager with unruly hair capered about, gripping a microphone in one hand and keeping the other wedged in his jacket pocket. His shoulders were stiff, his movements awkward and constrained. The hapless band battered away merrily behind him, giving 'Twist and Shout' a thrashing, and he yelled the tune with neither rhythm nor melody.

'His voice is *terrible*,' said his mother with an agonised laugh. 'He was eighteen. He didn't want me to see this video for years, he was so embarrassed.'

The film cut out suddenly, and she loaded the other. This one, in colour and much more competently shot, showed a big Italian wedding reception in a hall decked with balloons, flags and streamers.

'Look,' said Mrs Cinque. 'Joe's the MC.'

Again he was holding a microphone, but the scrawny, jigging youth of the first video had grown into a young man with the authority and the presence to run a large formal event. The messy schoolboy hair was cut now in a manly style, and severely, so that the hard lines of his well-shaped skull were visible.

While the video rolled, Mrs Cinque kept up a low murmur that required no response from me. Her tone kept changing, according to what was happening on the screen: she shifted from simple information to fond pride, from deeply possessive maternal devotion out into irony and savage bitterness, then back again to a gentle, sorrowing regret.

'That's the tie I put on him . . . *She* was invited to the wedding but she wouldn't go . . . Joe was so good with people. He couldn't stand smart-arses . . . Joe wouldn't buy take-away. I had to make his lunch. I used to peel his orange, cut it in four, then put the peel back on. And a man at his work say to him, *I can see that's a mother who did this lunch – a wife wouldn't do that* . . . He had beautiful hands, see? Loooooong fingers . . . but he always bite his nails. He always looked *young* . . . He could never stay still. I always tell him, *Calm down. Stop. Stay still.* He start to do architecture but he didn't want to stay inside – so he change to engineering. His sketches, I don't know how he did them because he couldn't sit still. When I saw him in his coffin – *then* he was still . . . I wonder if Crispin got a son like that . . . That scumbag, to make this decision. How can we accept this verdict?'

The newly-weds stepped out on to the floor and into each other's arms for the bridal waltz. They moved so slowly, enfolded in a blissful embrace, that they seemed almost asleep on their feet. Guests darted out to wind pink and lavender streamers round the dancing couple, cocooning them, mummifying them in love and paper.

A big black cat slid into the room and leaped on to Mrs Cinque's lap. She held it with tenderness, and stroked it.

'Joe had another girlfriend before he went overseas – Rebecca. After he passed away she came to see me. She put a big bunch of red roses on his bed. She said to me, "If only Joe would have loved me, I would've been the happiest girl in the world." What can you do. You can't tell your heart what to do. He was in love with *her* – I can't say her name. He was going to marry her. He was happy with her. Every time with her he laugh and smile. I called her a witch.

'I gave Joe a ring for his twenty-first birthday. He wore it to his uni exams, to bring him luck. I didn't put it on him, when he was ... when he ... *She* gave him a ring, her grandmother's wedding ring. He wore it on his pinkie. When I first see him at the – at the morgue – when I see that ring on his finger, I start screaming, *Get that ring off.*

'I didn't know till the trial that they had him for *three days.* When I hear that, I had another attack of screaming. For days, *for days*, nobody lift a finger.

'We went up and down to Canberra, just to hear *why.* What am I going to tell my mother, when I go back in Italy? Joe was the first grandchild on both sides of the family. He carried my grandfather's name. I don't know what I'm going to tell them.'

She sat with the remote in her hand and the dense cloud of darkness on her knee, and wept in silence. The tears slid off her face and disappeared into the weave of her jumper.

That first day, Maria Cinque and I spent seven hours in her kitchen, with the tape recorder clicking on and off between us. Her husband Nino came home late in the morning and took his place at the head of the table. He was a slightly built man of sixty or so, tanned and bespectacled, wearing a well-ironed open-necked shirt. He had kept his hair, though it was grey, and wore it combed back off his forehead in a wave. He was a smoker, with the cough to show for it. His manner was quiet and rather sweet, his natural expression a half-smile. Often, though, through the long afternoon, he would be overcome, and would have to leave the room abruptly and go into the garden, or step through the open archway into the living room and stand there for a moment, out of our line of sight; we could hear him, gasping and blowing out great lungfuls of air, like an athlete after a marathon run.

Their surviving son Anthony, a desperately thin young man in his early twenties, slept all day and rose desolate and paranoid, his face tormented with pimples: he drifted in and out of the room, smoking and seldom speaking. The big black cat, too, came and went. But Mrs Cinque stayed.

To call the encounter an interview would be to gild the lily. I was too bewildered by their story, and too shaken by their raging anguish and grief, to do much more than listen.

Yet the day was not shapeless. Underneath the machine-gun rattle of speech, the sobs and shouts of anger, the mourning cries, the curses, the incredulous whispers, and the long stretches of quiet weeping that sounded later, on the tape, like the soughing of a wind, there lay a solid foundation of courtesy. Wild with pain, half mad with it, they still thought to make a guest welcome. Mrs Cinque fortified us with brilliant espresso coffee. When I went to the toilet I found new soap and a fresh hand-towel. At noon she wiped her eyes, got to her feet, and asked with a smile if I would like something to eat. At five o'clock, Mr Cinque led me down the long, orderly back yard and we stood without speaking before his rows of shivering lettuces.

At half past five, as I was gathering up my things to drive back to Sydney, Mrs Cinque invited me to stay for tea. I hesitated, anxious that I had exhausted her. She pressed me. I accepted. While she cooked I got up from my place at the kitchen table and stood about, stretching my legs and watching her practised movements at the stove.

The time came for us to sit down. She called Mr Cinque and Anthony, but before they appeared, she whispered to me, 'Sit in *this* chair, Helen – sorry – don't sit next to Nino. That's where Joe always sit. Nino don't like it if anyone sit there.'

I looked at her in horror. For seven hours I had been sitting *in Joe's chair*, ignorantly making his father suffer; and they had been too polite to tell me.

It took me three days to transcribe the cassettes, hauling the tape back and forth, stabbing away at the buttons. I was appalled to hear my own contributions, the puny interventions I made, my impertinent attempts to inject hope, to modify savagery, to relieve tension. I sounded ignorant and shallow, a twerp with no experience of life. Mrs Cinque was three steps ahead of me the whole day. She had read my mind before I could open my mouth. She overmastered me at every point. Her voice was forceful, passionate, wild with bitterness and contempt, and heavy with the authority of suffering.

I had to take frequent breaks from transcribing, to run out of the building into the fresh air and walk fast up and down the hilly streets, because as I copied down their story, something inside me seemed to be breaking. Into my thoughts kept seeping fantasies of violent retribution. Of execution. What was happening to me? Like almost everyone I knew, I had always been 'opposed to the death penalty'. I had worn my 'belief' as a badge of decency and reason. But now I saw that I had never thought the matter through. I did not *want* to have to think it through. I didn't know how to start, and I was too scared of where I might end up. I put my head down and forced myself to keep typing.

❧

Joe Cinque and Anu Singh met in Newcastle towards the New
Year of 1995.

'Joe just came back from his overseas trip,' said Mrs Cinque, in
her husky, blurred voice. 'He start working for the same company
his father and grandfather used to work for. He was employed as
an engineering project manager. Couple weeks later, he went out
with his friends to the Brewery, a nightclub near the wharf here
in Newcastle. He met this Indian girl, who was studying in Canberra. She was home for the Christmas holidays. Her parents were
going to move down to Sydney.

'I got nothing against anyone, but when he said she was
Indian . . . I know the culture difference, I was worrying about it.
He says, "She's nice, I like her, she's very intelligent." And she
started to call on the phone.

'Joe used to come home from work about six o'clock for tea.
We haven't got a TV in the kitchen, because one thing I always
insist, we had tea together. Six to six-thirty was the special time –
we like to tell what happened to everyone during the day.

'But she start ringing up about quarter past six. Of course he
stop, he went to the phone for one, two hours. Every night. To
me was not normal to talk so long on the phone. One night he
went upstairs and I picked up the phone down here and I said,
very abrupt, "In this house we have tea from six to six-thirty – can
you please ring after that."

'That year, 1995, he started to go down to Canberra to see
her. He was going nearly every weekend. During the week he still
played a lot of sport, but he'd leave work in Newcastle on Friday
night, and come back Sunday night – two o'clock in the morning. I was worried sick about his driving all over, and he had to
go to work the morning after.

'She was very controlling, very bossy. She was calling at least

twice every night. Sometimes during the day I called his mobile and
he had it switched off. I go mad at him: "Why you have a mobile if
you have it switched off?" He never told me, but his boss told me
after that she was ringing and ringing, interrupting his work.

'I didn't meet her till the middle of 1996. Joe didn't tell me,
he just brought her here one day. They were going to play tennis.
They come to the door. I was doing the ironing. He say "This
is –" I can't say her name.

'When he came back that night he said, "What do you think
of her? Isn't she beautiful!" I said, "She's okay. She looks a bit
skinny." She *was* skinny. She was wearing jeans and a top. Even
though it was winter you could see her stomach. *He* thought she
was beautiful, anyway.

'Joe start to tell me at that time, she was having a problem
with eating disorder, she was throwing up, she was bulimic. He
took her to the doctor but the doctor could not find nothing
wrong with her.

'Before, Joe never miss one day university, one day work – but
couple of times he left work in the middle of the week to go to
Canberra and look after her.

'You know, the women talk more and the kids don't listen.
But Joe listen to his father. One time she call him, want him to fly
down there. Nino he say, "Look – her *parents* are doctor! Why you
want to go there?" "She sick, Dad." "Her parents can look after
her! *You're* not a doctor!" So that time Joe change the arrangement, he say, "I'm not gonna go."'

'Yes, but after another couple of weeks,' Mr Cinque broke in,
'she call him again, he go to the airport at Belmont, he take the
plane to Canberra – through the night! I was upset! Because he
working like a dog, here. First two years in a job, you got to put
your guts out, and he did! I say to him, "You are a man! Why you

go there for? Only because she whistle?" ' Mr Cinque sucked in a breath. 'Tssssssssss – I was so upset.'

'And the telephone!' said Mrs Cinque. 'I know when you're young and you're in love, but this was ridiculous! They were ringing and ringing each other – the phone bill go sometimes to seven, eight hundred dollars – just for *her*. Nino said, "I'm not gonna pay this phone bill!" and Joe goes, "*I'll* pay, *I'll* pay."

'Joe changed so much when he met her. He wasn't a happy, free spirit any more. I told my best friend Rosalba, "She's gonna end up taking Joe from us, from work, from his friends."

'That's the only time we argue, Joe and I, and Nino too – about *her*. I say, "She manipulate. She snap and you go."' She mimicked her son answering between clenched teeth. '"Don't *say* that, Mum! She *doesn't* do that." I say, "You're your own person. Don't let her control you like this." "Mum, please – don't make me choose. I love you but she needs me – I have to go there." But I say, "If she sick, and the doctor can't find nothing wrong with her, she just wants you there for *herself*." '

One of many things that enraged the Cinques about Anu Singh's defence was its stress on what they saw as the trivial problems of her early childhood, and its argument that these difficulties lessened her responsibility for her adult behaviour. Part of her father's evidence, for example, was that as a small girl she was unable to sleep except in her parents' room. The Cinques had their own story of childhood trouble: if the same reasoning were to be applied, they said, their two sons should be 'monsters'.

In 1979, when Joe was eight years old, the Cinque family had a very bad car accident. Another vehicle went through a red light and struck their car, which rolled. Joe was thrown clear, but Anthony was stuck behind his mother, bleeding and screaming; Mrs Cinque's left leg and foot were smashed (now, twenty years later, she still limps and has to take pain-killers every day), and Mr Cinque was knocked unconscious.

'People faint when they saw me in hospital,' Mrs Cinque told me. 'I was a mess. I was in intensive care, and then in hospital for three months. The boys had a lot of shock. I had to leave them behind so many times. When I went to Sydney for two months for an operation on my foot, a friend had to look after Anthony. He said, "Please, Mum, take me with you. Ask the doctor for a bed next to you. I will not do nothing. I'll sit there all day – please don't leave me behind." It nearly tore my heart out.

'Anthony had to have the light on in his room for years – he was scared of the dark. I took him to a psychiatrist in Sydney, because he remember how they had to cut the car to pull me out of the wreckage – he was only three years old. And now he's back in a mess again, because of what happened to his brother.'

Because they had no family in Australia, and because Mr Cinque, once he recovered, had to go straight back to work, Joe became 'the little man in the house'.

'He was only eight,' said Mrs Cinque, 'but he had to grow up quick. Anthony was a baby and Joe had to look after him. In a way I feel responsible. I was sick and in pain. I asked a lot of him: "You're older! You should know better than that!"

'He did it no problem, no complaint. He just *did* it. He could cook, he could do ironing. That's when he learnt to look after people.' The habits of care he was obliged to develop as a child, Mrs Cinque thought, fed into his relationship with the woman who was to kill him.

'He felt that she *needed* him. That he could take care of her and make her better. I think there was nothing wrong with her – she just pretended to be sick so she could hold him. It was the only way she could control him.

'When you're my age, you been through a lot. You know women, the way they act. *I'm* a woman – I'm not against. But you know the way they operate. I know exactly the way *she* operated. But Joe couldn't see that. He didn't *want* to see that. He was in love with her, and he thought he could make her better.'

The beginning of Joe's affair with Anu Singh was complicated by secrecy. 'Until he went down to live with her in Canberra,' said Mrs Cinque, 'Joe had never been to her parents' place. Her father didn't know about him. After she split up with the other man, Simon, her father said to her, "You gotta finish your study before you get involved with somebody." Joe warned us – in case her family ring up and ask who Joe was, we had to say he was "one of Tony's friends" – Tony's one of her brothers – he used to live with them down in Canberra. That was something I really could not accept.

'But around November 1996, when university finish, Joe brought her up here to stay with the family. She was polite and everything. She stay two, three weeks with us. She was perfect. Perfect girl. Dress properly. She help in the kitchen, wash the dishes. Joe tell me she didn't eat meat so I always prepare vegetarian food. Joe told her to look what I make – "That's what I like, dishes like that." And Joe tell Nino, "Just be careful when you talk to her. Don't say nothing chauvinist, because she's a feminist."

'Two months before he pass away, Joe wrote us a letter about the new car he got, how happy he was about it and his job, how much he loved us. "I can't wait till she finish her degree in November and then get married next year."'

'But deep down I knew she wasn't the right one for him. I tried very hard, but she just *upset* me.'

'You mean you kind of felt an instinctive thing?' I said.

'I swear to God I did.'

'Do you think maybe . . . When I look at the wedding photo I see those lovely Italian girls and I think . . . uhmmmm . . . what am I trying to say?'

'*I* know what you're trying to say,' said Mrs Cinque, very clear and loud. 'No! It was *not* because she was Indian. He had another girl before, Rebecca. *She* wasn't Italian. She was *Australian*. She was the most beautiful gorgeous nice girl. Used to work in the restaurant where he worked when he was studying. She gone to Sydney long ago, she's married now. Ohhh, she was wonderful. She like to get married and settle down. But Joe was only twenty-two. He was too young to get involved. He wanted to do a lot of things before – finish his study, go overseas. So when Rebecca was around he wasn't ready.

'When he came back from his trip we pick him up in the airport in Sydney, Nino and I, and he said, "Five dollars! That's all I got left!" He said he had the best time of his life. He says, "When your thirtieth wedding anniversary I'm going to send you to Greek islands! So beautiful! You gotta be there!"

'I dream of him only two nights after he pass away. And I said to him' – she imitated herself, strongly, like a mother – '*Where you been?* His hair was wet, just like he had a shower. *I told you, Mum – I been in Greece!* I said, *How did you get there?* He said, *Went by car!* Another time I dream of him and he said, *What happened to me, Mum?* I said, *She kill you, remember? After the party?* And he look at me, like he didn't know what happened to him.'

❧

Mr Cinque went out of the room and returned with a manila folder which he laid on the table in front of me. Confused, I opened it and shuffled through the papers.

'Whose are these? Phone bills? Credit card bills?'

'In court they tell,' he said, 'she never go nowhere, she stay home locked in her room, not eat, not go out. Not true. They went everywhere. See? Casino.'

'Joe told us,' said Mrs Cinque, 'they were going to the casino many times – at the casino, winning money, many times!'

'They went *everywhere*. They went shopping – in big shopping centre.'

'What about in court,' said Mrs Cinque, her voice rising. 'They say "She didn't look after herself, she didn't dress properly" – what rubbish that was! "Ten showers a day!" It's not true! She was here for two, three weeks, she never even had *two* showers a day. I can hear, when you open the water upstairs. She didn't have more than one shower a day. This pacing up and down – now I have to take a Valium to sleep, but before, I could hear a fly. If she pacing up and down, I could hear.

'And if she was bulimic, I never found any trace. When you're bulimic, you eat, you go to throw up after half an hour. She didn't. She sit here drinking –'

'Eating,' said Mr Cinque. 'Playing cards with us. In this house! At this table! She was laughing! We spent hours and hours. She wasn't going to the toilet to vomit. She was just going outside to have a smoke, because she never smoke in front of me — I *can* say that.'

'When she went out,' said Mrs Cinque, 'she dress properly. Elegantly! She put make-up. They went out, in the day and the night, and at least two, three times a week for tea. To restaurant. And what about holiday, Nino. They went on holiday. The Blue Mountains, Katoomba.'

I followed Mr Cinque's pointing finger, tracking the credit card entries: Jenolan Caves, Katoomba, Wentworth Falls.

'Jenolan Caves,' said Mrs Cinque, her voice quivering with scorn. '*I* never been there! Why they don't show *this* to the judge?'

'They didn't ask us nothing. We can't do nothing,' said Mr Cinque.

'When we saw her father go up there in the court, we were shocked. Because they told us the family cannot testify. Why was *he* allowed, then?' Mrs Cinque stood up at the table and began to shout. 'They say he could not talk as a doctor — so he had to talk as a father. *He's* a father — *I'm* a mother. Why not? *What's fair in this?*'

'We been at her parents' house one time,' said Mr Cinque, 'to a party. There was about a hundred and twenty, a hundred and thirty guests. We spent four hours there, from eight to twelve o'clock.'

'It was a beautiful party,' said Mrs Cinque. 'I know I say all the other things, but the party, I could not say otherwise — it was beautiful. The food, the service, the way they treat us. It was the first time I saw her dressed as an Indian.'

'Her mother was the one with the old idea,' said Mr Cinque. 'How you have to get married before you live with your boyfriend. But that night when we was over there at the party, she come and catch me and dance with me –'

'And *he* dance with *me*,' added Mrs Cinque.

'Ah, was beautiful. But this party was in April 1997. And in court we hear – one or two week after that, she ask Mancini and other fellows to get a gun for her! So she can kill herself and kill my son!'

'Around that time, March, April 1997,' said Mrs Cinque, 'Joe and her was here for the weekend. We had lunch on the Sunday. After, he came downstairs and said to me, "Mum, she wants to talk to you. Can you go upstairs on the verandah?" I was washing the dishes and he said, "*I'll* wash the dishes." I went upstairs.

'*She* could not sit down, but she say to me, "Sit down," and she started telling me about aaaaaaall her problems. She said, "I've had this thing crawling under my skin." She said her mother didn't understand her – said she felt close to me because I been sick for a long time so I could understand. And her leg was going like this all the time, jiggling. I thought, "She looks like she's on drug withdrawal." And I said to Rosalba the day after, "If I didn't know better I would say she's on drugs." That's one mistake I made – I didn't tell Joe.'

'Usually Joe rang me on a Friday,' said Mrs Cinque. 'But on the Friday before he pass away, 24th October, he didn't call. That Saturday he didn't call. Sometimes they used to go away on the weekend so I wasn't worried. Sunday the 26th I wait all day, then around five-thirty, I think if they gone away they must be home by now. And I rang his place.

'A strange voice answered the phone. I said "I must have the wrong number." He said, "Who you looking for?" I said, "Joe Cinque. I'm his mother – who are you?" He said "Constable Something." I said, "What the police doing in my son's place?" He said, "Just wait on the phone."

'And at the same time, somebody here in Newcastle knock on the front door. It was the police.

'I thought he was here to talk to my husband about an accident he had in the car that week. He says to me, "Are you Mrs Cinque?" I said, "Yes – do you want to talk to my husband about the accident? He's out the back." He said, "I want to talk to both of you."

'I called Nino and he came down from the yard. The policeman said, "Are you Mr and Mrs Cinque?" We say "Yes." "It's about your son Joe."

'Soon as he said that, I *scream* at him. "Go 'way. Go 'way. I don't want to hear you."

'The policeman says, "Your son has been overdose."

'Nino said, "*What?* Joe? You're joking. Not Joe. He never touch the stuff."

'Before the policeman say "A woman's been charged", I knew. I said, "*That witch has killed my son.*" I come inside screaming. I thought this – this – Let this *stop*.

'Nino didn't believe it till the day after. He was like a zombie walking around.

'Anthony comes home. He comes inside. There was all these people in the house. He put his fist through the door. He starts screaming, "*That bitch has killed my brother.*"'

'I've seen sometimes a documentary about the way the lioness defends the cubs,' Mrs Cinque said to me, that day in her kitchen. 'I was sitting here watching TV when my son was dying. I didn't do nothing. I didn't protect him. I should have stopped him. I should have broke his leg when he went down there to live in Canberra. He didn't want to listen to me.' Her voice loosened and broke into tears. 'She make me – she make me feel *like a failure*.'

'But – when they come here,' said Mr Cinque, with the strange gentleness that always softened his voice when he spoke of his son's visits, 'they look – happy. She say she love him, he love her, they was thinking to get married next year. When you hear things like this, when you see two young people kissing together all the time, touching together, what you think? You think, "Ah yes, my son is happy – good luck to him." If you start to go in between of them, it means you –'

Mrs Cinque cut across him: 'How many times I complain to you that Joe wasn't like he used to be? And you said, "Yes, but now he's a *man*. He's got *responsibility*." Every time I say something, Nino say, "Your son is not a little baby! He knows what he's doing. He's twenty-six years old. Why you calling him? Don't interfere! Don't ring too much!"'

'When *we* was married, you was twenty-one, isn't it?' said Mr Cinque. 'If something happen to us, why your mother have to know? You want to tell your mother?'

It was an unhealed wound between them, the difference between their styles of loving Joe: Mrs Cinque had had a gut sense from the start that Anu Singh was trouble, an instinctive bristling which her husband, wanting to respect his son's manliness and freedom, had put down to possessive mothering.

'When you are an adult, you are an adult,' he went on. 'She was twenty-five, he was twenty-six. They got their own life. They have to live together.'

'I knew she was no good,' said Mrs Cinque flatly.

'If she was no good, let *him* find out.'

'Yes,' cried Mrs Cinque with savage irony. 'We know that *now*!'

Her husband caught the charge of it, and fired up. He pounded the table-top with his flat hands. 'That's why she have to be *killed*! Because *nobody* can believe she done something like this – and she *did*. And she *say* "I did." She said "I killed him." She look at him dying. She look at him vomiting – people was disgusted when they see the photo – but *she* was there, she was around him, touching him – he was naked on the floor. We been in the house. We see all the blood on the floor.'

He was panting. The silence was electric. His voice dropped back suddenly to a gentle, almost plaintive note.

'My son haven't done nothing wrong. My son was innocent. Let them kill the son of the judge, the barrister. *Then* they understand.'

Silence, except for the hissing of the tape.

'When we talk like this to our friends,' said Mrs Cinque, 'they say' (she mimicked a tone of shocked rebuke), ' "That's *wrong*!"

'It's okay for other people to say "I don't believe in this! I don't believe in capital punishment!" I say to them, "Because *your* son hasn't been murdered yet. You wait till you're in *my* shoes, and *then* see if you think that." '

She was not ranting now, not shouting, but speaking quickly, lightly, firmly, with many pauses between her sentences; yet it would not have been possible to interrupt her, and one would hardly have dared, for she was laying out her deepest thoughts, the product of the long, dark brooding that accompanies unbearable pain.

'I can't even kill an insect. When I got a little grasshopper inside the house I took it back to the garden. I tried to get it drowned in the water but it kept coming back so I picked him up, I put him outside – I can't even kill that. But believe me – if I have my hands on *her*, nobody's gonna stop me. Not even the police gonna stop me.

'And if I find any of the Singhs on the street, I'm not gonna stop my car. They can put me in gaol – I don't care. Because they are responsible. They knew exactly what their daughter was like. If they took her to the psychiatrist, like they say they did, why didn't they tell us anything? My son was there with her. Why didn't they warn my son?'

'The next morning,' said Mrs Cinque, 'we got up at seven o'clock and they took us to the airport. We arrived in Canberra. Our godson Robert and his brother Nick were waiting for our plane. The detective Harry was there. He took us to the police station and talked to us. Then we met Gail, the policewoman.

'At the time I thought she just injected Joe and he die straight away. The police don't tell you everything. They tell you a little bit at a time.'

'Yes – it was only when I read the judgement,' I said, 'that I realised it took the whole weekend to –'

Mrs Cinque cut across me with great force. 'No no no!

The whole *week*! There was a party on the *Monday*. There were witnesses there who said they *went* to that party. They knew she was going to kill herself and Joe. And the judge dismissed that. He said not enough evidence. I don't know what's enough evidence. They gave Joe Valium. They tried to inject him.'

'What?' I stared at her. 'Even back then, on the *Monday*?'

'YES!' cried Mrs Cinque, frantic for me to grasp her point. 'Monday the 20th October! The day before that, on the Sunday, they were here and Joe asked me for some food, because they were going to have a party that night when they got back to Canberra, and he didn't have nothing ready. I said, "I haven't got nothing prepared – if you told me before, I make something" – but Joe said, "Don't worry, Mum, we'll get some fried chicken or something." They left here about two o'clock on Sunday the 19th, and that's the last time I saw Joe.

'He rang me the next day, on the Monday. I said, "How are you? You had the party last night?" "No, we didn't have one, Mum – we're going to have one late in the week."

'I don't think he even *knew* there was going to be a party on the Monday. Why did he tell me "late in the week" if he was going to have one that night?

'There were quite a few witnesses at the party on the Monday. Pappas asked one girl, "You went to the party, knowing she was going to kill herself and take Joe with her – you still went to the party?" And she said' (Mrs Cinque mimicked a tiny, feeble, girlish voice), ' "*Yes*." Pappas stand there, he says, "What kind of people are these?" '

'On Monday night,' said Mr Cinque, taking up the story in his careful English, 'when they had the first party, they give him just Valium tablets. When he was sleeping, he keep moving around – they can't reach, uhm –'

'Can't get the vein,' says his wife, holding back with an effort her urgent flow of words. 'This was said in court.'

Mr Cinque exploded again, beating his hand on the table in rhythm. '*They – said – this – in – court! Why the judge don't take notice of this?* On *Monday* they already made the first attempt to kill my son!'

'Joe wasn't stupid,' said Mrs Cinque. 'After the party on the Monday, if he knew she was trying to kill him, he would have left straight away.

'When we went to the house to get his stuff, the day after he passed away, we couldn't find his set of suitcases, his overnight bag, the hanger for his suits. None of this we find. My son dress beautifully. He had at least twelve good shirts, Country Road. But we only found two shirts. I said this to the police straight away: "Joe hasn't got his stuff. He was going to move out." '

'You don't think,' I said, 'that somebody just *stole* his stuff?'

'*When*,' said Mrs Cinque, challengingly.

'I don't know.'

Hard and fast she pressed me. 'When. She call the ambulance and the police come straight away. W*hen.*'

'Yes – okay,' I said, my voice fading.

'*When.*' She was fierce. '*WHEN.*'

I caved in. There was a pause.

'That's why I think he was gonna move out,' she said.

'You mean he was half moved out?' I asked. 'He'd started to move his stuff – he was trying to get away?'

'YES!' she cried. She limped into the next room and brought back a chunky appointments diary. 'Look. This is from his work. It was kept by the police till April this year. His diary said he was gonna leave her. On Monday 27th, here it is, look – "2 o'clock, get ready to move" – see? It's his own writing, you can see it right here. Then he's got an arrow down to six o'clock that night: "*Move urgent today.*" He must realise after the party on Monday 20th that there was something wrong. He was gonna move out. He was gonna move out, and she knew, and that's why she killed him.

'He didn't know nothing about the Friday party. If you had one on the Monday why you want to have another one the same week? So when he came home from work on the Friday, she had a party ready, and that's it. He never left.'

Towards tea-time Mrs Cinque got up from the table and set to work at the bench, preparing something for us to eat. For the first time her husband lost the shyness about his English that had been making him defer to his wife throughout the day: he began to speak at length, on his own account, into the tape recorder. His voice was low.

'We used to say in Italy, "Wifes and cows you have to buy from your own town" – because you know the girls, the way she look, the way she dress – and the cows, you know how much milk she make daily. You can't lie.

'When I was twenty I go to work in Germany. And then I read on the newspaper, if you like to go in Australia or Canada – you don't have to pay nothing. The ticket was free. So in the year 1967, September, when I was twenty-six and a half, I prefer to come in Australia. Maybe *this* was the mistake I done.' He uttered a tiny, soft laugh. 'The biggest mistake of my life.

'After one week I got a job as fitter in railway station in Red-fern. Time to see around. Sydney was beautiful. Then I change the job. I come here in Newcastle. On New Year's Day 1968, I been away to make some money so I can marry. I been in Western Australia for six months, and coming back to get married and start a family.

'At that time I was the only one fitter which was coming from Europe. In the year '69 they change all the inches in millimetric and I was on the top of everybody else.' Again the small, quiet, modest laugh. 'After all I wasn't a bad fitter. They try me, I was good.

'We try to grow a family, which we done. Every family suffer a little bit. Every family laugh, and every family enjoy, every family do things – but – never, never, never was I think anybody kill my son.

'I had an accident with a car. I saw people die on the job – falling down – I see a bottle of oxygen – When we were working, something can drop down, sometime wedges, sometime hammer, sometime a piece of steel. Anything can happen, and people get hurt.'

His voice dropped to an incredulous whisper. 'But you never – you think your family safe at home!

'You try to send your son into school, to change job – to don't do what *you* are doing, because you know your job is danger. You send your kids to school, to university. You suffer your life to help your sons.

'And then somebody else come in – a girl – and kill your son for nothing. *Wasn't* an accident. *Was* nothing burning. *Was* nothing in work. Just – she enjoy to kill my son.'

He laughed again, soft and ironic; he let out one of his shattering coughs, then took in a gasp of air and expelled it in a long, faint whistle.

'I think everything you can repair. But this – you can't do nothing – when you see your son dead and you can't help him. It's something which – I – I can't forget.'

From the bench his wife began to speak over her shoulder: the microphone picked up her words but the distance hollowed them. 'Nino one thing he always –'

But under her gush of confident, more fluent English, Mr Cinque lowered his voice and persevered, in a repeated whisper of disbelief: 'I can't forget. I *can't forget.*'

Part Four

Anu Singh had been found guilty of manslaughter, but two months passed before her sentencing hearing was held. On that day, 21 June, I flew to Canberra and ran into D-C Hains outside the Supreme Court, lighting a cigarette in the lee of the building. He was the sort of man who, when shaking hands, kept his elbow bent so you had to stand quite close to him.

'She could get as little as three years, you know,' he said. 'She's already been on remand for six hundred and three days. She could be out in a year from now.'

My jaw dropped and he laughed, then pulled himself up. 'Anyway it won't happen today,' he said. 'This is only a hearing. We're gonna hear more stuff. Another psychiatrist, and a parole officer.'

At that moment Anthony Cinque wandered up, in a loose dark jacket and sunglasses, smoking. There was something heart-stabbing in his smile. He was thin, wasted as if from within. He and Hains exchanged curt manly syllables.

'Is she really only gonna get three years?' asked Anthony.

'Mate. Mate,' said Hains quietly. 'Mate, you gotta keep cool in there. It's best for your family. Best for your parents.'

'I'm worried about Dad,' said Anthony.

'Listen,' said Hains. 'There's only one thing that'd change any-thing – if we could get Joe back. We all know that can't happen. So you gotta keep cool in there. It's what Joe would've wanted.'

'I'll keep cool,' muttered the young man.

'I know you will, mate. I know you will.'

I moved away, to let them talk in private. As I shifted my feminine sensibilities out of range, the detective's language coarsened. The boy stood nodding, nodding, twisting his mouth, tearing the smoke from his cigarette in great gulps.

What Joe would have wanted. It was only rhetoric. No one can know what punishment Joe would have thought fitting – the man who more than anyone, except her parents, had felt for his killer and pitied her, as she thrashed about in the cage of her own nature.

With what an urgent rush Anu Singh and her guard entered the court! They moved differently from ordinary people – a disturbance, a commotion in the air, and suddenly they were there. Behind me one of her family sighed as she whisked past them and seated herself. She was dressed in a charcoal trouser suit with a fitted jacket. Her toes, their nails glowing with dark red polish, peeped out of her high, strappy black sandals. Her hair in its thick club was banded in black. In one hand she held a dark blue handkerchief. Despite her sophisticated heels, her feet were placed neatly side by side, like a good little girl's.

The prosecutor who had conducted the Crown case, Terry Golding, was absent today. His job would be done by the Director of Public Prosecutions himself, Richard Refshauge, a tall, slender man in his forties with fair curly hair and long patrician cheeks.

I could not imagine what further material might be dredged up, but it turned out that three more people had something to say. As soon as Justice Crispin took his place, the Crown called the first of them, a man called Michael Ryan, a custodial officer at the Belconnen Remand Centre.

It appeared that Mr Ryan had 'come to know' Anu Singh at Belconnen.

'You see them every day,' he said. 'You wake 'em, you put 'em to bed, you feed 'em, you talk to 'em . . .'

One day Anu Singh had handed him a letter in the yard. He skimmed the first few lines and stuck it in his pocket, then later transferred it to his locker without reading it. From his locker it went, still unread, with other unsorted stuff to his garage, until a domestic clean-up in April 1999, when he had found it and read it properly at last. The next day he handed it to the police.

The five large, closely-written sheets were handed up to Justice Crispin. While he perused them, leaning his head on his hand, I glanced behind me and noticed that Anthony Cinque, instead of sitting beside his parents, was occupying the very end seat of the back row of the gallery, right next to Anu Singh's mother. I flinched at the thought of the psychic charge that must be zinging between them.

Justice Crispin explained that the letter was one Anu Singh had written, in some distress, shortly after certain other letters had been seized from her Belconnen locker and admitted as evidence in her trial. She believed that without the seized letters, which were damning, the Crown would not have had a case; in the letter now in the judge's hands, she had asked Custodial Officer Ryan to help her commit suicide.

This letter, said Mr Refshauge, was relevant to her sentencing in that it showed such a striking absence of remorse. Mr Pappas claimed rather wildly that just because no remorse was *expressed* didn't mean that no remorse was *felt*. 'A young woman,' insisted Refshauge, 'who has graduated Bachelor of Economics, who has arrived at final year in law, who has been highly successful in her academic and social studies, but who suffers from a personality disorder and a depressive illness, *and who writes that letter*, is not remorseful.'

The judge, with his head in his hands, pored over the letter. Anu Singh's mother sat in the back row beside the murdered man's brother. One would have described her as elegant had she not looked so traumatised. Her eyes were closed. Her tired face was tilted back on an angle of dumb endurance. The only sound in the room was the low roar of the air-conditioning. At last Crispin spoke. Nothing was said in the letter about remorse, and its contents were relevant – but it was not dated, and since he had admitted the earlier letters, written closer to the time of the offence, out it went, and out of the court went Custodial Officer Ryan.

The second person to give evidence was a Senior Parole Officer called Naomi Buick, a slender, fragile-looking blonde in her forties. She read aloud her report, which was based on over five hours of interviews with Anu Singh, and sketched briefly a fresh version of Singh's life story, adding a sprinkling of emotional details: during her affair with Simon Walsh, for example, she had become pregnant and had a termination, which had been 'traumatic' for her. 'Joe Cinque understood the cultural situation with her parents. She "misses him like crazy". He was possessive, constantly checking her whereabouts; she did not find this intrusive.' I remembered Mrs Cinque's complaints about the constant, driven, almost fanatical use of the telephone that had characterised their relationship right from the start. Perhaps they had been mutually obsessed, mutually anxious and distrustful; perhaps this was what they had thought of as love.

The account of her drug history that Anu Singh had given the parole officer was alarming. She had started in year ten with cannabis and alcohol, then at university moved on to acid, cocaine and speed. By June 1995, when she ended her relationship with Simon Walsh, she was taking drugs daily. She also used ecstasy and crystal meth, which caused hallucinations. Whenever she visited her parents (and Joe's parents too, I thought, recalling the twitchy scene on the verandah that Mrs Cinque had described to me) she ceased to use drugs; withdrawing had brought on depression – and perhaps, I wondered, also the behaviour that her father had found disturbing on her visits home: the pacing, the crying, the skin-pulling, the sleeplessness).

In 1996 she had entered a cycle of bingeing and purging. This was when she had started taking the ipecac. She had been 'too headstrong' to accept her parents' advice about getting psychiatric treatment. In custody, though, she had been taking a daily dose of Zoloft, and, in the words of the parole officer, 'she feels freer now between four walls than she ever has before'. Her family had been visiting her in Belconnen every second weekend, and she spoke to her mother every day on the phone.

'She says,' continued the parole officer, 'that she will still need to grieve for Mr Cinque.'

At this Mrs Cinque uttered a short sound of protest.

'She misses the victim and says that if this hadn't happened she would be married to him.

'She wants to write to Joe's parents.'

During her eighteen months in Belconnen Remand Centre, where male and female detainees are permitted social contact,

Anu Singh had had 'three romantic attachments'. Only one of these, she told the parole officer, was 'of any significance'. The officer found Singh to be 'an engaging, talkative, highly intelligent, educated young woman, but narcissistic. It is difficult to evaluate her expressions of remorse. She is self-absorbed and shows a paucity of personal resources.'

The Crown tendered a Victim Impact Statement written by Mrs Cinque. Mr Pappas, with a thoroughness that struck me as hard-boiled, objected to 'a large portion of that document'. Justice Crispin scanned it in silence, and admitted the document in its entirety, but I felt cheated by the fact that it was not read out loud. Journalists would not be able to quote from it as they would, if they chose, from the parole officer's potted history of Anu Singh's hard times. Oh, if only Maria Cinque could read out the statement in her beautiful accent, to show her strength of character, to give voice to her family's sorrow and rage in a public forum. I glanced at her. She sat silenced in the front row.

Now the defence called Dr Fatma Hadiye Lowden, a consultant psychiatrist whose qualifications were gained in Turkey and Australia. She was a blonde in her forties, pleasant-faced, broad in the beam, wearing a tailored jacket and calf-length skirt. The Canberra winter was chilly, yet under her high-heeled black sandals her legs and feet, like the prisoner's, were bare.

She had made nineteen professional visits to Anu Singh in Belconnen Remand Centre, she said, flashing her a smile across the court. At their first meeting, Singh had presented as superficial, with great difficulty in expressing emotion. Since then, however, Dr

Lowden had established greater trust with her patient, who had what was called 'an *as if* personality': she was able to put up a good facade. Dr Lowden had diagnosed 'a borderline personality disorder which was complicated by either an eating disorder, or depression, or substance abuse, and maybe brief psychotic episodes'.

The psychiatrist, too, depicted Singh as 'very upset' about Joe Cinque, full of loss and remorse, and sure that if only she had accepted treatment earlier, she would now be 'happily married' and getting on with her life. Dr Lowden had asked her, as part of her treatment, to keep a diary. Often Anu Singh was so intensely emotionally distressed that she could barely read aloud to the doctor from this journal. The parts of it that made her 'choke up' were those to do with her pain, guilt and remorse 'about *what happened*'.

Anu Singh would benefit, said Dr Lowden, from extended and intensive psychotherapy. Three to five years was the period over which she would require medication for her depression, that is, the biological part of her condition; and alongside that, she needed at least seven years, maybe more, of psychotherapy.

'The core of the whole tragedy,' said Dr Lowden, 'is that due to her mental state she was not able to accept treatment. She is now ready. Given *what happened to her*, I suggest three to six months of hospital treatment. I believe she will recover from her condition.' She would not, the doctor said, be a danger to herself or others in the future.

Maria Cinque, filing up the carpeted stairs for the lunch break, muttered to me, 'Another one, eh. Another big pay cheque. This is all an act. The judge has already made his decision.'

D-C Hains pulled papers and tobacco from a pouch as he walked out the glass front doors of the building. He grinned at me. 'What do you reckon?'

'I don't know how the Cinques can sit there and take it.'

'Yes, there's certainly something wrong with her,' he said, skilfully composing a cigarette. 'I'd be the first to admit that.' He stopped on the path, took a big, grateful drag on his rolly, and laughed, emitting a column of smoke. 'I understand that the Cinques want revenge. I don't believe in it, of course. I know you can't get it. But still – if anyone hurt *my* son . . .'

While we were talking, Anthony Cinque in his sunglasses was sitting on the ground with his knees bent to his chest and his shoulders pressed against the pale grey outer wall of the Supreme Court. He too was smoking, desperately, as if his life depended on it. What was he to do? Where was he to put himself? His pain and loneliness were terrible to see.

In a cafe at lunchtime I ran into one of the young journalists. We compared notes. Her sympathy for Anu Singh had lessened further, if that were possible. 'What *she* needs is a good kick up the arse. And her *silly* friends. It was all a big game.' She put on a thrilled, girlish, singsong voice: '*Anu's* having a *muuuurder* party! *Oooooh!*'

'I might write a book about it.'

'You're going to write a *book*? About *that*?' She jerked her thumb at the court across the road. I nodded. She laughed scornfully. 'Huh. Anu'll *love* that.'

Under cross-examination by Mr Refshauge, Dr Lowden continued to avoid using the simple expression *'what she did'*. Again and
again, with a spontaneous discretion, she dodged it.

'She has never had time,' said the psychiatrist, 'to deal with
what happened. Once the legal part is over, that will be the hardest
time for her – coming to terms with *what happened* in her life.
Exactly *what happened* on that day in 1997 she described to me as
"a blur". The bit she could remember was Joe gasping for air and
she was trying to do CPR and there was blood everywhere, and
eventually she rang an ambulance and –'

Mrs Cinque made a wordless sound of contempt.

'At that session she was in tears, telling me how much she
misses Joe – how much she wished this *didn't happen* in her life.
She told me about her constant thoughts of him, her sense of guilt
and self-deprecation.'

Justice Crispin listened faithfully, his wigged head leaning low
on his hand, his face solemn and thought-worn.

Anu Singh had not yet acknowledged to her psychiatrist that
she had injected Joe Cinque with heroin and killed him. 'There's
a difference,' said Dr Lowden, 'between logically accepting *what
happened* and emotionally coming to terms with it. I expect to
work on that a lot more, to get to the core of *what happened*.' She
made a delicate gesture, touching the pads of her thumb and forefinger together, as if deftly taking hold of a tiny, elusive thing.

The psychiatrist was warm, she was motherly, she was professional. The way she spoke about her patient was tinged with
possessiveness. 'I think she *trusts* me,' she said earnestly, and a little
flicker of spite ran through me: So you have gained the trust of this
'witch'. You have tamed a wild, glamorous creature whom others
fear and see as evil. *You* are not afraid of her. She will peck grain
from your hand.

She told the court about a 'love poem' that Anu Singh had written about 'very tender important moments' with Joe, her love and longing for him, and the meaning of their relationship to her. 'She couldn't read it. She asked *me* to read it out. As soon as we scratch the surface, great emotional distress is underneath. She talked about her nightmares. Joe is always there. In one dream she found out that Joe was married to another girl – major distress and sense of loss, and then tears again.'

'*Huh*,' said Mrs Cinque loudly.

When Mr Refshauge pressed her for examples of remorse, however, Dr Lowden was obliged to paint with a very broad brush. She interpreted as remorse the fact that Anu Singh missed Joe very much, that 'never a minute passes without her thinking of him', that she wished she had had psychiatric treatment before '*all these things got out of hand*'.

'"Remorse"?' said Mr Refshauge. 'In that she regrets that he is no longer here? Has she ever indicated what she might *do* as a result of these expressions of loss, guilt or remorse?'

'She discussed with me writing a letter to Joe's parents,' said Dr Lowden. 'I supported her in this. I don't know if she's actually written it.'

Mrs Cinque shook her head.

'She felt that Joe's parents were so angry with her that they would tear it up or not even read it. But she was really aware of the pain caused to the family.'

When Mr Refshauge asked Dr Lowden to explain how Anu Singh's mental abnormality had caused the offence she was guilty of, the psychiatrist shifted up a gear. 'If she didn't have this disorder,' she declared, 'she wouldn't have ended up in this predicament. It's well known that ten to fifteen per cent of people who suffer from this condition end up killing themselves. I don't think anyone else in this room' – the pretty doctor turned her head and cast a glance at the people in the public gallery – 'would like to be in her shoes.'

Mrs Cinque uttered a loud, guttural scoffing sound.

'Is there a risk,' asked Refshauge, 'that she will reoffend?'

Dr Lowden turned her torso forty-five degrees clockwise, and addressed her fervent argument not only to the judge but to everyone in the court. 'Let's say she gets into drugs again,' she said, 'and if she's suffering from severe depression – there's always a ten per cent risk. But *anyone in this room*, if they suffered from borderline personality disorder, if they had episodes of depression, if they had substance abuse – every single one of us would have that risk! We *all* carry that risk, if we're suffering from that condition!'

The psychiatrist had picked up the antagonistic vibe. She was challenging our hostility, trying to crack us open: she was fighting to keep her patient out of prison. But people in the gallery sank lower in their seats. Some folded their arms across their chests and scowled at her under their brows. Mrs Cinque jutted her jaw. Her cheeks went hollow, and her face took on a bitter stubbornness.

The pitch of Dr Lowden's voice rose. She sounded almost tearful. 'This person is *very severely ill*. Being in gaol is like being constantly *punished* for being ill. Remand is not a therapeutic environment. If she'd come to *me* as a patient before these things happened, *I* would certainly have admitted her. I'm telling you!' She swung back to the judge and threw out both hands to him, arms wide, in a passionate gesture of supplication. 'She is severely ill! She needs treatment in the structured environment that a hospital provides – not a gaol! She was physically attacked at the Remand Centre, but she wouldn't tell anyone about it – because in that culture –'

'Objection!' cried Mr Refshauge.

Dr Lowden sat back, flushed and unhappy. Again I thought how lucky Anu Singh was in not being at the mercy of a jury. If the body language of the listeners in the gallery was anything to go by, the psychiatrist's ardent plea might have fallen on deaf ears; perhaps it would even have further hardened hearts already closed and locked against her.

Mr Pappas argued vigorously for a minimum sentence that would allow rehabilitation. 'She accepts the tragedy of what she has done. This was not a man she disliked. This was a man whom she had planned to *marry*.'

Mr Refshauge invited Justice Crispin to impose a severe penalty. He asked the judge not to throw up his hands – not to decide that because nothing would bring back Joe Cinque, he would focus on rehabilitation. Hospitalisation, as proposed by Dr Lowden, would not do. The outrage of the community must be expressed. The taking of a human life, he said, was the ultimate crime, and there must be denunciation of it in the sentence.

By now Mr Cinque's head was down on his arms, which were outstretched over the fence of the gallery. Beside him his wife was weeping.

Justice Crispin stirred on the bench. 'They're profoundly difficult cases to sentence, are they not?' he said to the barristers in a quiet, almost conversational tone. 'It's obviously impossible to put oneself inside the head of someone who is seriously ill psychiatrically – and to make a judgement about what they were thinking, and why, and what measure of responsibility they had for their actions.'

He called for his diary: he would announce Anu Singh's sentence on Thursday. But it was only Monday. Where would the Cinques go, in the meantime? What would the Singhs do? Would they go back to their devastated homes, and wait it out there?

At half past six that evening I walked across the tarmac in the dark. In a black sky hung half a moon, very high. The air was cold and smelt of wet grass. The fatigue I felt after the long day in court was also a kind of gratitude. I had been granted the inestimable privilege of looking into other people's lives. What I had found there had absorbed my intellectual and emotional attention for many hours. Unlike the Cinques, unlike the Singhs, I could walk away.

As the small plane blundered along the runway and into the air, I suddenly remembered *Facing the Demons*, an Australian documentary I had seen on TV about restorative justice, the movement that sets up conferences between the perpetrators of crimes and their victims, or the families of their victims. The person I recalled most vividly from that hour of excruciating realness was a relatively minor figure, the mother of a young crim who had taken part in an armed robbery at a fast food outlet, in the course of which his mate had shot dead an innocent boy working behind the counter.

The mother, probably about fifty, had struck me as one of those mild women who are defeated by their sons' destructive wildness. She had the demeanour of a church-goer, a dutiful, kindly neighbour: timid, thin, with short grey hair and big pale-rimmed glasses. She took her place in the ring of chairs and sat in a neat posture with her shoulders cramped. Her cheeks burned with an uneven flush. Her whole body was trembling.

The conference began. The murdered boy's parents poured out at last their pent-up rage. His killer's accomplices (the killer himself having declined to take part in the documentary) choked out maimed gobbets of speech or sat in shamed and brutish silence with their forearms across their thighs.

This mother waited for a pause, then began to speak. She stammered. She whispered. She tried to say that she felt herself partly to blame for her son's character, for the terrible thing he had done, or helped to do, or allowed to be done. But the dead boy's parents jumped on her. They came down on her like a ton of bricks. 'It's not *your* fault, Mrs X. He made his own choices. It's *not your fault.*' The woman subsided, unconvinced, unshriven, her entire face in spasm. Her son, a hulking, tattooed, low-browed boy in prison greens, sat silent beside her, holding her hand, his eyes fixed on the floor.

On the Thursday morning I took an early flight to Canberra. A man detached himself from the line of long black coats in the taxi queue outside the airport, and approached me.

'Excuse me,' he said. 'I have the advantage of you – but would I be right in thinking I used to know you at Ocean Grove State School?'

Ocean Grove? I went to that school in the late 1940s. 'You might. What's your name?'

He said it. It was an unusual one, and at the sound of it I saw in a flash of shock a scene from my childhood: an angry man gripping a boy in short pants by the scruff of the neck, pressing his head down over an ugly grey cement basin where water streamed, and filling his mouth with foam.

'I remember you! You had your mouth washed out with soap for swearing!'

He stood there in his good dark coat, holding his briefcase, and the smile faded from his lips. 'Not me,' he said. 'That never happened to *me*.'

'But I saw it! I've told the story about a hundred times! I've dined out on it! I've never forgotten it!'

He kept shaking his head, looking at me in a puzzled way. 'No, it wasn't me. How could I have forgotten something like that?'

'But I was there! In my double desk! The classroom door was

open and we were all watching! It was awful! I remember you *vividly*! You were really clever! You had a brother! You were British migrants!'

'Yes, I did, and we were. But I never had my mouth washed out with soap. No. Never.'

People in the taxi queue were listening and smiling. I gave up on it and stood impotently staring at him. We both began to laugh.

'I married a girl who was in your class in Geelong,' he said. 'We're about to move to Oxford. I'm going to take up a chair.'

We parted with expressions of good will; but his flat denial of the mouth-washing incident troubled me, and it still does. Nothing he said could expunge the scene from my memory, or even dim it: it shines as shockingly bright today as it ever did. If memory is not to be trusted, what can courts rely on? How can they establish what 'really happened'? How can things from the past, even the relatively recent past, be *proved*?

The television crews were already loitering on the steps of the Supreme Court. Inside, Joe Cinque's parents in their front row seats were surrounded by an intense group of police and Victim Liaison workers; but they seemed terribly vulnerable and alone. Of their son Anthony there was no sign. In the back row of the gently raked gallery, Anu Singh's father wiped his eyes and nose on a big clean hanky. His wife sat very still, dark-faced, thick-haired, severe, her cheek twitching faintly.

The court was packed. There was a hum of subdued excitement. People bent to each other's ears, hissing and whispering. Where had they been during the trial itself, its long arguments, its hours of tedium, its occasional flurries of drama? Why do people want only to be in at the kill?

Suddenly Anu Singh materialised between two women guards, one of them gripping her by the arm. Under her charcoal jacket she was wearing a striped cotton T-shirt, like the one she had on in the photo of her and Joe in the Cinques' kitchen, that the papers ran and ran. She sat neatly on her chair and bowed her head.

At ten-fifteen a silence fell. It was like the moment before a funeral starts. I looked down at the Cinques. Mrs Cinque was crying quietly, wiping her eyes with a hanky, blowing her nose.

The tipstaff banged on the floor. We sprang to our feet and in stepped Justice Crispin to the bench, pausing only to make his sombre bow. He began to read aloud.

'A profoundly tragic case . . . Ms Singh's mental condition began to deteriorate . . . a bizarre and dark plan to kill herself, extending to killing Joe Cinque . . . a decent young man so full of promise . . . caused almost incomprehensible pain to those left behind . . . her parents blameless . . . tried to have her committed against her will . . . a tragedy for Anu Singh herself . . . lost her mental health . . . her plans for the future . . . sentencing unusually difficult . . . impossible to see clearly into the mind of the mentally ill and assess moral culpability . . . uncertainty about how long to serve . . . seriously ill psychologically . . . further psychiatric treatment in prison . . .'

Then, while the other fifty of us held our collective breath, he leaned forward across the bench and looked at Anu Singh, a few metres away on her metal-legged chair between the guards. She raised her chin and he spoke straight at her.

'In the next few years,' he said, 'you will have to come to terms with the fact that you killed the man you loved. You have caused immense pain.'

The young woman wiped her eyes, but she kept her face up and continued to return his gaze, like a schoolgirl being hauled over the coals.

'If you find the moral courage,' he said, 'you may be able to rebuild from this wreckage, to repay the trust people have put in you.'

Trust? Who had put trust in her?

The judge, for one. 'Ten years,' he said. Ten years with a non-parole period of four years. Back-dated to 26 October 1997, the day Joe Cinque died. I did the sum in the margin. She could be out by 26 October 2001. Two and a bit years from now.

The court let out its breath, and drew another.

'I recommend she be considered a prisoner at risk. I publish my reasons.'

Pappas was on his feet. 'May it please your Honour.'

'The prisoner may be removed. We will now adjourn.'

The judge bowed and swept out. The wiry little blonde sheriff got down on all fours to yank open the trapdoor. Anu Singh descended once more into the hole. Once more Maria Cinque's voice, solitary, thin at first, then gathering a hoarse strength, rose in the hushed court and spewed out curses. People stopped in their tracks and turned towards her. Transfixed by dread and by a strange, breathless need, we listened once more to her jeremiad: 'You demon. Rot in hell forever. I'll never ever forgive you. She's a demon. My son – that's *all*? Four years? How can you sleep at night? *Four years?* Is *that* all my son is worth?'

D-C Hains pushed through the frozen crowd in the aisle and stepped into the well of the court. He walked briskly along in front of the gallery railing, stopped before Mrs Cinque, seized the weeping, cursing woman by her upper arms, and gently kissed her cheek. The Victim Liaison people gathered around the Cinques and led them away, up the stairs of the courtroom and out into the lobby, along the carpeted hall past staring strangers, towards a place of shelter within the building. The supporters moved in a cluster, tightly jammed, like soldiers carrying two wounded comrades off the field; and the hot core of the group was Maria Cinque, stiff with anguish, staggering with her head back, wailing, weeping beyond shame. D-C Hains followed ten paces behind the stumbling group. Her sobbing cries streamed back to him. His face was closed.

Beside me in the lobby, watching this, stood a young TV reporter in a dark suit. Her smooth fall of blonde hair turned under perfectly at her shoulders. Her face was masked with make-up. She glanced at me.

'Four years,' she said.

'She could be out in two and a bit.'

'Before she even hits thirty,' said the girl. '*I'm* nearly thirty. My whole *life's* still in front of me.'

'Still,' I said. 'She'll have to live with what she did. They *all* will.'

The journalist said nothing. She was not convinced, and neither was I. We turned and walked out the big glass doors to the steps where the media crews were waiting in the bright, cold air, keeping themselves amused while the Cinques and the Singhs, in retiring rooms at opposite ends of the building, tried to compose themselves for the onslaught.

The doors opened and the press stirred, but it wasn't the Cinques. A bearded man in his thirties with a hard face, square and mean, and a thin, ratty little plait hanging down the nape of his neck, emerged into the light. Beside him walked a broad woman who was obviously his mother. A car with a panel-beater's logo stuck to the rear window screeched in to the kerb on the road behind the media. The pig-tailed man leapt with youthful vigour down the steps and across the footpath, yanked open the door and dropped sideways into the passenger seat. He lounged there, defiantly at ease, with one leg stretched out over the gutter. His mother, left like a shag on a rock at the top of the steps, saved her dignity by catching my eye and calling out, 'Must be somebody important they're all waiting for!'

'What are *you* here for?' I asked.

'My son,' she said. 'That's him, in the car. *She* says he come to her place and bashed her. Hit her in the mouth. But he wasn't anywhere *near* the place!' She smiled as she spoke, with an odd mixture of resignation and hollow bravado. 'I've come up here to give him some support. You don't like some of the things they get up to, when they're grown – but you gotta back 'em, when they're in trouble! The jury's out. We're just waiting.'

She fell silent. Together we watched her son blowing smoke out the open car door, sprawled there cursing and laughing coarsely with his invisible friend the driver. What sorrow or fear did her good-natured stoicism hide? Or did she really believe in this sleek, muscular thug with his nasty little pigtail?

'Here they come!' called the young woman from the ABC.

Maria and Nino Cinque stepped out on to the broad stage of the top step. A tide of cameras, microphones and shouted questions surged to meet them. The couple, squinting in the light, stood still for a moment, then Mrs Cinque began to speak.

'For me,' she said, 'the sentence should be *Hang on that tree over there.* I know it's not possible, but – for me, thirty years. When she come out, she's sixty. That's not possible, but it's fair.'

Usually in public her husband stood quiet and let her do the talking. But one of the reporters shouted at him the hackneyed question: 'Mr Cinque. How are you feeling?'

Nino Cinque stepped forward. 'She write letter,' he said, his voice trembling. 'She say' (he mimicked a falsetto tone) ' "*I love him.*" If she do good thing, why she don't go to the other world and find him?'

The journalists closed in on him. His fragility was unbearable. I turned and ran away down the steps.

At the bottom I met D-C Hains, just hanging about. 'What do you reckon, Haitch?' he said, with his dry grin. 'My wife was cryin'. She's a police officer. She got upset because Maria got upset. Still . . . she got more than I expected.'

'She could be out in two and a half years?'

'Don't be so sure!' he said. 'The parole board has to take her psychological condition into account – her own *shrink* said she needed seven years.' And off he went with a wink and a wave, in his AFP jacket and tie-clip.

I set out for my hotel, but almost at once I spotted the Cinques across the stretch of unnaturally green grass that separated the Supreme Court from the Magistrates'. They had gone from the ordeal on the steps to sit out in the wintry air, on the terrace of the court cafe. I approached their table and stood at a respectful distance. When they noticed me they smiled and offered their hands. I leaned over and we exchanged formal pairs of kisses.

I was awe-struck by Maria Cinque's composure. Nino Cinque maintained his place, with few words and a sweet expression, alongside the huge, elemental drama of his wife's persona; but such power dwelt in her that others shrivelled in her presence, became wispy, insubstantial. She never grand-standed or behaved falsely; yet as their suffering and outrage intensified, there rose from the depths of her a tremendous, unassailable archetype: the mother. We recognised it. It answered to a need in us as well. Her outburst after the sentence was not a rupture of protocol. On the contrary, we had waited for her to speak, holding open a space for her to utter. It was an honoured and necessary stage of a ritual: a *pietà*. We listened in respect, almost in gratitude. We needed to hear the sufferer cry out against her fate, although we knew that for this pain and loss there could be no remedy.

❧

That night I sat by myself in the empty hotel bar. The weight of the trial hung round me; I couldn't shrug it off. Justice Crispin had said it was impossible to see into Anu Singh's mind, to determine her moral culpability. But didn't the fascination, the terror of her story lie in the fact that she embodied a barbaric force in each of us that we must at all costs control? I thought of her arriving at Silverwater in the dark, being bundled out of a horrible van. I tried to imagine her parents, how they must be suffering now at the thought of their only daughter in that place teeming with harsh, wild people who would corrupt her. Eighteen months in a provincial remand prison was one thing, but now she was being delivered to the very centre of punishment in this country to which her family had migrated, where they had thrown in their lot.

But she had killed someone. Perhaps she was already as corrupted as the worst of them. What *is* corruption? Is corruption 'sin'? What is sin? Is it the inability to imagine the suffering of others? Surely she belonged in prison. Surely, now, she would pay for what she had done.

At last someone had cut through the euphemisms, the circumlocutions, and had stated it bluntly, in front of everyone, right to her face: '*You killed the man you loved.*'

PART FIVE

I still had no idea how Madhavi Rao fitted into this story. I did not understand exactly what she was supposed to have done, or how it was that she had been charged with murder. She would not be tried for months yet. I would have to go back to Canberra and read the transcript of the aborted double trial. But before I could organise it, I received a phone call, late one winter afternoon, from a funny and friendly young doctor I had met the year before at a consulate party. At the time he had made me laugh with his rueful caricatures of the problems encountered by children, like himself, of Indian immigrants. 'There are two acceptable things you can do,' he said. 'You can either be a doctor, or you can open a restaurant.'

Now, however, he was in a serious mood. 'I hear you're writing a book about a murder,' he began.

'I might be.'

His voice dropped a few tones. 'They're family friends.'

'Who – the Singhs?'

'No. Rao.'

I didn't need to ask a single question: he threw himself into it with feeling. He had known 'Madhu', he said, since they were small children. He was fond of her. He said several times that he could not *imagine* her doing any such thing. (*What*, though? What was she supposed to have done?)

'They put more blame on her than she deserves,' he declared. 'Madhu was in the wrong place at the wrong time. She was with the *wrong people.* She won't be able to practise as a lawyer with this charge against her. She'll have to leave the country – change her name.'

He sketched out her family situation. The Raos came from Hyderabad. Madhavi was an only child till the birth of a much younger sibling, who was disabled. The family hopes then focused on Madhavi. There was a lot of pressure on her. She was a very good tennis player – second in the state. Her HSC score, in the upper nineties, was not quite high enough to get her into medicine, so she repeated the year, but got a similar score, and enrolled in law. Her mother was a doctor, her father a teacher: he in particular was held in affectionate regard by the Indian community. They had both retired, but had had to go back to work to pay for Madhavi's defence.

The Raos were a rather unworldly family, the young man told me – a *pious* family. There was no smoking, no drinking, in their house. Madhavi herself, he said, had an endearingly formal way of speaking, 'without contractions or slang – like she'll say, "I was interested to hear the latest album by the Beastie Boys, so I approached the store with the intention of purchasing it".' He laughed affectionately.

Everything he said was suffused with a protective tenderness. 'If *your* daughter was mixed up in a thing like this, would *you* want a book to be written about it?'

I said nothing. I dropped my pencil and listened to his version of another family distorted, shamed, brought low. I was affected by it. What further hurt might I inflict? What right did I have?

Yet surely if you kill someone – if you are intimately involved in a situation that ends in a death – you forfeit your right to a polite turning away. You have blazed your way into the collective awareness. The rest of us *have* to think about you. We need to work out what you mean, what should be done about you.

How could I unpick the ethics of it? It was a confused drive that had been firing me, so far – first, curiosity, then a repelled fascination – even an identification – with Anu Singh; then, as I came to know the Cinques, a contagion of horrified grief.

Now, though, while the winter afternoon faded outside and the clever young man's voice murmured urgently on and on in my ear, the urge to witness and to understand drained sadly out of me. It was replaced by fear.

'You think that book about sexual harassment got you into trouble?' he said. 'This would be much, much worse. The person who's murdered stays the same, or even gets better – becomes a martyr. But the person who's killed somebody goes on and on being speculated about.'

After we hung up, I went out into the cold kitchen. It was already dark. From the high window I could see the lights of a ship, way out at sea. While I washed and stripped a bunch of spinach, I tried to think with purpose. I had a stubborn attachment to the story. I did not want to put it down. I wondered if I could find ways to fictionalise the events, to disguise the characters and their ethnic groups, to break the whole mess of it down into a series of short –

But wait. Hang on a minute.

Joe Cinque was murdered. Justice Crispin in his judgement had declared it manslaughter, but in his slip of the tongue from the bench that day, and in the speech of any ordinary person, what Anu Singh had done was called murder. And not a spontaneous stroke of revenge for cruelty or betrayal or abuse, but a carefully planned killing. His family was smashed: his brother driven half mad, his parents' hearts broken and trampled, their future hopes flung into outer darkness.

At the end of every argument, every doubt, stood the fundamental fact of the matter.

Joe Cinque is dead.

In the third week of July 1999 I went back to Canberra, to read the transcripts of the trials in the office of the Director of Public Prosecutions.

Australians used to love to joke about the awfulness of their capital city, its social bleakness, its provinciality, its grandiose, curvaceous street design in which the visitor strives in vain to orient himself. The jolly Croatian who drove me to Sydney airport that morning told me, when he heard my destination, that he and his wife had made a one-day visit to Canberra in the early 1960s, to contemplate it as a possible place to live: 'But the streets were empty! Like there has been a war, but no bombs! Only the gas!'

Because I had spent many happy student holidays in Canberra in the 1960s, as the guest of a family I was deeply fond of, I had always loved the place, found it beautiful with its cloudless skies and dry air, and looked forward to every visit; but now, with my new sombre purpose, it seemed to change its nature. When I sprang into the back seat of a taxi, in my heavy overcoat and minus my suitcase which, on the short flight from Sydney, the airline had managed to mislay, the middle-aged driver ignored my greeting and barked at me, '*Do* up yer seatbelt!'

'Oh!' I said, flustered and complying at once. 'Sorry!'

He took off towards the city. 'If you're caught,' he said, 'it'll be an instant fine of $750.'

'Yikes!' I said. 'You wouldn't want *that* to happen!'

'Don't worry,' he said in a sour, ominous tone. 'It wouldn't be *me* who'd have to pay. It's not *my* responsibility. It's *yours. You'd* have to pay the fine. And that's *only fair.*'

I subsided in my seat, irritated, and looked out the window; but the driver, having crushed my fleeting *joie de vivre*, now took it on himself to play the tour guide. He ground out between his narrow lips a list of statistics, which continued all the way to town, to the effect that Canberra was cleaner, better policed, less polluted 'in air or water', culturally richer, and athletically better equipped 'than any other capital city in Australia – in the *world*'. Long after I had ceased to make even the most perfunctory response he droned on and on, in an aggressive and huffy tone, as if defending his city against some disobliging remark I might be about to make. What on earth was biting the fellow? Was it because I had come from Sydney? Or because I had got into the back seat instead of taking the egalitarian spot up front? Sitting behind him with my arms folded, I grew more and more cranky. His litany, thickly studded with percentages of new house construction, kilometres of bike track and the like, was so endless, tedious and smug that I could barely control a desire to cut across it with my own catalogue of facts: 'Listen, pal – Canberra is also the hard drug capital of Australia. Heroin is cheaper and more readily available here than in any other city. Its suburb of Fyshwick is the porn video supplier to the nation. There are more bored, under-occupied tertiary graduates here than anywhere else in the country. *Plus,* the people who empty the syringe disposal units have stated that the fullest ones are to be found in *your famous Parliament House.* So shut up and drive, you gormless provincial bore.'

I maintained an icy silence till we reached Civic, then said, 'Drop me at the Department of Public Prosecutions, please. Do you know where it is?'

'Not exactly, no.'

'It's near the Law Courts. In the Reserve Bank Building. Do you know where the Reserve Bank is?'

'Of *course* I know where the Reserve Bank is,' he said, scrambling to recover his advantage. 'Huh. *Funny place* to have the Department of Public Prosecutions.'

We pulled up outside the Magistrates' Court. I handed him the money, rounding it up twenty-five cents to the nearest dollar, and asked for a receipt. He inspected the coins in his palm, turned for the first time to look me in the eye, and whined in a wounded tone, 'I was only trying to be *helpful*!'

But I had already lost interest in our petty struggle, for I had spotted three barristers charging across the road, headed for the Supreme Court. Jack Pappas stood out among them, with his anachronistic red cheeks and dark clipped beard. From behind, the queue of each man's wig and the curve of his shoulders under the pleats of his black gown called irresistibly to mind a shark or a currawong – a creature highly evolved for attack, plunder and flight.

The people in the DPP set me up at a spare desk near a window in an outer office. A helpful young prosecutor dumped on to my table the material I would need to read: four coloured binders bursting with the typed records of the court proceedings. I had never laid eyes on a transcript before. There was *so much* of it, over a thousand pages: first, the 1998 jury trial of Singh and Rao together, which had been aborted; and then Singh's solo trial – everything that had happened before I got there, and the official version of what I *had* seen. I lined up the binders with their spines towards me. Excited and hopeful, I opened volume one of the jury trial, took the lid off my pen and carefully labelled my brand-new exercise book.

I must have had a childish fantasy of the transcript as a text of wonderful clarity and simplicity, a coherent document in dialogue that would lay out the story from go to whoa. I thought it would answer the questions I was still too confused to formulate; and I hoped that somewhere in its pages I would find Joe Cinque. But it was a mess, full of senseless fast forwards and flashbacks. Just as a narrative got rolling, it would be cut short and abandoned, and the story taken up at a different point by a new speaker. People stammered and repeated themselves. Witnesses hesitated, got muddled, huffy, panicky, asked for a break. Barristers stood on their dignity, made pedantic interruptions and ponderous jests, launched themselves on bombastically long and archaically complex sentences. And what was a '*voir dire*'? A 'Basha inquiry'? How the hell did one *read* this stuff?

As I thrashed along, unable to discern the overall shape of the story or grip with my memory the sequence of events, but continuing to take notes with a sort of helpless conscientiousness, the prosecutors strode in and out of their offices, calling to each other cheerfully, making efficient phone calls, donning and doffing robes and wigs. Occasionally one or two of them would stop by my desk to gossip. They spoke with irritation of the defence's psychiatric experts, of what they saw as 'the creation' of Anu Singh's borderline personality disorder and her 'masked depression'. They were particularly annoyed by Justice Crispin's manslaughter decision.

'It was a wrong decision,' said one of them.

'And very bad for the victim's parents,' said another.

'He *could* have called it murder —'

'— Which it *was* —'

'– And *then* talked about diminished responsibility – and given her the same sentence.'

By lunchtime I no longer had a handle on the rightness or wrongness of anything. I kept nodding off over the folders. I went outside for a sandwich and a walk in the cold air. Far below Canberra's high, clear sky, along its de Chirico colonnades and across its open plazas, moved a host of fast-walking bureaucrats whose long black coats, unbuttoned, flew out behind them. On my way back to the DPP I passed a splendid modern legal chambers whose frontage was cheekily emblazoned with the name *'pappas, j'*. A sign on a window advertised *Legal advice on most contentious matters*. As I picked up speed to walk on by, an insignia on the glass door caught my eye: a fighting cock armed with spurs, and underneath it, elegantly lettered in a curve, the legend, *Every knot was once straight rope*.

It wasn't till my third day among the documents that I came upon the crime scene photos.

I found them pushed into one of the folders I had been given: there was no reason why I shouldn't look at them. But furtively, hunching my shoulders and keeping my back to the room, I flipped open the cheap little plastic album. The police photographer was uninterested in argument and immune to ideas of art. He had roamed through the house and into the mortuary, brooding on detail. I followed his eye, and this is what I saw.

A colour snap, propped on a shelf against a little wooden jewel box, of a merry young man standing in front of the Trevi fountain. He is wearing a dark bomber jacket unzipped over a very white T-shirt, and a dark peaked cap. He is grinning, gesturing dramatically with one hand: *Look! It's me! I'm in Rome!*

A black briefcase stuffed with prescription drugs still in their packets: Capadex, Tilade, Becloforte, Zantac, Fybogel, Imodium.

The bar of a mechanised treadmill.

A window shielded by diaphanous net curtains.

A pink leather lounge suite. A dining table with six chairs. Another chair made of white plastic.

On the table a single plate of food, a glass of wine.

And on the kitchen bench, half a dozen Granny Smith apples: it was jarring to see their intense, gleaming green, the fresh green of childhood – as if these people, with their poisoned 'dinner parties', their horrid dramas, could never have performed an act as ordinary as cutting, peeling and eating an apple.

A framed print, hung high on a bedroom wall: Van Gogh's starry sky above the terrace of a lamplit cafe.

Two tan suede men's workboots, carelessly dropped on the carpet.

A pair of dark green corduroy men's trousers slung over a cast-iron chair, with a tan leather belt still threaded through the loops.

A young man stretched out on his back, naked, on the bedroom floor. He is as relaxed as a sunbaker. His body is healthy, smooth and strong. His uncircumcised penis lolls to one side. His arms lie loose against the carpet. But he is already livid: blood is pooling in his thigh muscles, a dark, uneven flush. And behind him the sheets of a double bed are wrenched askew, dragged halfway to the floor, and stained with streaks of black fluid.

On the floor beside the wrecked bed, a mug half full of pale milky liquid – instant coffee? – with two cigarette butts floating in it, part-submerged.

A bare left arm on the metal surface of a mortuary table, its elbow crook showing the discoloured, swollen entry mark of a needle.

A bare right arm, similarly punctured.

And another shot in the bedroom, a close-up of the young man's face taken from directly above, as if the photographer were standing straddled over him. Yes, it is the young traveller from the Trevi fountain. The youth and tenderness of his face, with its smooth curves. His thick, dark, curly hair, not harshly shorn as in the wedding video. The springy hair. The beauty and freshness of the hair. The only sign that he is not simply dozing on a beach is a thin trickle of black muck running from one corner of his gently closed mouth and disappearing under his left earlobe into the dark.

This is Joe Cinque.

Joe Cinque is dead.

After wandering for days along the forking, criss-crossing paths of the transcripts, I started to piece together a narrative of the week that ended with Joe Cinque's death on Sunday 26 October 1997.

Two dinner parties, not the single one of glamorous rumour, had been held that week at the young couple's rented townhouse, 79 Antill Street, Downer. The first took place on the evening of Monday 20 October. Maria and Nino Cinque, in their interview with me, had railed bitterly against the court for letting slide the evidence of a failed murder attempt that night. The Crown, I now learnt from the record, had certainly had its suspicions. According to the Prosecutor, Terry Golding, there may have been 'preparatory conduct' on the Monday evening. Someone had certainly given evidence about a syringe in which heroin had congealed, rendering it unusable. But, said Golding, *because it cannot prove it'*, the Crown did not press its claim that an attempt had been made that night to kill Joe Cinque.

The very next morning, however, on the Tuesday, Madhavi Rao went to work and spoke provocatively to two puzzled colleagues about a party she had been to the night before. She told them that 'the worst thing in the Crimes Act' had been tried, and would be tried again the following weekend.

On the Friday evening, 24 October, a second set of guests was assembled for dinner at the Antill Street townhouse. Those of them who gave evidence described it as a pleasant enough evening. Anu Singh was 'acting bubbly and vivacious'. She and Joe Cinque were seen to behave affectionately towards each other. But at some stage during the meal, Anu Singh had laced Joe Cinque's coffee with Rohypnol and, after all the guests but Madhavi Rao had taken their leave, she tried – and failed – to inject him with heroin.

One young woman who was present at the Friday dinner, a student friend of Madhavi Rao's who lived out of town, had left the party early, soon after midnight, and gone back to Rao's share house where she was to stay the night. Rao returned at dawn and related to her bewildered visitor the events of the night. Astonished and frightened, the visitor went home, but later that Saturday morning she made a phone call of protest to Rao and Singh. She threatened to go to the police unless she was assured that no harm would come to Joe Cinque. Anu Singh got angry, then burst into tears on the phone. She told the worried girl that she had sat watching Joe for two hours while he slept; she had realised that she loved him and would never do anything to hurt him. She begged the protesting guest not to interfere – not to ruin her relationship with Joe.

Joe Cinque did not wake from his Rohypnol sleep till early evening that Saturday, the day before he died. He was still very groggy. Suspecting that something weird was going on, he stumbled around the house throwing out all the drugs he could lay hands on. When Madhavi Rao came over to Antill Street that evening, bringing food as requested by Anu Singh, and intending to do some study with her friend – these people were bright students about to sit their final exams – Anu Singh accused *her* of having spiked Joe's drink. Rao got upset and went off to spend the rest of the night with a bunch of her other friends at the Art School Ball.

Meanwhile, back at Antill Street, Anu Singh once more spiked Joe Cinque's coffee, this time with a massive dose of Rohypnol. When he passed out, she got the needle into his arm.

By dawn on Sunday 26 October, he was deeply unconscious. At about eight a.m. Singh drove round to Rao's place, woke her, and hauled her back to Antill Street. Rao went into the bedroom and saw Joe lying on the bed, slightly blue, but breathing. Singh pressured Rao to drive with her to an ATM, where Rao withdrew $250 from her account and handed over the money. Then the two women quarrelled. Rao got out of Singh's car at the lights and walked home alone.

It was now just after nine-thirty on the Sunday morning. Anu Singh drove on to the house of the law student who had previously scored heroin for her and taught her how to inject it. The police had given this witness indemnity from prosecution, and his name had been suppressed, in order to spare his ill, widowed mother, who was unaware of his addiction: in court he was referred to as 'Mr T'. (He had told Anu Singh's trial that Singh had been in the class ahead of him at their Newcastle secondary school; she had stuck in his mind because she wore shoulder pads under her uniform shirt, and came to school in high heels.)

When an agitated Anu Singh presented herself at the front door of his Canberra flat in a long white flowery dress and brandishing a fistful of cash, Mr T was already up and dressed, waiting for his mate to call for him, so they could go together to their appointments at the Woden methadone clinic. Anu Singh had several times in the past confided to Mr T that she wanted to kill herself with a heroin overdose. She had also told him that 'someone else' was coming with her. Still, on this unseasonably warm Sunday morning in October, Mr T took the cash from her and went out to score, leaving his mate, when he turned up, to 'make small talk' with her. Singh was restless. She came and went several times while they waited for Mr T. She said to his friend, 'I've done something I shouldn't have.'

Mr T returned in a while with a half-weight. He helped himself to the taste that was his reward. Anu Singh said to him, 'Today's the day.' He told her to relax – not to be silly. He cooked up the balance of the heroin for her and sucked it into a syringe. Off she went, carrying barely concealed in the palm of her hand a fit loaded with almost $250 worth of heroin.

What Singh did next has not been established. But just before noon she made the famous phone call to Bronwyn Cammack that so exercised the psychiatrists during her trial. She told Cammack that Joe's lips were 'a tiny bit blue', and that he was 'still taking a breath every ten seconds or so'. Cammack, showing the kind of crude common sense that the story conspicuously lacked, refused to be dragged into Singh's mess, told her she was 'a selfish bitch', and bluntly ordered her to call the paramedics at once. And in the end, as we know, Singh did dial 000. But at one-fifty p.m. on Sunday 26 October 1997, Joe Cinque's life was pronounced extinct.

The transcripts may not have offered me the simple chronology of events that I craved, but as I shifted back and forth between the aborted double trial and Singh's solo trial, I found the differing versions were rich in extraordinary passages of dialogue that witnesses had recreated under the pressure of counsel's questioning – scenes of strange drama which gave the flavour of the social, moral and emotional world these people inhabited.

In October 1997, for example, a young woman called Robin Mantoszko had a placement as a student social worker in the Community and Health Services Complaints Commission, in Civic, where Madhavi Rao was doing work experience. According to the evidence this witness gave in the aborted jury trial, Madhavi Rao had said to her on Friday 17 October, 'I've got a friend who's suicidal. She smothers me.'

Then, on Tuesday 21 October, the day after the first dinner party, a flustered-looking Madhavi Rao had launched a conversation with Mantoszko and her work-mate Russell Baker.

'Canberra's such a strange place,' she began, according to Mantoszko. 'My friend asked me to get twenty people together for a dinner party by nine-thirty. I just drove around and knocked at people's doors, that were acquaintances. It was amazing. They said "Oh yeah – I've seen you at uni – I'll come." The party was really strange. Something really serious happened. It was bizarre. I've been looking over my shoulder for the police.'

'Why?' asked Mantoszko. 'What happened? Was it something to do with sex?'

'Look at me,' said Rao with a sort of a smile. 'Do you think I look like a sex goddess?'

'I don't know. Was it something to do with drugs?'

'If it were that, I wouldn't be worried.'

'Was it some sort of game, like Dungeons and Dragons?'

'No,' said Rao. 'I'm not into that. It was really strange. It was . . . something really serious.'

'Was it something to do with the occult?'

'No. It's the major crime of the century since 1901. Since the turn of the century.'

'Was someone raped?'

'No. It's the worst thing in the Crimes Act.'

Mantoszko looked at Russell Baker and asked, 'What's in the Crimes Act?' Baker shrugged.

'It's the worst thing in the Crimes Act,' insisted Rao. 'The *worst.*'

'Murder,' said Mantoszko.

'Murder,' said Baker.

'Do you mean murder?' asked Mantoszko.

Rao turned away.

'Were animals involved?' asked Mantoszko.

'No,' said Rao. 'I wouldn't let that happen.'

'Was someone murdered?'

'No,' said Rao. 'I don't want to talk about it any more.' She threw her hands in the air. 'I'm not going to talk about it any more.' She said this several times, quite assertively, then sat down at her desk. A few minutes later she spoke again: 'It's got something to do with revenge.'

'Was someone hurt?' Mantoszko asked. Rao did not answer.

Mantoszko asked again and then again, more forcefully. Rao did not reply. She kept looking down at her desk with her back to Mantoszko. Mantoszko wheeled her chair over to Rao's left side and tried to look her directly in the eyes. Rao would not meet her eye. Peering round, trying to look into her face, Mantoszko said directly to her, 'Was someone hurt?' Rao gave no reply. She turned her chair away from Mantoszko, then stood up and started tidying her desk.

'Can it be reversed?' asked Mantoszko.

Rao shook her head and hesitantly said, 'No.'

Frustrated, Mantoszko said to her, 'What's going on? If you can't tell us what's going on, is there someone else you can talk to?'

No reply.

'What about the police?'

'Oh no,' said Rao. 'I'll be thrown in gaol.'

'What about a university counsellor?'

'No. I'd be locked up as well.'

'If you're really serious about this,' said Mantoszko, 'perhaps you need to see a lawyer.'

There was a pause. Then Rao said there was a university professor who specialised in criminal law whom she could perhaps see and talk to.

'I strongly encouraged her to do this,' Mantoszko told the court. 'I told her to go and see him, to tell someone what was going on. And I told her to cover her own arse.'

Two days later, at lunchtime on Thursday 23 October, Madhavi Rao said to Mantoszko, 'It looks like it's going to happen again this weekend.'

'What's going to happen again?' said Mantoszko, who was in a hurry to leave the office. 'Can you stop it?'

'No.'

'Then tell someone who can.'

The July nights in Canberra gasped with blue cold; mornings were stiff with frost. Before dawn each day, right outside my window at the erstwhile government hostel where I was staying, a magpie let loose a bubbling burst of song. I would force myself out along the flat streets to a football oval, and tramp round it three times. The grass crunched under my shoes. The breath of singing birds shot out of their beaks in tiny white puffs.

When I got to my desk at the DPP, I would slide Joe Cinque's photo out from its hiding place among the papers, prop it against a folder, and contemplate it quietly for a while before I started work. I had an urge to greet him, to say, 'Here I am, Joe. I haven't forgotten you.' His eyes were closed. In death he looked young and tender, pure-faced, even slightly child-like. I felt protective of him, though it was too late. He seemed to me an innocent who had fallen into a nest of very complicated evil.

But I didn't know what 'evil' was. I didn't know whether such a thing existed, though in an anxious corner of myself I stubbornly believed it did. I kept thinking about a remarkable book by the British writer Tony Parker that I had once read, *Life after Life: Interviews with Twelve Murderers.* I remembered the sense I had got, from even the most laceratingly remorseful of those candid speakers, that 'evil' or 'violence' or 'the urge to kill' is like a storm that rushes in from outside. The killer's nature is weak, or porous. He lacks resistance. For whatever reason, his defences are down. And this force inhabits him, uses him as its tool, destroys, then rushes on, leaving its host empty, limp as a glove.

Is this primitive? Is it a fantasy of possession? Yet it still has a hold, otherwise there would be no such defence as 'diminished responsibility'. One lunchtime I went down to Garema Place and emailed a friend who was a Jesuit priest. 'I think there is good reason,' he promptly replied, 'for the long tradition which speaks of evil in the third person, even gives it a name. It seems to treat the human as a kind of host, like a parasite. I do believe there is such a thing as diminished responsibility. But the hardest thing is to get an aggressor to accept what responsibility is appropriate.'

In the transcript of the aborted jury trial I came upon a terrible cross-examination by Mr Pappas of one of Madhavi Rao's friends, a young woman called Olivia Pipitone. According to this witness, Madhavi Rao had confided in her that Anu Singh, needing practice for suicide, had injected Rao with heroin. 'Madhavi showed me the mark in her left elbow,' Pipitone told the court, 'and said, "This is where Anu injected me." She said it wasn't an amazing experience.'

When Rao invited Pipitone to the Monday night dinner, she explained that the reason for the party was so Singh could kill herself. Pipitone had at this stage never met Anu Singh, but she accepted the invitation, and it was very hard for her, in court, to explain why.

'Now,' said Pappas, 'you were left with the impression that Madhavi Rao believed her friend Anu Singh might well commit suicide?'

'Yes,' stammered the witness. 'I – I don't really agree with that. Like all I had to go on was what Madhavi was saying to me, so therefore whatever she believed I pretty much believed. So –

because *I* didn't believe, then I don't think *she* would have believed either. If she'd have had belief she would have imparted that through the way she would have told me.'

'There was nothing about the way she spoke to you, was there, in her demeanour or her manner, to suggest that she was treating this simply as a joke?'

'No, not as a joke.'

'And she never said to you, did she, "I don't think she is going to do anything of the sort"?'

'No.'

'You believed that Madhavi and Anu had a degree of conviction about these plans but you yourself were sceptical about it?'

'That was only an impression. I don't know.'

'When you got to the party you found that there was a lot of food and only a few guests?'

'Yes.'

'And it was Anu Singh who said, "We've got to find more guests. We've got too much food"?'

'Yes. It was Joe as well because he was cooking. Like, they were both cooking.'

'It seemed a bit odd to you, surely, that you'd turn up to a party and there's only a few people there, to the house of a person you'd never met, and yet then you're sent off on a door-knock looking for more guests?'

'Yes, it is strange, yes.'

'That must have struck you as particularly odd?'

'Yes, it was quite odd.'

'And this was the party you'd been told was to celebrate Anu Singh's intended suicide?'

'Yes, the whole thing was quite strange.'

'You didn't know of any other reason for the party, did you?'

'Yes, I did.'

'There was some other reason, was there?'

'Yes. Yes.'

'What was that?'

'It was for Anu to kill her boyfriend as well as herself.'

'Well, that made it perfectly normal, then, did it? It wasn't just a suicide, it was going to be a murder as well? I mean – you weren't told that it was someone's birthday, were you, when you got to the party?'

'No.'

'Or that someone was going overseas or just graduated from university?'

'No.'

'You were told that this was a party to celebrate a murder/ suicide, and when you got there you were told by the hostess you'd never met that there was too much food – "Go and get me some more guests"?'

'Mm.'

'And you said to Madhavi Rao, "Why are you doing this?" And she said, "Anu asked me"?'

'Yes.'

'Did you say, "Why are you playing along with this?" '

'Yes, but I don't recall any answer.'

'And Madhavi Rao was telling you all this in serious, sober, sombre tones, wasn't she?'

'I really wouldn't use those words to describe it –'

'What words would you use?'

'It's just so hard to say. It's just not – just nothing – all I can say, it was just nothing. No overly impressive tones. Like, no – nothing overly – sort of light and fun and not overly serious and sombre. Just – but not – not carefree either.'

'There wasn't a word spoken by Madhavi Rao on the evening of that party which led you to the view that it had all been some bad joke?'

'No.'

'Because the very next day you went round to ask her what happened?'

'Yes.'

'You had some morbid curiosity about whether there'd been a suicide or a murder, did you?'

'I suppose I would've, yes.'

'You certainly posed that question, didn't you – "What happened last night?"'

'I did, yes.'

'What did you mean by that? – "Was someone killed?"'

'Yes, that would have been what I meant.'

'She had conveyed the whole story to you with sufficient conviction to cause you to ask the question the next day?'

'But I still didn't really think that anything would happen.'

'Well, why did you ask the question?'

'It's sort of like, you know – I'd, you know, "Did anything happen", sort of, as if it would have, sort of.'

'That was a little joke, was it?'

'No, I don't think it was a joke.'

'And once you'd confronted Madhavi Rao and asked what happened, the talk about this suicide dropped off a little bit?'

'It just sort of dropped off, yes. It was the end of uni and I didn't – I didn't – yes.'

'And the next conversation you had on the subject, you were told by your friend Madhavi Rao that there was going to be another party?'

'On some occasion, yes.'

'And she was again telling you that Anu Singh was suicidal?'

'That was the implication, I suppose, yes.'

'And she told you that Anu did not have in mind, at that point, the killing of Joe Cinque?'

'I remember Madhavi saying that Anu isn't going to kill her boyfriend, like she's decided not to and there's going to be a party, there's not going to be another party – that's just sort of hazy.'

'Did all this seem perfectly normal to you, did it?'

'Well, no, but – it was something that had been coming up in conversation for a couple of months, and –'

'Had your friend Madhavi Rao been talking about it so much that you'd become a little desensitised to the whole subject?'

'Yeah, perhaps. But it's not that I was highly sensitised from the start.'

Olivia Pipitone's memory of this cross-examination, so unbecoming to her, may have been rendered slightly more bearable by the benevolent treatment she received next, for his own purposes, from Mr Adams, counsel for Madhavi Rao. Deftly he let her off the whole row of nasty ethical hooks from which Mr Pappas's questions had suspended her. He reminded her of previous evidence she had given to the effect that Madhavi Rao, when inviting her to the Monday night murder/suicide dinner, had 'rolled her eyes' in a manner he called 'symptomatic of disbelief'. Eagerly Pipitone agreed that this 'rolling of the eyes type of response', which conveyed what Mr Adams called 'a sense of exasperation about Anu Singh going on and on and on', had characterised all of the discussions between her and Madhavi on the subject of Anu Singh's suicide. And though she didn't actually recall having said in conversation, 'People who are going to do this sort of thing don't just talk about it – they go ahead and do it,' she now agreed that 'this does sound like a sentiment I would have had and would have expressed at some point.'

If Pipitone had really taken the talk seriously, Mr Adams went on, 'you wouldn't have put yourself in a position to go along to a party to witness a murder and a suicide, would you? You didn't understand Madhavi to be telling you that that was going to happen on a particular night – because you simply wouldn't have gone along to it, would you? You certainly wouldn't have gone out to get additional guests, to get a bigger audience to witness this murder and suicide, if that's what you knew or thought was going on?'

'No. No. No,' said Pipitone.

'And the dinner party was perfectly normal, if not boring? You saw Joe Cinque and Anu Singh there behaving like an ordinary couple who were obviously affectionate to one another?'

'Yes. Yes. Yes.'

'You didn't expect anything to happen? It doesn't seem logical, then, does it, that you would be asking the question "What happened"?'

'No. No.'

'Can I suggest to you that when you saw Madhavi Rao the following day, you said "How did it go?" It's a more logical thing to have asked her, isn't it?'

'Yes.'

And as for when Madhavi Rao had shown Olivia Pipitone the needle mark on her arm – 'I think you'd agree with the proposition,' said Mr Adams, 'that the fact that it was practice for suicide is more likely to be a conclusion drawn by you than something that Madhavi told you?'

'Yes,' said Pipitone.

'And when you asked Madhavi, "How could you let Anu do that to you?" she said "Anu pleaded with me and was terribly insistent and eventually I let her do it"?'

'Yes,' said Pipitone. The girl's relief lit up the page. '*That's* it. *Yes.*'

One of the props of the adversarial system, I began to see, is a curious charade that memory is a clear, coherent narrative, a stable and unchanging source of information, so that any deviation from a witness's original version of an event can be manhandled to look like unreliability, or the intent to deceive. Thus, I saw how a Crown witness of what seemed to me transparent sincerity and desire to do right – the only person who had made any real attempt to break through the ghastly, paralysing spell that hung around Anu Singh and her plan to kill Joe Cinque – could go to water under the sustained onslaught of a defence cross-examination.

Because this witness's family belonged to a historically traumatised ethnic group and would have turned her out of home if they knew she had had dealings, no matter how innocent, with the police, her name was suppressed by the court; I shall call her Tanya Z—. According to her evidence-in-chief at the jury trial, she had met and had social contact with Madhavi Rao early in 1996 when they were both residents of a university college. Her acquaintance with the morbid concerns of Singh and Rao began around July 1997, when she ran into them at the university library. It was the first time she had met Anu Singh. Rao asked Tanya Z— to lend her some money so she could photocopy an article for a law assignment. Tanya was surprised to notice that the material was about suicide.

Early in the week familiar to us as the one leading up to Joe Cinque's death, Madhavi Rao phoned Tanya Z— and invited her to a dinner party that 'a friend' was having on the following Friday, 24 October. Tanya Z— was pleased to accept.

On the Friday evening, Rao and Singh picked up Tanya Z— from a bus stop. When Singh hopped out of the car in Braddon to buy something in a shop, Rao turned to Tanya Z— and said, 'I've got a big story, bigger than you've heard before. It's a secret. I'll tell you about it later.'

They dropped Singh off at 79 Antill Street, then drove on to Turner, to pick up another guest. During the twenty minutes when they were alone in the car, Rao told Tanya Z— that the dinner party was to be a send-off for Anu. She was going to kill herself afterwards, because she was suffering from a muscle-wasting disease caused by 'a syrup called ipecac that makes you vomit if you've eaten too much'; Rao said Singh had heard about the ipecac from her boyfriend Joe. Singh and Rao had researched the means of suicide. They would inject several hundred dollars' worth of heroin, and it would take two seconds.

Tanya Z— panicked. She told Madhavi Rao that it was morally and legally wrong to participate in such a thing.

'I've taken care of that,' said Rao. 'I'll be downstairs when it's happening.'

'Anu can't be serious if she's using that method,' said Tanya Z—. 'If she was serious she'd try other methods like, for example, a gun.'

'She's tried that,' said Madhavi Rao, 'but she couldn't get one.'

Having picked up the other guest, they headed back to Antill Street for the party. On the way, Madhavi told Tanya Z— she might as well stay the night at her place after the dinner, instead of making the long trip home to the township where she and her family lived.

Another guest, a friend of Singh and Rao called Len Mancini whom Tanya didn't yet know, would give her a lift back to Rao's share house later. Tanya should be ready to leave with him when told to.

Tanya Z— was not asked to give the court an account of her state of mind during the party, which was already in progress when they reached the house. She said merely that she met Joe Cinque and others, that people ate and drank, that there was conversation round the table, and that she recalled nothing unusual about the dinner. She stayed at the party till sometime between midnight and twelve-thirty, at which point Len Mancini drove her back to Madhavi Rao's house in Condamine Street and left her to spend the night in Madhavi's room.

At about six on Saturday morning Tanya was woken by the noisy arrival home of her hostess. Rao, she said, was ruffling angrily through her things, jerking them this way and that, apparently getting ready for bed.

'Hi,' said Tanya Z—. 'You seem upset.'

'Yes,' said Madhavi Rao. 'Just go to sleep. I'll tell you about it later.'

'You seem *really* upset,' said Tanya Z—. 'Do you want to talk about it?'

'It didn't work,' said Rao.

'What – you tried it?'

'Yes.'

'How could it not work? She's an idiot. If she really wanted to kill herself she'd do it. How hard is it to do? She's not a good friend to you. Just stay away from her.'

'Well, it's okay with her,' said Madhavi Rao, 'but Joe's the problem. She wants to take Joe with her.'

'What?' said Tanya Z—. 'I didn't think they were that close.'

'No – it's because she blames him for her condition.'

'What kind of idiotic rationalising is that? *She's* the one that took the ipecac!'

'Yes,' said Rao, 'but he used to roll round in his sleep saying, "You're such a slut, Anu."'

Madhavi lit a cigarette for Tanya Z— and another for herself.

Tanya asked her whether she'd ever had heroin. Madhavi said she had tried it with Anu, to practise injecting, at the house of a student friend. This man had given them stern advice about dosages: he said, 'You don't fuck around with things like murder and suicide. If you do it, you do it properly.'

'We had a party on Monday night as well,' Madhavi went on, 'but the heroin had been left in the syringe too long. It congealed in the syringe.'

'So was the party for Joe?' asked Tanya.

'Yeah. It was to get him drunk.'

'That's just too elaborate,' said Tanya. 'Anu can't be serious. How hard is it to get your own boyfriend drunk?'

Madhavi began to talk about spiritual things. She said, 'It's amazing – it wasn't his time to go. Even though he'd had that many Rohypnol, he was still moving. Anu couldn't get the injection into him. She wanted to put it into his arm muscle. I told her it wouldn't work – it wouldn't kill him.'

'Did Joe take the Rohypnol deliberately?'

'No – would *you* take ten Rohypnol deliberately?'

'How did you get him to take it?'

'Anu put it in his coffee.'

'Did you know that Joe was supposed to go as well?'

'Yes,' said Madhavi. 'That's why I couldn't look him in the eye when he was talking about the conspiracy book I'd lent him.'

'So are you still going to try and kill Joe,' asked Tanya, 'or is this all over with?'

'I'm not going to have anything more to do with it. Anu doesn't want me to. She said, "No offence, Madhavi, but I'm going to have to do this alone – it's just not working." '

It was by now seven-thirty on the Saturday morning. Tanya Z— was due to start work at noon. After their disturbing conversation, Madhavi Rao made Tanya a cup of tea and drove her to Civic so she could catch her bus home.

I had read a compressed account of all this in Justice Crispin's judgement; but in the transcript of the jury trial, Tanya Z—'s dismay and fear seemed to leak out between the words. Even without having seen her or heard her voice, one could feel her sense of the crazy unreality of what she had been told. I tried to imagine her in the bus as it trundled along, that warm Saturday morning, heading out of the city. She had slept badly in a strange house, in the bed of someone she hardly knew, and had woken to find herself in the middle of a tale so lurid, so absurd, that she might have thought she was still dreaming, or the butt of a practical joke.

As soon as she got home, she picked up the phone and dialled Madhavi Rao's number.

'Madhavi,' she said, 'I'm not comfortable with the situation. I think Len Mancini will know how to handle this. I just can't. I don't know what's going on. I'm going to either tell Len about it, or I'm going to tell the police. I want you to give me Len's phone number.'

'You can't tell the police!' said Madhavi. 'What are you doing? It's none of your business. Joe's going to be okay. Don't tell the police. There's no evidence, anyway.'

'If I tell the police and there *is* something going on,' said Tanya, 'they'll be able to do something about it – and *you'll* probably be okay.'

'If they talk to Anu,' said Madhavi, 'they'll talk to Anu's parents. They'll ask Anu's parents who her friends are, then they'll come round to my house asking questions. I don't need the police asking me questions.'

At this point in the conversation, according to Tanya's evidence, the phone was abruptly taken from Madhavi and another voice said, 'It's Anu here. What are you doing?'

'Madhavi's told me about Joe and the heroin and the suicide,' said Tanya. 'I don't know how to deal with it. I want to tell Len about it. He knows you better. He'll know whether you're serious. If you don't give me Len's phone number I'm going to call the police or the Mental Health Crisis Centre.'

'You don't know anything,' said Anu. 'What are you going to tell the police?'

'That you have heroin, that you tried to kill Joe, that you gave him Rohypnol and you tried to inject him –'

'You don't have any evidence,' said Anu, and started to cry.

Tanya Z— kept talking right over her tears. '– And that you blame him for your medical condition.'

Anu Singh's crying intensified. 'I love him, but there's that. What can I do?'

'If there's something wrong in the relationship,' said Tanya, 'you just leave. You don't murder people to punish them for what's going wrong.'

'Leave this alone!' said Anu. 'Nothing's going to happen. I won't do anything to him. If anything happens it could ruin my career!'

'Look,' said Tanya. 'Just let me tell Joe about it, then I'll leave it. I won't tell anyone else. You needn't worry about your career.'

'No!' screamed Anu. 'You'd ruin him, you'd ruin us! We're engaged. We're in love. I couldn't do anything to him! After I tried it, I sat there looking at him for two hours when he was asleep – I realised that he'd been the one who stuck by me, and that I loved him. Please don't tell anyone! All this is over with Joe, but I can't go on, knowing that some time in the future he'll find out about it, and our relationship may be ruined and possibly my career. I can't live comfortably day to day with this hanging over me.'

'Right,' said Tanya. 'Give me Len's phone number and I'll tell him about it. He'll know what to do and I'll stay out of it. I'm going to tell him that you blame Joe for your medical condition, that you wanted to kill yourself, that you had heroin, that you gave him Rohypnol and that you tried to kill him too. If it's out of character for you, if it's a result of stress and you're unlikely to go through with any of it, Len will know. He knows you better than I do. I'm really uncomfortable in this situation. I don't know you and I can't judge what's going on, but I feel somehow implicated. I have to do something.'

Singh and Rao must have taken Tanya Z—'s threats seriously, for within the hour, that Saturday morning, they had arrived at Len Mancini's house, where the phone apparently had an extension and a complex conversation was possible. Rao dialled Tanya's number and handed the receiver to Mancini.

When Mancini greeted her, Tanya Z— announced to him, 'Anu tried to kill herself and Joe last night. She was using heroin and Rohypnol.'

But Mancini's reaction was not what Tanya had expected. 'Yep. Yep,' he said. 'Okay, yep.'

'There,' said Anu, butting in on the line. 'Are you satisfied?'

'No, I'm not,' said Tanya. 'He obviously doesn't believe me.' She tried once more, and got the same off-hand response from Mancini.

Anu cut in again. 'Are you happy now?' she said. 'You've told him twice. Are you going to leave this alone?'

Tanya Z— stuck to her guns. 'No. I'm not satisfied.'

'How about *I* tell him,' said Anu, 'and you hear me tell him, so he understands everything – will that do?' Tanya agreed. Anu said, 'Okay, Len. I've been really depressed for the last couple of months – but aren't I always?'

'Yes,' said Len Mancini.

'I thought about killing myself and I thought about taking other people with me, but –'

'What's new?' said Mancini.

'I got some heroin and I considered it but I didn't do it – I never do.'

'No,' said Mancini. 'You don't.'

'There,' said Anu to Tanya, according to the transcript of the jury trial. 'Len heard everything. Is that it? Are you going to leave it alone?'

'I don't know,' said Tanya. 'I'm still not satisfied.'

'What else can I do?' said Anu. 'I can't have this hanging over my whole life.'

'I don't know,' said Tanya. 'I don't know what to do about it.'

'This is none of your business anyway,' said Anu. 'Just stay out of it. Nothing's going to happen to Joe. Len loves Joe and I love Joe. We wouldn't let anyone hurt him. Look – how about I call you tomorrow morning? You think about it and then you let me know.'

Tanya Z— agreed to this, and they hung up. But later that same morning, before she left for work, Tanya phoned Anu Singh once more and said, 'Okay. I'm going to leave this alone – but just know that if anything does happen to Joe, your friends are now implicated.'

And so this unfortunate young woman Tanya Z—, her resolve 'to be moral', as she put it, worn down by frustration – and per-haps by a suspicion that she was making a fool of herself, *being uncool* – released her terrier grip, hung up the phone and went to work.

But the story had not quite finished with her.

When Tanya got home from work at six-thirty that same day, only a few hours before the events of the fatal Saturday night would begin, Madhavi Rao pulled up outside the Z— family house in Anu's car and came to the front door, keen to talk.

'I just wanted to thank you for what you did this morning,' said Madhavi. 'Anu has told Joe how depressed she was, and every-thing is going to get better. I wanted to give you a hug and thank you for it.'

But Tanya was expecting friends over; and anyway she had plainly had a gutful. 'How can I trust you,' she said, 'after all the lies you've told me? I'll give you back your books. I don't want you to have an excuse for us to have contact again. It's better that we don't have anything more to do with each other.'

'Okay,' said Madhavi, as she was being hustled out the door, 'but this doesn't need to be dinner conversation for you and your friends.'

❧

Who else in this story was bold enough to try to alter its course, to hold up her hand and say, '*Stop!* What on *earth* do you think you're doing?' Tanya Z— came so close to blasting a hole in the force-field around Anu Singh that one can hardly bear to think of the moment when the news reached her that Joe Cinque was dead.

It was awful, too, to read the transcripts of the days of mauling cross-examination she had to face, in both the trials: to see the erosion of her certainty about herself and her memory. Again she was outmanoeuvred by heads cooler and wills tougher than hers. Tanya Z— was an earnest witness, eager to co-operate and to get things exactly right; but she was easily rattled, and defence counsel showed no mercy. Lex Lasry, Madhavi Rao's QC, yanked her story this way and that, repeatedly asking her whether she was – that word so insulting in a legal context – 'emotional'. He launched long, convoluted questions and then, when she lost her way, became irritated. He made much of the gaps in time – as long as seven months – that stretched between her bouts of memory of the incidents: she had kept notes for herself, thrown them away, spoken several times to people at the DPP, remembered further details after having given evidence at the committal, and added things to her original statement. Lasry hinted that her shocked, confused and angrily ironic responses to Rao's early morning reports of the failed suicide attempt were signs of a hard heart and a lack of care. He suggested that she hesitated to go to the police that Saturday morning because, as he put it, she had had 'three or four drinks the night before, probably looked like some kind of drunk' and was 'not dressed up'.

Tanya Z— struggled to clarify this. 'I hadn't really slept,' she said. 'My eyes were red and I was in a state of shock. I was ruffled up, and I was upset. I wasn't dressed in a suit or anything, and I thought the way I appeared would contribute to the police not taking me seriously. They would have asked me whether I'd been drinking. I would have had to say yes. I was all roughed up and I was in a panic.'

But shade had already been cast on her character; she was being made to look trivial and callous.

Anu Singh's counsel, Mr Pappas, put Tanya Z— through an equally pounding ordeal. He battered away at her about what exactly she had said to Len Mancini during the frustrating four-way Saturday morning phone call, and what precisely she thought Mancini had understood her to be telling him. At one point in Singh's solo trial, while the distressed and exhausted witness was given a short break, the judge remonstrated mildly with Pappas: 'I do not propose to stop the cross-examination, Mr Pappas, but I must say, being the jury in this case, I can tell you that I do not see it turning on fine distinctions about the extent of this lady's anticipation of the depth to which this comment had percolated into Mr Mancini's brain.'

'Your Honour,' replied the chastened Mr Pappas, 'I will cease bashing my forehead.'

But the forehead being bashed, of course, was Tanya Z—'s.

When a serious charge is laid against a person, a preliminary inquiry called a committal proceeding is held before a magistrate, who decides whether the accused should face trial. Only one side of the case is heard: the evidence that the Crown will rely on. Individual witnesses give their evidence and may be cross-examined, but no findings of guilt or innocence are made. Its purpose is only to test the sufficiency of the evidence against the accused. To read the record of it, specially after one has ploughed through the transcript of the trial proper, is to be flung back into the same story when it was in a much more sprawling, undignified state, before the Crown and defence teams had taken hold of it to smooth away its rough edges and trim off damaging or uncontrollable bits that did not fit their respective 'case concepts'.

Thus, when a young prosecutor laid before me the transcript of the Singh/Rao committal, I opened the sky-blue folder and found a document of raw human richness, clanging with artless voices, shot through with colour and marked by a sort of fabulous crudity. The proceedings are slowed down by Mr Pappas's need to keep taking notes – 'Your Worship, I am not a writing machine!' – but they are also a showcase for his old-fashioned glorying in the performance of it all. 'Madam,' he says, 'let me beg to differ . . . I am growing old at the bar table while my learned friend . . . Let us not exhaust your memory so quickly . . . If you'd be so kind . . .'

Surly, resentful-sounding witnesses, certain of them distinguished by unabashed histories of drug use, affect a world-weary tone. 'Okay,' drawls one, when questioned about recreational drugs, 'LSD, cocaine, speed, ecstasy. I've tried them all.' Another remarks that he does not go to Garema Place to score after dark: 'Canberra's a very ghost town,' he adds poetically, 'when night hits.' Others bandy words with Pappas and have their knuckles rapped for it: 'You think you've made a joke, do you, sir? Is that why you're laughing? *Is that why you're laughing?*'

One young man who unwisely attempts to spar with counsel is Jonathan Bowers-Taylor, an ex-squeeze and former housemate of Anu Singh's, and the possessor of two bachelor degrees. A few days after the murder, he tells the committal, Anu Singh called him from the remand centre and asked him to look up and bring out to her 'relevant High Court cases', and cases on insanity. Bowers-Taylor is a peevish witness, insolent and evasive. He has to be asked count-less times to stop mumbling and speak up. He comes the bounce with Pappas, who looses thunderbolts upon him. On his way out of the court at a morning tea break he calls Mr Adams, Rao's counsel, 'an imbecile'. When brought to heel he becomes aggrieved: 'I felt like I was being harassed and nitpicked.' He doesn't enjoy giving evidence, he says: indeed, 'the whole thing has been quite distaste-ful for me. I, as a young person, have a natural inclination not to dob in my friends.'

Bowers-Taylor does, however, have at his fingertips a certain amount of information about the build-up to the events in ques-tion. I had read in his evidence at the jury trial, that in late September 1997 he gave Singh and Rao an injecting lesson using a water-filled syringe. He was also, some weeks later, asked by the women to unblock a syringe in which heroin had congealed. On Saturday 25 October, the evening before Joe Cinque died, Anu Singh called Bowers-Taylor as many as eight times. She was still phoning towards eleven o'clock at night, pestering him with questions about injecting: 'Why can't you shoot up in your legs? Can you use the veins in the back of your arm?' He was 'terse' with her, he says; she kept hanging up and dialling again; and she abruptly terminated one of the calls with the words, 'I've got to go – that's Joe moving around.'

Bowers-Taylor's live-in girlfriend, an erstwhile waitress by the name of Jasmin Kent, is another of those called to the witness stand. This young woman is also, as it happens, an ex of Mr T, the law student who scored the second dose of heroin for Anu Singh on the morning of Joe Cinque's death. Kent seems unenthusiastic about being required to give evidence, and responds to Pappas's questioning with reluctance. She tells the committal that Singh often used to ring up their house and talk about killing herself. 'I told her that OD'ing from heroin was like an easy way to go, because I'd done that once. She said she couldn't kill herself with heroin because of the social stigma attached to the Indian com-munity, so that kind of killed that one.'

When I traced Jasmin Kent through to the jury trial, I found that she had been present on the September day when Singh and Rao came over for their injecting lesson, bearing as a gift some Danish pastries. 'They came to my house,' Kent reports. 'They brought me food. I asked, because I was starved. I was pretty happy about that. I said hello. I sat down and chatted to them. They were there because Jon was showing them how to shoot up. I wasn't really listening to the conversation between Jon and Anu. I was kind of watching TV. I was eating. I wasn't really switched on to it. Jon had a syringe. She put her arm out. He was showing her which vein to go in. He showed her how to draw back to get blood, that you should hit the vein. She was really squeamish. Jon would put the needle out and she'd go no, no, no. Like I said, I wasn't switched on to it. I mean that's what they came round to do.'

Still later, Jasmin Kent tells the jury trial that she had discussed with Anu Singh a range of suicide methods: 'Shooting herself. Overdosing. Running into a tree with a car.' Kent articulates, in her bolshie way, a belief that seems to have been common among many of the young people in this extended social milieu, namely that if someone wants to kill herself, it is her inalienable right to do so and scant further inquiry is called for. 'Well, if she was sick and she was dying,' says Kent under cross-examination by Mr Pappas, 'and she wanted to kill herself, that's *her* business.'

Several of the students who attended the Monday night dinner tell the court, in the jury trial, that they were informed 'quite categorically' by Madhavi Rao, as she drove them home afterwards, that 'the suicide was going to happen that night', and that she herself 'had to help'. They asked her if they should call an ambulance, or get some help, but she told them not to. The three young men speak with fervour of their concern. 'We took what was said to us extremely seriously,' says one of them, 'and we did not sleep that night.' The whole thing seemed 'so strange, like a joke or something – melodramatised, a little bit unreal'. They thought hard about whether or not it was their business. They tried to determine 'what would constitute a good action, here'. They considered ringing the police. But in the end they 'took the view that if she wanted to kill herself – and because she had deliberated this over a long period of time – it was the best action for us not to get involved'. If it had been her choice, adds one of them, 'then it would have been okay by me'.

How has it come about, this ready acceptance by people so young of the idea of suicide? Is it just mutinous rhetoric, or does it signal a new loss of heart, a collapse of shared meaning and hope? When I was twenty or so I was gripped by a novel called *Bright Day,* published just after World War II and written by

J. B. Priestley, a writer who had gone out of fashion long before I ever heard of him. The only sentence from it that had stuck in my mind over the intervening forty years was its epigraph: 'The bright day brings forth the adder.' But now, when I went looking for a copy and reread it, I came across a pertinent observation: 'As we grow older we are apt to forget that the despair of the young is even more gigantic and immediately overwhelming than their hopefulness: we never again face such towering blank walls of misery.'

The video of Anu Singh's charging at the police station, which I had seen in court and which, like the phone call to Bronwyn Cammack, had been decoded so variously by the psychiatrists, was not the only film this matter had produced. The police interviews with the two women had also been videotaped. In the DPP conference room I loaded the first cassette, dated 26 October, the day Joe Cinque died.

It had been shot by a high, fixed camera in a room whose paintwork of crimson and intense blue seemed to have been chosen with film in mind. For a moment the soundtrack was drowned out by a coarse electronic buzz, and I found myself watching a mime show, dramatic in a primitive, frightening way, all gesture and posture and grimace; then the noise cleared and it became a comprehensible official record.

Anu Singh sits at a bare table with three men in suits: D-C Harry Hains, a second detective, and her solicitor. Her long hair is up and she is wearing an ankle-length white dress with thin straps, in a silky synthetic material printed with tiny flowers. D-C Hains informs her of her rights. She replies in a light, low, ordinary voice: 'Yep. Right. Yep.' While Hains reads in a monotone from a sheet of paper, she keeps getting up and moving round the room in a fretful manner. Glancing down at herself, she notices that the skirt of her dress is stained with long streaks of black liquid. She fusses with it, trying to fold it so as to cover the marks, and returns to her chair, but her veneer of self-command is breaking up. Hains intones the words 'the death of Joe Cinque'. She lets out a stifled cry of protest, then states in a clear, measured voice, 'I'm not comprehending death, yet.' She springs to her feet. She paces and pants. She wanders to and fro in the small, brightly painted room. She covers her face with her hands, fiddles with her hair, grazes the wall with her shoulder. She drifts out of shot, then veers right up against the camera lens so that she looms into close-up, bringing to the scene a brief flash of cinematic life. The men ignore her as they would a distracted toddler. They begin to discuss her mental state and the risk of suicide. They negotiate among themselves in slow, formal voices, as if the young woman weren't there, as if she weren't brushing and rustling and bumping around the walls behind them like a moth in a lampshade.

The second video, shot two days later, shows Madhavi Rao in the same setting. It was my first clear sighting of her image. I had imagined a plump, untidy, even motherly creature, but here she is, seated at the table in the coloured room with the two detectives and a different solicitor – and at first glance she could be mistaken for a ten-year-old boy. She is small and slight, soft-faced, without make-up. Her thick black hair is cut to ear-lobe level and lies in a smooth curve against the nape of her neck. She sits very still, with her fore-arms laid on the table. Only her fingertips peep out of the cuffs of an enormous, loose, cream cotton jumper. Her posture is attentive, like that of a co-operative pupil: listening, concentrating hard. But when the detective tells her he is going to charge her with murder, a jolt of energy straightens her spine. Her eyebrows go up. She asks him to repeat himself. He does so. On the table-top her forearms fly apart in a gesture of amazed innocence. One hand, palm up, stops at the first detective's notebook, the other at the second's. She freezes, mouth agape, pointing with each open hand at a notebook. Then she lets out a short harsh breath of indignation: '*Hoh!*'

The detectives do not speak.

'I tried,' she gasps. 'At every stage. To intercede –'

The men caution her again. She subsides. She closes her mouth and rests her head on one hand. She is silent.

What deep, deep trouble Rao was in! How much she knew, how little she did! I had read only that morning, in the transcript of Singh's solo trial, how Mr Pappas and the two defence psychiatrists had strongly hinted that Rao ought to carry a certain degree of responsibility for Singh's acts. A cold draught blew across my shoulders. Would *she* have to carry the can, the tiny, indignant girl swamped in her cotton sweater, spreading her hands to the detectives with a gasp of disbelief – this polite, vague, spineless creature who preached the saving power of yoga and meditation, who stepped over columns of ants? I wanted to turn back the clock, the calendar, to 19 October 1997 – to grab her by the arm, sling her into my car, hustle her back to the house for her stuff, talk right over her protests, drive like the wind to another city, enrol her in a different university, straighten her out, *wake her up*, get her away from voracious Anu Singh, her nemesis. Too late, too late. She was going to get more time than Singh *because she wasn't mad.*

But if the judge gave so much credence to the evidence of Anu Singh's psychiatric disturbance and to the force of her delusions, where did he see them stop? Did he think of people as discrete bubbles floating past each other and sometimes colliding, or did he see them overlap, seep into each other's lives, penetrate the fabric of each other?

Where does one person's influence end, and another's responsibility begin?

In *The Silent Woman,* her book about the way public opinion has always taken the part of the suicidal poet Sylvia Plath against her husband Ted Hughes, Janet Malcolm makes the Freudian point that we side with the dead 'because of our tie to them, our identification with them. Their helplessness, passivity, vulnerability is our own.' Whatever the reason, I sided with Joe Cinque. I searched for him in all the documents. But every place where he should have been was blank, without scent or colour: a point where nothing resonated. His direct speech is rarely recorded. He is forever upstaged by Anu Singh. As the transcripts' tapestry of versions unfolds, she kills him again and again. Attention always swings back to *her:* why she did it, what sort of person *she* is, what will become of *her.* She gets bigger, louder, brighter, while he keeps fading. He blurs. He sinks into the shadows and leaks away, until all that is left of him is his name, and the frozen, saintly lineaments of a victim.

The famous twenty-minute 000 call enacts the whole tale in miniature. The foreground action is all Anu Singh's: garish, loud, full of obsessive movement, jangling with her histrionics, her hysterical demands for reassurance, her towering sense of entitlement. She babbles, she swears, she invokes God, she invents a name and gives a false address. The ambulance dispatcher, as helpless as everyone else in the face of her antics, does his utmost to calm her, to get sense out of her. He tries to force a path through her flamboyant racket, but she is busy setting up a wall of sound behind which lies Joe Cinque on the messy bed in the upper room, quietly turning blue, quietly losing his pulse; then vomiting black muck, then choking on his vomit; then quietly dying.

What was he *like?* What made him laugh? Was he grouchy or cheerful in the mornings? Did he use after-shave? What did he drink? Did he like to dance? Who did the washing? What football team did he follow? Why did he 'love' Anu Singh?

Would he ever *really* have married her?

Did he get on with Madhavi Rao, or were they rivals for Anu Singh's attention? Did Anu play them off against each other? And what did her cool friends make of Joe? They were law students; he was a scientist, an engineer. Did he cut it with them socially? Did he care, or did he draw his sense of self from a different, deeper well?

What were *his* friends like? What did they think of *her?* How did he manage, living so far away from them, and from his family?

I raked over the transcripts for scraps. I picked them up and shook them, listening for echoes of his voice.

Tanya Z— told the court that, after the dinner party on the Friday evening, people were standing around outside Joe and Anu's house, talking about what to do with the rest of the night. Anu Singh said, 'Maybe we can all go to the casino.' And Joe said, 'The women can dance and the men can gamble.'

Anu Singh's erstwhile best friend Rachel Fortunaso told the police, 'I thought that Joe was a very nice person and he was obviously smitten with Anu. Anu however regularly put him down by telling me that he was not intelligent, and would make fun of him even if he was there. I recall one instance when Anu and Joe came up to Newcastle and joined myself and a friend for dinner. Joe said something and Anu nudged me and rolled her eyes, mocking what he had said. I thought this was cruel but Joe did not seem to react to these actions or comments from Anu. He appeared to be totally devoted to her.'

Perhaps it was at the same dinner in Newcastle that the subject of ipecac first arose. Rachel Fortunaso had told the committal hearing that when Anu spoke about her weight, Joe said, 'I've heard of a substance that models overseas use, called ipecac. Apparently it induces vomiting. It's used to suppress appetite.' Anu appeared very interested. 'She said, "Can you tell me more about this?" And Joe said "No".' It wasn't hard to imagine the way in which a man – certainly any man *I* have ever known – would mention such a drug and its misuse in the service of vanity: in a tone of incredulous disgust.

Shortly after that Newcastle evening, Singh called Fortunaso to tell her she had got hold of some ipecac and was taking it. Sanjeeva Tennekoon, a chef who was at that time a house-mate of the couple, gave evidence in the jury trial that he had come home from work, towards the end of 1995, and seen Anu Singh 'dry-retching'. She told him she had taken ipecac which, she said, Joe had brought her from Newcastle the previous weekend. 'I took that bottle of ipecac,' said Tennekoon, 'and I threw it out.' Four or five days later he found a new bottle on top of the fridge where Anu Singh's colossal array of medications was kept. 'What's ipecac doing up there?' he asked. 'I got Joe to bring it,' said Singh. 'Did you?' he said to Joe. 'Yeah.' 'Why did you bring it?' 'Because Anu wanted it.'

Mr and Mrs Cinque, I knew, were enraged by this evidence. They refused to believe that their son, who never even took a Panadol for a headache, would have supplied someone else with such a stupidly damaging drug. To me, though, it fitted the overall picture of Anu Singh, and of other people's helplessness before the force of her erratic will. I remembered the Crown psychiatrist Dr Diamond, with his analysis of the ceaseless drama Singh scripted and starred in, to make her collapsing life bearable. She could have walked down to a pharmacy at the local shopping centre and bought herself a bottle of ipecac over the counter; but instead, the ailing princess commands her lover to bring the potion to her, all the way from the provincial city. I thought about her well-attested ability to get her own way, to coax people to act against their better judgement and even their moral code. She could get her father, a doctor, to make an appointment for her with a liposuction specialist, even to pay a deposit, when by his own admission she was virtually a skeleton with skin hanging off her. This was a woman of formidable coercive powers.

Sanjeeva Tennekoon told the jury trial that he and Joe went to the same gym, where they saw each other nearly every night. At the Friday night dinner party, Sanjeeva and Joe talked together at some length about Joe's new car, and about holiday plans: Joe wanted to go to Queensland in January, and he and Sanjeeva were thinking of going to Melbourne in March for the Grand Prix. Tennekoon also told the court that Joe and Anu 'used to call each other maybe sometimes about twelve to fifteen times a day'. There was no pattern, he said, as to who called whom.

What was the meaning of these neurotically frequent phone calls? Why didn't they trust each other? The stereotype, of course, is the besotted lover who in his jealousy hounds the free-spirited woman, never letting her out of his sight, always checking up on her and demanding that she account for her movements. But I remembered Mrs Cinque talking about Anu Singh's demeanour at the beautiful party her parents gave, six months before Joe was killed, and at which the Cinques had such a happy time: 'Nino and I we comment later how she cling to Joe. Even with her relatives there, she didn't leave him one minute alone all night.' And, she added, 'it was the same when they came up to visit us. No chance for us to speak alone with Joe. She was always with him.' Which of them was the more possessive?

When Mr Golding slashed Professor Mullen's psychiatric report at Singh's trial, he seemed to be stripping it of her descriptions of Joe. Tantalising fragments flew through the air: *'fairly straight . . . materialistic but protective . . . inflamed by jealousy . . . with another man'*. How I longed to read that report in its original state! Mullen had laughed charmingly as he was being censored – 'All my best lines are going!' – but he evened the score the very next day, under cross-examination, when he tossed into the ring his offhand remark, 'To the extent that she was utterly terrified of this man . . .'

Had I completely misread Joe Cinque? Was my gut feeling about him only an identification with the helpless, harmless dead? Had I been taken hostage by his parents' suffering and love?

Professor Mullen's aside made it sound as if she had been intimidated by a violent brute. Yet everybody knew what she blamed Joe for: she had told anyone who would listen that it was the ipecac. Granted, her trial heard evidence that Singh had complained to a university counsellor, a month before she killed Joe, that he had hit her and 'verbally abused' her. She could not leave him, Singh told the counsellor, because she was rendered financially and emotionally dependent on him by her 'medical condition'. But anybody who had sat through her trial would be tempted to see her approach to the counsellor as one more scene in the narcissistic melodrama she was staging. Nowhere else in any of the evidence does a witness breathe a single word about Joe's having raised a hand to her. The suggestion that she was harbouring a terrible secret about domestic violence simply did not stack up.

I walked back along Ainslie Avenue to my tiny hostel room, crept under the doona, and went to sleep. When I woke, night had fallen. I opened the window. The air outside was cold. The magpies had stopped singing. It was only six p.m.

PART SIX

At the end of August 1999, home again in Sydney, I called Dr Singh at his medical practice and told him I was interested in writing the story.

'What sort of *conclusion* do you intend your book to have?' he asked.

'I don't know, yet.'

'Because whether this judge – Crispin – whether he's put my daughter in prison for punishment or for treatment – I don't know! I don't know! Because why do you punish someone who's sick? This girl is back to normal, now! She is back to normal! That Professor Hayes – she said my daughter was coming off drugs! If you are in professional bloody Behaviour medicine – God forbid you should treat someone! My daughter is much better now! She's even looking after the other girls in there! And Helen – she is thinking of writing something herself! She says, "Dad, people in here, they shouldn't be here! They don't belong here! They don't need here!" She is an intelligent girl! She's not stupid! One girl is an arsonist! You know – burns things? And she's getting no psychiatric treatment! Nothing! Because her parents can't afford it! My daughter is getting psychotherapy! Once a week she is getting psychotherapy! Because I can afford! But these other girls – they get nothing! They are punished for being sick!

'These people, though, Joe's parents – they are still angry! They haven't got over their grief! You saw the mother – she was

185

angry! I don't want to do anything that will hurt them even more!'

'No,' I said. 'That's very important.'

'I'll speak to my daughter. I'll ask her if she will have a chat with you! You know, I think that being in gaol may even improve her! Perhaps the guilt will die out in her! I have a feeling she will become a normal person!'

I phoned him again several days later, as we had arranged. He invited me to come to their house on the following Tuesday. 'My wife will also be there. We will sit down and have a chit-chat. I have not yet made up my mind. I want to know what your ideas are and how you are going to tackle such a book. And it all depends on whether my daughter agrees.'

On the appointed spring afternoon I took a train out to their suburb. I was early, and loitered for a while in the station shopping centre, which had a marked Asian flavour. In one shop I bought a white china bowl patterned with blue twining leaves in a vaguely oriental style. Later when I turned it over and examined the base, I saw a couple of squiggles that looked Chinese; but to this day I persist in thinking of it as Indian, and as an accidental memento of my first real contact with the Singhs.

I had never been to that part of Sydney before. Three things about it surprised me: first, its old, established, bourgeois solidity; next, its splendid trees; and third, the fact that its wide streets were full of Indian and Southeast Asian people *on foot* – not strolling or taking exercise for the sake of it, as one would see morning and evening in the suburbs where I lived, but carrying shopping, walking fast and purposefully towards a destination. I too walked, along leafy streets studded with the odd grand old mansion, from the station to the Singhs' Federation house.

The two doctors welcomed me into an agreeably furnished living room. They were a good-looking middle-class couple, with the gloss of their profession on them. They called me by my first name, but gave no guidance as to how I should address them. Mrs Singh was a quiet-mannered woman, curvy and warm. She wore jeans and heeled boots, and her thick hair was cut shortish, but her presence was intensely feminine: her black mohair top was discreetly appliquéd with sparkles, and she had knotted a little scarf round her neck, 1950s style. Her face was serious, shadowed perhaps by years of sadness. Her husband, in a sweater, wool trousers and black lace-ups, wore a gold Sikh bangle on one wrist. He was a big man, spontaneous and outgoing, with a heavy, forceful energy.

While Mrs Singh was out of the room getting tea, Dr Singh dived in at the deep end. He told me that on one of his visits to their house Joe had said, in front of his daughter, 'Dr Singh – if Anu died I'd want to die *with* her.'

'He meant to tell me how much he loved her – but I took him aside. I said, "Listen, Joe – you must not mention dying in front of Anu! She has talked about suicide!"'

Mrs Singh returned with a tray and invited me to sit on the sofa. She and I drank tea, but Dr Singh could not seem to settle. He crossed the room to a small table against the wall behind me. I could hear the clink of glass. Still out of my eye-line, he suddenly burst out, 'Is there anything in this for us?'

'What do you mean?' I said.

'Any money? If it should be a best-seller?' He came back to the other sofa with a glass of scotch in his hand and sat down, planting his feet on the pale green rug.

'I don't think so,' I said. 'I make a living as a freelance journalist. This book could take me years to write. I don't want to get
an advance from a publisher, in case I find I can't make it into the
book I want.'

'We could do the book together.'

'I wouldn't like that,' I said nervously.

'Why not?'

'Because I wouldn't be independent.'

He began to question me with a gusty intensity on what I
planned to write.

'What I want to do,' I said, surprising myself, for until that
moment I had not managed to articulate it, even in my thoughts,
'is to enlarge my imagination to the point where it can encompass
truths as widely separated as your version of events and the
Cinques'.'

Mrs Singh, who had been listening to this with courteous
attention, nodded and brightened, as if she had readily grasped
what I meant. She caught my eye with a flash of intelligence and
opened her mouth to speak, but her husband cut across her and
declared roundly, 'You must tell the truth! The main character is
my daughter!'

Mrs Singh subsided and so did I. I sat quietly, meeting his eye,
while he spoke with vigour and at some length about how sick
Anu had got, and how he and his wife had tried so hard to get
help for her. Mrs Singh told me, having to sustain her line of
thought against his excitable interruptions, that when she had
called the Dean of the ANU law school to ask whether her
daughter was going to class and handing in her work, the Dean
had replied that since Anu was an adult, he could not report on or
discuss her progress with Mrs Singh. We all agreed that, whatever
the law said about the rights of adulthood, this was ridiculous.

They had become so concerned about Anu's state, Mrs Singh went on, that they had made an application to have her hospitalised against her will. The application had to be heard by a magistrate, however, and before the process could take place, Anu had killed Joe – or, as Mrs Singh put it, *'this thing happened'*.

In the remand centre, no psychiatric treatment had been provided. Her parents tried to bail her out. Their application was refused. They considered making a second application, but decided not to, since they both had to keep working, and thus could not give her at home the twenty-four-hour care she needed.

'And I think she was always a headstrong girl?' I said.

'Always,' said Dr Singh. 'Always.'

So they engaged and paid for the psychiatrist who treated her in Belconnen Remand Centre, Dr Fatma Lowden. Otherwise, said Dr Singh, she would have had no treatment at all 'for her psychosis'.

'She is studying now,' he said. 'She is about to sit her final exams.'

'Will she still be able to practise law, though?' I said. 'With a criminal conviction?'

Dr Singh sprang to his feet. He propped one elbow on the mantelpiece above the empty fireplace, and rapped at the air with the forefinger of his hand not holding the glass of scotch. 'She *will*! She *must*!' he said loudly. 'I will see to it! If she is *not* allowed, I will take it all the way to Human Rights! When she's served her time, she must not be punished further! That's discrimination! I will fight it!'

Mrs Singh said nothing. Her eyes seemed to darken. There was a pause.

'Which of her friends from university is she still in touch with?' I asked.

'None,' said her father.

I was surprised. 'Not a single one?'

'No. You see, Helen, to her now they don't seem very *mature*.'

'That's one question I would like to find an answer for,' I said. 'Her so-called friends. Why didn't they *do* something, when she started obsessively talking about suicide – let alone murder?'

Dr Singh did not reply to this, but raised his eyebrows, looked me right in the eye and held out one hand in a palm-up gesture.

They asked me if I was going to talk to Joe's family.

'I've already spoken to them.'

'That poor woman,' said Dr Singh, 'is still very angry! But what can you do?'

'I suppose,' I said carefully, 'they will be angry forever. Their family is smashed. Joe's brother is terribly wounded.'

They nodded. They did not appear to be offended. We sat for a moment without speaking. Then Mrs Singh sighed.

'We loved Joe,' she said. 'They had a marriage account. They put money into "Anu and Joe's Marriage Account".' Her face had become bleak, filled with a pained darkness.

I suddenly recalled having glimpsed, at the Cinques' house when they were shuffling through a folder of documents they wanted to show me, a letter that Mrs Singh had written to them after Joe died. They flipped past it in their search, pausing only to identify its writer, but in that one flash I had seen the strickenness of the handwriting, the way each line started level then plunged as it approached the right margin, as if the hand pushing the pen were barely able to keep moving under its load.

Someone knocked at the front door. It was a maths tutor for Anu Singh's younger brother: we must vacate the room. As her parents led me through a modern kitchen and into a small TV lounge lined with books, they spoke about Anu's amazing ability to do brilliantly in exams with a bare minimum of study. 'She could look at one page,' said Mrs Singh, 'run her eye down it, and know it by heart. She has a photographic memory.' In any other circumstance I might have quoted a deflating (and haunting) remark that my grandfather had made to me when I was a bright and bouncy schoolgirl: 'You are quick on the uptake, my girl, *but that is not enough.*'

The phone rang in another room. Dr Singh went out to answer it and returned to tell his wife the call was for her. Mrs Singh hurried off. While she was away, Dr Singh said, 'It's Anu. We haven't told her you're here. We don't want to upset her, or worry her. She is doing her exams soon.'

He explained that his daughter was in Mulawa, the women's section of Silverwater gaol, a mere five-minute drive from their house. This information, and the fact that she could casually call home, stunned me. I sat in silence, sunk in the leathery depths of an armchair, until Mrs Singh returned.

The couple remained standing, leaning against bookshelves, plainly waiting for me to leave.

'Anu has the job of librarian at the gaol,' said Mrs Singh. 'She's teaching an Aboriginal girl to read and write. One hour a day.'

'Shouldn't they have tutors?'

'They have tutors,' said Dr Singh. 'But the girl wouldn't ask them for help.'

'She came to Anu and asked *her*,' said Mrs Singh. 'She said "Because you're Indian". She wouldn't ask anyone who was . . .'

The word *white* hung in the room, unspoken.

The Singhs were due at a medical meeting in Liverpool. They kindly offered to drive me to my train. Because her husband had drunk two scotches while we talked, Mrs Singh took the wheel, and off we went in a softly rumbling, high 4WD. They delivered me to the station. We said goodbye. It was already dark. A train came and I got on it. In my carriage several crazy-looking, stupefied people sat slumped in their seats. All the way to Central a small, wiry, tattooed fellow paced up and down the aisles, foully raging and cursing, trying to pick a fight. The other men ignored him, but the air in the carriage hummed with fear.

❧

Thinking next day, in a troubled way, about Dr Singh's unqualified backing of his daughter, I remembered one of my sisters telling me about a conversation she had had, years before, with our mother. 'Mum said, "You can always come to me and Dad, you know, if you're ever in trouble. We'll always help you – unless, of course, you've done something *really* bad. Like murdering someone." '

We both laughed; it was typical of Mum, a diffident woman, to make a splendid offer then hedge it round with conditions.

'I said thanks and everything,' my sister went on, 'but actually I was furious. I was thinking, Wouldn't that be when I'd *really* need help?'

I related these things to my close friend, a Jewish mother of three. Perhaps I meant to amuse her, but she didn't laugh. She looked at me seriously. 'The world ends,' she said, 'at your children's skin.'

In early October 1999 Maria Cinque called to tell me she was back from Italy. She gave me a rapid account of the ankle operation she had undergone in a Bologna clinic, another attempt to repair the botched surgery she had had in Australia after the car smash twenty years earlier. The surgeon had found a small piece of bone pressing against a nerve, and removed it: she was hopeful.

I asked after Anthony.

'No good. He come to Italy with me, he come back, Nino kick him out, I don't know where he is. I hope he's gonna get over this and have some sort of life.'

She asked me if I had interviewed *her,* if I'd visited *her* in prison, if I'd seen *her* parents. I replied that I had been to the Singhs' house to discuss with them the possibility of an interview with their daughter, but that they didn't want to ask her till she had finished her exams.

'So,' said Maria Cinque bitterly. 'She's gonna do her exams, is she. She gonna be a lawyer over my dead body. She ruin my family. My son is dead – who cares. I'm a very angry person at the moment. They can go on with their life, but my life is shit, if you'll excuse the language. I'm gonna make trouble for them. If I ever see *her* walking down the street I'm gonna –'

'What?' I said anxiously. 'What are you going to do?'

She forged onwards, in a voice dark with irony. 'If there's no justice,' she said, 'you gotta make your own justice, eh?'

'I'm worried about you.'

'If *she* can kill an innocent person and get only ten years because she's not sane, why can't I? Do you think *I'm* sane, at the moment? *Do you think I'm sane?*'

'Are your friends still around you?'

'*Yes*,' she said impatiently. Then her voice thickened and weakened. 'Two years ago he was here . . .'

With horror I realised what month it was. 'Oh – it's almost – it's coming up to the anniversary! No wonder you feel so terrible!' I heard myself babbling and winced, expecting her to bite back savagely, as my widowed sister did: *What do you mean? I feel terrible all the time. I don't need an anniversary to feel terrible.*

But she only said, rehearsing the precious fact, 'Two years ago he was here, he stayed the weekend . . .'

I could hear her slightly accelerated breathing. There was a pause. I asked her if they would be going to Canberra in November for Madhavi Rao's trial.

'Of course we'll be there,' she said. 'Of course we will. She's gonna talk, we're gonna find out more things. They're gonna do it with judge alone too. We hope we get another judge because we hate that one. He's a bastard. I'm very angry. I'm *angry*. Singh's probably got her degree by now. I saw on TV last week the thing about the women's gaol. It's a hard life they have there, eh. A little room, a TV, a computer – yeah, a very *hard life*, isn't it.'

Under her flailing sarcasm I began to panic. Nothing I could think of to say or do would ever be of any use to her. I was helpless, only a vessel into which she would pour forever this terrible low fast stream of anguish. The pressure of her pain was intolerable. I would give way under it. I too would fail her. I did not know how to bring the phone call to an end. But then she got a grip on herself. Once more she drew on her deep reserves of formal grace, and let me off the hook. We would see each other – yes, we would meet again in Canberra. I asked her to give Nino my best wishes, and offered the same to her. With dignity she accepted my timid crumbs. We said goodbye. I hung up, exhausted, in awe. I longed to know her, but I was afraid that I would not be strong enough.

PART SEVEN

I flew to Canberra on the evening of 23 November 1999. The plane was almost empty. A silent taxi driver took me into town. We sped along the dark, quiet streets under a raving moon. Dry air rushed in through the open window. Where would Madhavi Rao spend this perfect summer night? When your murder trial starts, do you just *stay in a hotel*? Would her family be with her? Would she have to take a pill to go to sleep?

The small dark girl in the outsize cotton jumper, who might have saved Joe Cinque. Tomorrow I would see her for the first time.

When I walked into the court at five to ten, Rao was sitting by herself on a chair near the bar table. She was so tiny, in her cream trouser suit and black loafers, her spectacles and neat haircut, that one could almost have missed her. Like the sweater in the police video, her suit looked too big for her: she resembled a child in adult's clothing. She wore no make-up. She sat still with her hands in her lap and her feet squarely planted. She was not in custody and her status showed in her demeanour: she seemed ordinary, as quietly respectful and patient as any onlooker. She was alert to the minor dramas that unrolled in the court before the judge arrived, while counsel settled themselves. When a loud-voiced sheriff barged in and started throwing her weight around about note-taking, mobile phones and the wearing of sunglasses, Rao turned on her chair like the rest of us to see what the fuss was about. Beside her on the floor she had placed a large, flat-based, brown leather shoulder-bag. It looked brand-new. Its straps stood vertical in a stiff double curve, like things frozen in motion.

The housekeeping part of the proceedings had begun two days earlier. I bailed up one of my two young journalists, who hissed to me a rapid précis of what I had missed. On Monday Rao had pleaded not guilty to all four charges: murder, unlawful and felonious slaying, attempted murder and administering a stupefy-ing drug. To speed the whole thing up, many of the original witnesses from the aborted jury trial would not be called again: the judge had spent Tuesday in his chambers rereading the relevant evidence in transcript. Judge and jury, despite Mrs Cinque's hopes, were to be combined once more in the person of Justice Crispin.

Once he strode in, things went with a swing.

The Crown called its first witness, 'Mr T', the man who had sold to Anu Singh, and loaded into syringes for her, the heroin that was to kill Joe Cinque. I had imagined someone sleazy, but the young man who stepped on to the stand looked serious, even severe. He must rue the day he let his fellow-students Singh and Rao cross his threshold; but he was now a law clerk, which meant, I supposed, that the immunity from prosecution he had been granted had worked its magic, and that he had been admitted to the next stage in the process of becoming a lawyer. He was tall and slender, pale, thin-faced, with dark eyes and hair, and dressed in a suit, blue shirt and maroon tie. On his right hand he wore a silver ring.

In early August 1997, he said, Anu Singh came to his flat with

Madhavi Rao. Singh confided in him about her ipecac symptoms and suicide plans, and asked him to help her get hold of a gun. Mr T's attempts to console Singh in her troubles, and his mention of his own dark times and suicide attempt, rolled right off her back. He had no idea if she really had the money to buy a gun, and he didn't care either way: he thought it was 'too silly for words'. A few days later she changed tack and asked him to explain the mechanism of a lethal heroin overdose.

'I said it was very easy to overdose and die,' said Mr T. 'I told her how long it would take. She – or a person – would stop breathing fairly instantly and be dead in a number of minutes. She asked how much heroin would be needed. I told her fifty to a hundred dollars' worth, for someone who wasn't an addict. She said, "I don't have the money now, but when I do, I'd like to get some."'

Around this time Mr T had bumped into Madhavi Rao in a lecture hall. She said to him, 'Don't worry about Anu. I don't think she'll go through with getting the heroin.' A week or so after that, Anu Singh called him. She had the money, and wanted to buy half a gram. 'I said, "I can arrange that – come around."'

The two women turned up at his place with $250. He went 'elsewhere' and scored half a gram. Then, at his dining room table, he showed them how to prepare a hit. 'I mixed it in a spoon with water,' he said, 'showing and explaining what I was doing.' After he had injected himself – 'because that would have been the first thing on my mind,' he added, with what could have been either hip irony or the harsh self-contempt of the reformed junkie – 'they said they wanted to have some too. I injected Anu first, then Madhavi. I used the same syringe. Madhavi said, "That's nice."'

Mr T raised his eyebrows in a wry grimace. But his lesson, I thought, must have gone in one ear and out the other; only weeks later, the women had applied to Jonathan Bowers-Taylor for a refresher course in the use of the needle.

In October 1997, Anu Singh showed up at Mr T's flat with $500, wanting to buy a full gram. He went off and scored two half-weights, injected a small amount into her, then at her request loaded the balance of it into two syringes. 'I asked her why she wanted so much, and in two syringes.' Mr T sighed. He spread his hands on his thighs. His face was white and tense. 'She said, "Someone's coming with me." I said, "What! You mean someone wants to commit suicide with you? Who?" We both said, at the same time, that I didn't need to know who.'

And then Mr T's last sighting of Anu Singh, on the day Joe Cinque died: the Sunday morning visitor in the long white dress with $250 in her hand, her purchase of another half-weight, her grand statement, 'Today's the day', his replying, 'Don't be ridiculous', and her flurried departure with the loaded syringe.

Madhavi Rao's counsel, Lex Lasry QC, was a big fair solid fellow with a tanned face, who wore his wig tilted forward over his brow. Cross-examining, he stressed that at the time in question Mr T was using fifty to a hundred dollars' worth of heroin a day, and suggested that his addiction must have affected his memory as well as his judgement. Mr T kept trying to protest this point, but Lasry repeatedly squashed him: 'Your job is to *sit there and answer questions.*'

Mr T subsided with a twist of the mouth and a sigh, and resumed his laconic manner. Yes, Anu Singh had been the instigator of the whole business with the heroin. Madhavi Rao was plainly not an addict. Even after such a small taste, she 'tried to stand up and fell over'. Mr T believed Anu Singh was using the heroin 'for pain relief and enjoyment'. He never thought she would commit suicide. 'I didn't believe she'd go through with it,' he said. 'I didn't believe a word of it.'

And indeed, I thought, in his hard-eyed way he had read Singh correctly. As for how he had read Madhavi Rao, nobody really asked him, and he did not say. She was hardly even present, in his account. Anu Singh might have been sent to gaol, but she was still right up front, in full colour, playing the lead. Rao was the blur behind her.

During the morning break, Madhavi Rao wandered at large in the Supreme Court hallway. She appeared to be quite alone, except for a tall, kindly-looking woman in her forties whom I took to be her counsel's solicitor and who occasionally hovered near her in the lobby. I could not get used to the fact that Rao could go, for example, to the public toilet unescorted. When she brushed past me in the doorway, I glanced down at her – she must have been barely five feet tall – and saw her smooth face, her small pearl ear-rings, her thick cap of dark hair, the fine gold sides of her glasses. Her uncoloured mouth was closed without strain. I was struck by her self-possession. Anu Singh had been instantly recognisable as that classic type, the sex bomb round whom the air crackles with an agitating static, but Rao was a different proposition altogether. She was closed and quiet. I could not read her.

She sat down on a bench in the lobby. A young man with cropped hair and an ear-ring, dressed in a baggy green T-shirt and flares with embroidered hems, wandered in through the glass doors and strolled up to her.

'G'day, Madhavi!' he said with a tentative cheerfulness.

She glanced up and smiled at him.

He moved closer. 'How you goin'?'

'You're a witness,' she said in a clear, carrying voice. 'I'm not allowed to talk to you.'

His face faded. 'I just wanted to make sure you . . .'

She lowered her eyes, and he drifted away.

Madhavi Rao at university had had plenty of ordinary friends. The next Crown witness, Rebecca Lord, was one who had been close to her: a slender, bright-faced girl whose ponytail and leotard-like black top gave her the look of a dancer. Like many other peripheral characters in this story, she claimed to have expressed real concern about Madhavi Rao's passivity towards her devouring friend Anu Singh. Madhavi, she said, was always taking Singh here and there, looking out for her, even being called by Singh's mother about Anu's problems.

'I told Madhavi,' said Rebecca Lord, 'that Anu was exerting a lot of pressure on her – that she should tell Anu to back off.' Madhavi tried, but Anu didn't listen: she just kept coming round.

Rebecca had no time for Singh. She spoke about her with a wary distaste. When Singh big-noted in her presence about the heroin she was going to buy, Rebecca warned her: 'You're going into the dark.' Madhavi had told Rebecca that Anu was planning to kill herself, and that she was going to throw a send-off party before she did it. One of Madhavi's tasks, in preparation for the Monday night dinner, was to get hold of some syringes from a chemist.

'Why are you *doing* all this?' Rebecca asked her.

Madhavi explained to her Anu's reasons for wanting to die. She added that Anu was upset because Joe didn't trust her 'fidelity-wise', and that Anu was angry with Joe because he had been the one to break up her relationship with her previous boyfriend, Simon Walsh.

By this time, Rebecca had made it very clear to Madhavi that she wanted nothing to do with Anu Singh's 'last night on earth party'.

On Saturday 25 October, the night before Joe Cinque died, Madhavi Rao had arranged to go with Rebecca and Olivia Pipitone to the Art School Ball. The three women were supposed to get dressed for the ball at Madhavi's place in Condamine Street, but when Rebecca arrived there with her outfit, Madhavi wasn't home. Rebecca hunted her down by phone, and located her at Anu and Joe's place. Eventually Madhavi rushed home, distracted and odd. She advised Rebecca and Olivia to forget all the things she had told them about Anu; she said she didn't want to get them into trouble. The three friends got dressed and took a taxi to a nightclub in Civic called Heaven, where they stayed till about eleven-thirty, then walked to the Art School where the ball was in progress.

Rebecca saw Madhavi on and off throughout the evening, and occasionally greeted her in passing. Sometime after midnight she noticed Madhavi sitting on the floor, looking upset. She went to her. Madhavi told her that when she had been at Antill Street earlier in the evening, before she had come home to dress for the ball, everything between Anu and Joe had seemed to be resolved – but that Anu had suddenly turned on her, and accused her of having put something in Joe's drink.

'Something's not right with her,' said Rebecca. 'If she doesn't trust *you*, her best friend, there's nothing you can do to help her any more. You should call her parents.'

'I can't,' said Madhavi. 'She'd come after me.'

'Go to the police, then,' said Rebecca. 'They might be able to take out a restraining order or something.'

The friends stayed at the ball till 'around dawnish'. Soon after that the group dropped Madhavi Rao at home in Condamine Street.

Rebecca Lord was a Crown witness, but even so, like almost everyone else, she didn't have a bad word to say about Madhavi Rao. Indeed, under cross-examination she willingly drew a very affectionate picture of the accused. She was fun-loving, said Lord, and always available to help – in fact she would go out of her way to help people. She had some difficulty in standing up for herself, but she was warm, she was 'deeply caring', not at all the sort of person who would be interested in doing harm to anyone. The time she spent with Anu Singh caused her a good deal of annoyance, and she had tried many times to break away from her. Anu overwhelmed her, but Madhavi felt an obligation to help Anu if she could, specially regarding her physiological complaints, which Rebecca herself, however, was 'dubious about'. Rebecca considered Anu Singh to be 'a very manipulative person who put on shows'. Her talk about buying heroin had struck Lord as 'a bit of a production'. Madhavi, however, had persisted in trying to be helpful: she did things like taking Anu to yoga, though Anu had told Rebecca on the phone one day that yoga was 'a lot of crap'.

The lady who lived next door to 79 Antill Street was a retired public servant called Ms Josephine McLaughlin. This witness recalled that in January 1997 new tenants had moved into the adjacent townhouse, and that one of them had been 'an Indian girl' with 'her hair on top of her head'. Ms McLaughlin had had little to do with her neighbours, apart from saying hullo, but she had sometimes been able to hear their conversation, specially at night when both houses had their windows open. On one occasion, perhaps three weeks before Sunday 26 October, the day Joe Cinque was killed, she had heard raised voices from next door – 'yes, but not a *nasty* raised voice': usually when she heard her neighbours they were happy and laughing.

Ms McLaughlin had been woken early in the morning of that Sunday by the sound of a car being started very close to her fence. The previous night had been the change-over to daylight saving: was she absolutely certain about the time? 'I've got thirteen clocks in my lounge room,' said Ms McLaughlin stoutly, 'and I adjusted every single one.'

Dismissed, she marched out of the court in her black suede heels and loose striped pyjama suit, her brows pinched in an efficient frown.

Now the Crown called Wholly High Dunstan, another skinny little Audrey Hepburn figure in a black top, with her dark hair in a ponytail, and clear, glowing ivory skin. In one of those tiny, creaky, nasal modern voices, she told the court how Madhavi Rao had moved into her share house, in Condamine Street, Turner, and taken the room closest to the front door. The household phone was kept in the hallway of the house. Once Madhavi moved in, however, it began to ring at about seven every morning and continued through the day and into the night. The frequency of the calls, which were more often than not from Anu Singh, drove the other residents crazy, so eventually the phone was moved into Madhavi's room each night and left there till morning.

Towards midnight on Saturday 25 October, Wholly Dunstan saw Madhavi Rao at the Art School Ball. Because she was concerned about Madhavi's relationship with Anu, she asked Rao if she was all right, and 'told her to knuckle down and study hard'.

Wholly came home from the ball well after sunrise on the Sunday morning. As she came down the hill towards the Condamine Street house, she saw Anu's car parked at a dangerous angle on the road in front of the house. Madhavi was standing on the porch, and Anu was walking towards the car, wearing an off-white empire-line dress.

'I'm sorry,' said the judge, 'what is an "empire line"?'

Eagerly Wholly Dunstan turned to him to describe it – something the young woman knew more about than any of these men. Making illustrative gestures at her own torso, she said, 'It's where the sort of waist of the dress is up *here*, and it goes *up* and *out*.'

'Jane Austen's heroines were fond of wearing them, as I recall,' said Mr Golding, 'if your Honour pleases.'

'I'm afraid my experience with heroines has been somewhat limited,' said Justice Crispin, 'but I will defer to your obviously greater experience in life.'

Wholly Dunstan agreed, under cross-examination by Mr Lasry, that whereas she and her friends tended to go out to clubs, the people in the social group Madhavi shared with Anu Singh were in the habit of going to dinner parties at each other's houses. She described Madhavi Rao as gentle, concerned at all times to make other people happy; maternal, open, caring, occasionally talking round in circles; and 'very giving'. Being nice meant that Madhavi was popular, but it also meant she had a lot of crazy friends – like the obsessed and peculiar Anu, who constantly dominated her time. In fact, Madhavi had expressed envy of Wholly Dunstan's ability to confront people over some domestic issue: 'I wish *I* could stand up to people,' she had said to Wholly, 'the way you do.'

Madhavi Rao, said Dunstan, was 'in the *nicest* possible way someone who couldn't plan her way out of a paper bag'. Here even the judge laughed. The witness, emboldened by his human response, risked an unsolicited comment. 'Oh,' she said, fluttering her hands round her face, 'I think this whole idea of her being the mastermind is *very* far-fetched. She was *scatty*. She gave too much of her time to other people.'

Several other witnesses, young men coming home at dawn on the Sunday from the Art School Ball, had seen Madhavi Rao and Anu Singh in the street outside the Condamine Street house at about six-thirty a.m., looking 'pretty strange' and behaving as if they had quarrelled. The bloke in the embroidered flares whom Madhavi Rao had rebuffed in the Supreme Court lobby said he got back to Condamine Street at about two a.m. and stayed the night with his girlfriend, who lived there; from 'sun-up' on, he had heard the phone ring several times, but had not bothered to answer it till after eleven-thirty a.m., when his girlfriend had left for work. When he did answer it, at about noon, the caller was Anu Singh. She asked if Madhavi was there. He thought she was, but because she had had 'a big night out', he told Anu that she wasn't. Ten minutes later she rang again, and again he protected Madhavi by saying she wasn't there. At some time during the afternoon he met Madhavi in the Condamine Street kitchen. 'She looked like she just got outa bed. I told her there'd been a call from Anu. She said, "If Anu calls again, let me know – I've got to ask her sumpthin'."'

Dressed in T-shirts, necklaces, baggy cargo pants and coloured runners, the young male witnesses slouched in and out of the court with their hands thrust deep in their pockets. They shared an odd demeanour – resentful, wry, even defiant, though Justice Crispin was always gently courteous to them, giving them eye-contact and smiling down at them when he spoke to them. They were like sulky children. It was as if no formal demeanour were available to them. One would hardly have been surprised to hear them address the judge by his first name.

'You're free to go,' said Justice Crispin to the one who had answered the Condamine Street phone.

'Cheers,' he replied, and shambled off.

Next morning as I came round the corner of the Magistrates' Court, heading for the Supreme, I saw Mr and Mrs Cinque talking under a shady tree with a man dressed in combat gear. I approached to greet them and realised the man was D-C Harry Hains. We teased him about his macho get-up. He told us cheerfully that he was working with the Water Police while he waited for a transfer to Christmas Island; meanwhile, he had to undertake weapons training.

'Oooh!' I said. 'Which weapons?'

He affected a scowl and recited deadpan, '*Remington 870P pump action shotgun.*'

Mrs Cinque, mother of sons, rocked back on her heels with laughter. 'You look younger than you are,' she said to him affectionately.

But once Maria Cinque returned to her post in the courtroom, her face lost its softness and went grim. Things for Madhavi Rao, too, despite the glowing character studies that Mr Lasry had drawn from her friends, now seemed to darken.

Detective Sergeant Gregory Ranse, balding, tanned, in gold-framed glasses, told how he and D-C Hains had taken out a search warrant on Monday 27 October, the day after Joe Cinque's death; at about eleven o'clock that night they had gone, with six other police officers and a tape recorder, to the house in Condamine Street. They had searched Madhavi Rao's bedroom, where they found, along with Anu Singh's torn-up diary, a Rohypnol packet still bearing its prescription label, some apparently used syringe packs, some alcohol swabs, a quantity of printed material, pamphlets about drugs, drug dependency, veins and arteries, and seven foolscap pages, hand-written in pencil, on the subject of Rohypnol.

D-S Ranse came under heavy fire from Lasry's junior, the clear-voiced Mr Brady, about whether he had properly cautioned Rao and observed all her legal rights during the search of her house that night. Telstra records showed that no one had phoned out from the Condamine Street house after nine p.m., but the detective main-tained that he had heard Rao speaking on the phone, and had assumed that she was 'accessing a legal practitioner'.

At this, Madhavi Rao drew a quick breath of indignation, and swung her head towards the gallery. Her eyebrows went up and her mouth fell open in the expression of someone about to say, 'Did you hear *that*?' The eyes that her glance met were mine. For a second or two we stared each other right in the face. Then she turned back to the action.

'Are you saying,' said Mr Brady sarcastically, 'that a solicitor *just happened* to ring Ms Rao?'

'Funny you should say that,' said the detective. 'I don't know. But that does happen – I've known it to happen – at the police station. It was a flowing conversation between her and me. Maybe the questions were back to front, but *she* was the one who kept talking.'

Madhavi Rao pulled an ironic grimace, almost a smile, full of bitterness. She uncrossed and recrossed her legs, and her face settled back into its smooth reserve.

A year earlier, when Rao and Singh were being jointly tried before a jury, their friend Len Mancini was called as a witness. What he said had caught both Crown and defence off guard: indeed he had casually thrown a rather large spanner into the works. His evidence suggested that Anu Singh, rather than being driven to kill by her psychiatric condition, had had 'a rational motive' for killing Joe Cinque: that late on the Saturday night Joe had told Anu he was going to leave her. This piece of information had been passed to Len Mancini by Rao, who told him she had heard it from Singh herself. At that point Justice Crispin, for complex legal reasons, had decided to dismiss the jury and abort that trial.

Len Mancini, then, was a crucial witness – a close friend of both Rao and Singh, and the repository of a great deal of relevant information. He was also, of course, the man whom the unfortunate, honourable Tanya Z— had thought of as 'a steady sort of person', and to whom she had addressed her fruitless plea, on the Saturday morning before Joe Cinque died, for assurance that Joe was not in danger.

In my experience, few men have the emotional stamina to sustain a friendship – as distinct from an affair – with a high-maintenance histrionic like Anu Singh: I was curious to see Mancini. Now, in Rao's trial, he was to be called again. But first, the Crown called his parents.

Tony Mancini, from Griffith, New South Wales, was a big, broad, slow-talking man with an Australian accent and a farmer's profound, almost blackish tan. On Sunday 26 October 1997, he said, he and his wife were on their way from Griffith to Sydney, where Mrs Mancini was to have an operation. They travelled via Canberra to stay a night with their son. They got to Len's place, he said, at about three on the Sunday afternoon, and found him waiting for them, with Madhavi Rao. The young people, 'very nervous, very upset', told Len's parents that the paramedics were at Anu's house – that 'Anu had tried to kill Joe.'

Mr Mancini, having met Anu Singh several times in the past, responded to this news with predictable scepticism. He thought it was 'more of Anu's melodrama – unbelievable'. But he urged them to phone the Canberra hospitals and check whether anyone by the name of Cinque had been admitted. Madhavi made the calls, and reported that nobody had. She seemed, said Mr Mancini, under pressure, disturbed, agitated.

Mrs Kathy Mancini, an imposing dark-haired woman in a navy blue blazer, jewellery and gold shoes, said that she and her husband had encouraged Madhavi to make a further call, to Joe and Anu's house. Madhavi dialled the number, listened for a moment without speaking, then hung up abruptly, saying, 'That was Joe, and he was very angry.' Mrs Mancini had taken this to mean that Joe was all right.

But a horrible feeling crept through me. *Some time after three* she made this call? And Joe *spoke* to her? But hadn't he been declared dead just before two o'clock? I glanced at Madhavi Rao. Her face was still, and closed.

Mrs Mancini completed her account of their late Sunday lunch. At the table, Madhavi told Len's parents that Anu had accused her, the night before, of having put drugs in both her drink and Joe's. She said she'd had a 'massive fight' with Anu;

Madhavi had really stood up to her, and told her she never wanted to be her friend again. 'I'm going to see Joe first thing tomorrow morning,' she declared, to the approval of the assembled Mancinis, 'and tell him to leave Anu.'

✂

Now Leonardo Mancini himself stepped into the witness stand. What a curly-lipped, heavy-browed, chubby-cheeked, olive-skinned, soft-mannered young man! Madhavi Rao kept her eyes down as he began to speak.

He had met Rao in 1992 and Singh a year later. They were all law students together and he knew the women 'fairly well'. He had had many conversations with Anu, often in the presence of Madhavi, about her illnesses and grievances. There had been talk of suicide, and of techniques and methods she was contemplating: guns, heroin. Late in September 1997, on his way to a lecture, he ran into the two women 'wandering around the Law School carpark'. Standing side by side they said to him, 'Len, we've taken heroin.'

Mancini was a guest at the second dinner party, the Friday one. Anu had phoned from Sydney to invite him. No, she hadn't told him the purpose of the party. He went to Antill Street at eight-thirty on the Friday evening and found there Joe Cinque, whom he already knew, Anu, Madhavi, Tanya Z—, and five or so other people. During the evening he found himself briefly in the kitchen with Anu. He remarked that she seemed 'bubbly' and she told him she had taken some Rohypnol. Len left the party with Tanya Z—, dropped her off at Madhavi's house, and was home in his own bed by twelve-thirty.

At nine-thirty the next morning, Saturday, he was woken by

Anu and Madhavi banging on his door. They came hurrying in all anxious, saying, 'Len, you've got to speak to Tanya.' Madhavi dialled Tanya's number and handed him the receiver. As he listened to Tanya's report, he turned aside from the phone and asked Anu, 'Did you give Joe sleeping tablets last night?'

'Yes,' she said, 'I did. I gave him three.'

'Why did you?'

'She goes, "I wanted Joe to be asleep while I killed myself." She took the receiver off me several times. She said to Tanya, "My life's in your hands. Please don't tell Joe. My relationship will be over. Please, please, please, you can't tell. You'll ruin our relationship. I love him."'

In the front row of the gallery Nino Cinque lowered his head. Maria Cinque sat bolt upright but her face was wet with tears.

'I said to Anu, "What are you going to do now?"' continued Mancini. 'She said, "I'm going home to tell Joe."' Mancini took this to mean that she would confess to Joe what she had done, and the whole matter would be resolved.

All this happened on the Saturday morning. At ten-thirty on Saturday night, Anu Singh phoned Mancini. Part of the call was accidentally recorded on his answering machine and the tape had been admitted into evidence at the earlier trials. Having read its contents in the transcripts, I understood why Justice Crispin, in the presence of Mr and Mrs Cinque, did not order it to be played again: Singh tells Mancini she is worried about the sleeping pills she has given Joe the night before; they have kept him asleep till early Saturday evening and are still affecting him. There is some talk about taking him to hospital to get the drug 'removed from his system'; but then Joe's voice can be heard on the tape, blurrily murmuring, 'My mind's a hundred per cent functional – my body just wants to sleep like crazy! Anu's worried for nothing!'

An hour or so later, around midnight on the Saturday, Singh called Mancini again. Telstra records show that they spoke for nine minutes. Oddly, Mancini couldn't remember what they spoke about. Sorry, he couldn't recall any details – no, not even the thrust of the conversation. But at around noon on the Sunday – at either elevenish or twelvish; he was uncertain because of the switch to daylight saving – Mancini called Rao and said, 'What's going on? I got this strange call from Anu last night. Have you heard any developments?'

'Len,' said Madhavi, 'something's happened. I might come over. I don't want to talk about it on the phone.'

It was a five-minute walk from Condamine Street to Len's place, but Madhavi didn't arrive till thirty or forty minutes later. She came in looking upset and anxious, and told him that the paramedics were at Antill Street. 'Anu tried to kill Joe last night,' said Rao. 'With heroin. She injected him with heroin.'

'I was in shock,' Mancini told the court. 'I was rambling – I was saying "I can't believe Anu's actually *done* this."'

Mancini and Rao got it into their heads that they ought to call Anu's mother and tell her that her daughter had 'done some-thing very bad'. They were concerned that Anu would get away with it – that she would tell the paramedics Joe had done it to himself. Madhavi picked up the phone, but for some reason, instead of calling Anu's mother in Sydney, she dialled the Antill Street number.

Anu answered. Madhavi asked, 'Are the paramedics looking after Joe?' Mancini could not discern actual words, but Anu's voice came blaring out of the phone. Her screaming intensified when Madhavi told her they were about to call her mother. Madhavi hastily hung up and said to Mancini, 'Anu's hysterical. We shouldn't tell her mother. She told me not to tell anyone.'

'Was she mad?' asked Mancini.

'She sounded really, really angry,' said Rao.

What if she came over? The last thing the two friends wanted was to have to face a furious Anu Singh. They got into Mancini's car and went for a drive to South Canberra. As they motored along they marvelled to each other that Anu had had the nerve to try to kill someone. This time, they agreed, she had really gone off the deep end.

Mancini couldn't understand it. '*Why* did this happen?' he kept asking Rao. Anu had sounded so remorseful on the phone last night – *why* had she done this?

Madhavi knew why, and at last she told him. Anu did it, she said, because during the night Joe told her he was going to break up with her. Madhavi knew this because when she got home from the ball at dawn, Anu had called her 'heaps and heaps and heaps' of times; and during one of these calls she had also told Madhavi that she had given Joe heroin.

The court was breathlessly still.

'Eventually,' Mancini went on, 'Madhavi told me, hesitantly, that Anu had come and got her from her place at about eight that morning, and taken her back to Antill Street. Madhavi saw Joe. He was lying on his bed. Madhavi said he seemed pale, or blue, but stable. He was breathing.'

Madhavi Rao sat expressionless on her chair. Her face had turned grey.

'I asked her why she didn't call an ambulance,' said Mancini. 'And she said, "Anu wouldn't let me."'

❧

After lunch at Len's with the Mancinis, Madhavi went home; but she and Len were on the phone to each other 'pretty well all afternoon, going "I can't believe Anu's done this, I wonder where she is, God, I wonder what Joe's doing, I wonder if they've broken up."' Mancini slept that night on the couch. On Monday morning his parents resumed their drive to Sydney and he went to his classes. On the Monday evening his friend Rachel came over. They saw on the TV news that Anu had killed Joe – that Joe had actually died. A few moments later Madhavi Rao walked in.

'We were all in shock,' said Mancini. 'And Madhavi said, "I think I'm in trouble. If this ever gets to court I'm going to plead duress." She kept saying, "He seemed stable. He was breathing. He seemed pale – or blue – but he seemed okay."'

'When was the last time you spoke to Madhavi Rao since then?' asked Mr Golding.

Mancini dropped his eyes. 'I don't think I have, actually.'

Outside at the morning tea break, the young women journalists were quieter, much less scornful. Madhavi Rao puzzled them. 'She comes across as a complete *victim*,' said one of them. 'Anu Singh you can almost understand, but this one's so *passive*.'

Len Mancini, citified in his loose, fashionable suit and professional's haircut, stood about the lobby in the protective circle of his family: his confident-looking parents had been joined by two more large, brown-faced farmers in their thirties, perhaps Len's brothers, who planted their feet wide and kept their powerful arms folded across their chests.

When Mr Lasry rose to cross-examine him, Len Mancini's demeanour underwent a certain change. He turned spongy. His voice dropped so low that he had to be asked again and again to speak up. He agreed with Lasry that he had not had a romantic involvement with either Rao or Singh, and that he felt his contact with Singh to be 'one of life's liabilities'. He described her as 'psycho', and 'fixated on her own problems'. But soon he began to exhibit a fading of memory that was quite striking. His evidence today, it seemed, differed from the account of events he had given a year ago during the aborted jury trial; but when Lasry pointed out these differences to him, Mancini would turn his mouth down at the corners and shrug, or say in an uninterested voice, 'Probably.'

What could Mr Lasry do with such a passive, forgetful witness? He tried to refresh Mancini's memory of his own evidence by reading aloud to him from the transcript of the jury trial, but in vain: the times and contents of certain phone conversations he had had with Madhavi Rao on that deathly Sunday had flown clean out of Mancini's head. Most vexing to Mr Lasry was that Mancini couldn't recall Madhavi's telling him on the phone that, during her eight a.m. visit to Antill Street, *she had told Anu Singh to call an ambulance*, and that *Anu had gone downstairs to do so*. No, Mancini couldn't remember saying that. Nor did he remember Madhavi's telling him on the phone that Joe's breathing had been *regular*; that she had looked at Joe, checked his breathing and *put him on to his side* before she left the house. Mancini kept shaking his head.

Lasry took him again to the transcript of the first trial: 'You asked Madhavi why she didn't ring an ambulance. She said she was going to, that she wanted to, but that Anu said *she* would ring an ambulance.'

Mancini sat there on the witness stand, vague, slow, stumped. He let a long silence fall. He turned his mouth upside down.

'Madhavi said,' he repeated, with a sort of dreamy stubbornness, '"*Anu wouldn't let me.*"'

Lasry pressed and pressed Mancini to confirm that Madhavi Rao had left his house that Sunday afternoon declaring that as soon as she had 'gathered up the courage' she would call Joe Cinque and get him away from Antill Street. Once again Mancini's memory lost precision. He couldn't seem to make a clear statement on that point.

But there was one thing he was very firm about. In August 1997, when Singh had told him she wanted to get a gun or some heroin, in order to commit suicide *and* to kill Joe Cinque because of the ipecac business, he had taken the view that this was ludicrous, that Anu would not kill either herself or Joe. Having made this clear, Len Mancini was dismissed, and departed, his curly lips widening in a smile of relief.

What was Mr Lasry doing? He hadn't a histrionic bone in his body. He seemed to be labouring to haul up into the light, from the dim recesses of witnesses' minds, every available skerrick of behaviour or thread of speech on Rao's part that might conceivably be construed, in retrospect, as *action* – but his presentation so far was lacklustre, turgid, without pace or rhythm. Or was his unaggressive performance merely echoing the personality of his client, the young woman herself?

Where *was* she, in the tale?

Sitting there in court she was real enough: she had shape, she had colour, she took up space. But in the last days of Joe Cinque's life she remained a phantom. One's imagination strained to picture her, as the story circled back and round and back again towards the unbearable moment of Joe Cinque's death. It was wearying, it was exhausting – and yet somehow, appalled and incredulous, one went on swallowing it down.

Joe Cinque's parents sat shoulder to shoulder in the front row, macerating in their grief and rage, firing shafts of dull, violent hatred at Madhavi Rao where she sat side on to them, almost within arms' reach, exposed to their gaze.

When the court rose for lunch I wanted to go outside, lie down on the grass under a tree and fall asleep. But I bought a sandwich in a bag and sat at a table on the terrace of the court cafe. It was a dry day, bright, with a fresh breeze. At the next table a bunch of law students who had been listening to Rao's trial sat eating and loudly chattering.

'They were just *entertaining* themselves with these nutters,' opined one young woman in a colourful T-shirt. 'Then suddenly the police are involved. They never realised it would go that far.'

'I reckon I could drug *my* husband,' said another, earnestly, 'and then explain it away, and he'd believe me. 'Cause that's why you're *with* them. 'Cause you *trust* them, and *they* trust *you*.'

'If you call the ambulance, you don't go home, do you? You wait with your friend?'

'If *you'd* killed someone, what would you do? First thing *I'd* do is, I'd go straight to the cops.'

'I tell you what – in a thing like this, heroin's the least of your worries.'

I threw my paper bag in a bin and went for a walk through Civic. Garema Place, the very centre of the city, swarmed as usual with junkies – gap-toothed, lank-haired, tattooed, with bruises and scabby lips. Many of them wheeled babies or toddlers in pushers. They didn't bother to cover their scarred, wounded elbow crooks, but slunk or barged about blatantly. The city's heart

belonged to them now, their 'chasing', their buying and selling
and using. Some civic hope had been abandoned. It was a plague
that raged unchecked.

I had pictured Bronwyn Cammack, from my reading of the transcripts, as a wiry little toughie with spiky black hair and a snaky
manner; but when her name was called, the person who responded
was a slim, matte-skinned, languid young woman in a tight white
shirt and grey trousers. Her lank brown hair was cut in an exagger-
ated bob, very short behind, then dropping steeply at the sides to skim
her jaw-line, and held back off her face by a thin band. Her lower lip
was pierced by a silver stud. She had a face out of a Vermeer, well-
shaped and regular, like a large smooth river stone; if it had been
animated it would have been striking, but it remained, throughout
her entire appearance in court, almost completely without expression
except when, very occasionally, she pressed her lips together in a line.
As Madhavi Rao's manner could, according to one's attitude towards
her, have been described as either 'reserved' or 'affectless', so might
Cammack's demeanour have been called either 'relaxed' or 'limp'. She
took her seat on the stand and at once twisted one leg over the other,
laid her forearms on the bench in front of her, and twined her fingers
together. Something about her was doughy. Her life spark was turned
down to pilot. Time after time counsel and judge had to ask her to
speak up. Her voice was feeble, as if she couldn't be bothered projecting it: as if nothing happening here was worth expending energy
on. She was not stupid. She was not angry. She was not resentful. But
what *was* she? She was 'unemployed at the moment'. She had been
an addict, yes, but her most recent use of heroin was six weeks ago.

No, she was not on methadone. She just stopped. Was she hanging out? No – she had been, for five or six days after stopping, but she wasn't hanging out now.

As her version of the tale unrolled – she volunteered little: in her profound passivity she had to be led, led, led, all the way – her mother was mentioned several times. It appeared that Bronwyn Cammack could call home from Civic and her mother would come into town in the car and pick her up, take her to where she wanted to go, come back and collect her afterwards, give her friend a lift to wherever she was going, and then drive Bronwyn herself home. Her family had not given up on her, then. Perhaps they even danced attendance on her, the stone-faced girl who carried, buried deep inside her, more of a practical moral sense than did many another in this story. Suicide she may have casually countenanced and even been ready to abet, but when it came to murder, when the chips were down she got angry, she gave tough advice, she took it right up to Anu Singh, she drew a line – too late.

Cammack was a distant acquaintance of Madhavi Rao's. In early 1997, when Cammack was a regular user of heroin, the two young women would run into each other every now and then around town or in Civic. In August 1997 Cammack saw Rao sitting on a seat in Garema Place with a girl whom she introduced as Anu. Without preamble Singh began to talk about wanting to get hold of a gun. When Cammack pointed out a dodgy character she knew who chanced to be walking by, Singh buttonholed him and asked him on the spot whether he could get her a weapon. No transaction was concluded, and Singh offered to drive Cammack home. On the way she spun out the ipecac scenario, and explained that she wanted a gun to kill herself with. Cammack remarked that if *she* wanted to kill herself she wouldn't use a gun. She would overdose on heroin.

Some time later Anu Singh got hold of Cammack's phone number from Madhavi Rao, and called to ask her where one could buy heroin and how much it cost. It was readily available at Civic, said Cammack – you could 'just get it off someone in Garema Place'. She explained the forms and quantities in which it was usually bought.

On Tuesday 21 October 1997 (the day after the first dinner party), Madhavi Rao phoned Cammack and put Anu Singh on the line. This time Anu wanted to know how to get hold of some Rohypnol. Cammack told her you could buy that in Civic too, but if she herself wanted it she would get a prescription from a doctor by saying she was 'having difficulty overcoming her addiction to heroin'. Anu said she didn't think she could deal with a doctor. She asked if Cammack would do it for her in exchange for some heroin. Cammack agreed to this, and made an appointment with a GP in the suburb of Farrer.

The following morning, Wednesday 22 October, Anu Singh picked Cammack up from her house to drive her to the doctor's. On the way they pulled over and Singh showed Cammack a little box with two syringes in it, each one containing a half-weight of heroin. Cammack extracted from one of the syringes the equivalent of a $50 deal and hit it up, right there in the car. Off they drove to Farrer.

The GP responded to what the Crown politely called Cammack's 'fib' by writing her a script for fifteen Rohypnol. Cammack didn't have the money on her to complete the process, but she said Anu wouldn't have any trouble at a pharmacy. Cammack's Health Care Benefits card was about to expire; she gave it to Singh so she could get the script filled more cheaply. While Singh was driving Cammack to her bus, she explained that she wanted to use the Rohypnol to 'knock her boyfriend out while she committed suicide'. She milked Cammack for information about the effects of

Rohypnol combined with alcohol and heroin. Cammack said that she personally would be rendered unconscious by one or two Rohypnols followed by a hit of heroin. Having offered this advice, Cammack hopped out of the car and caught a bus home.

Her next real contact with Anu Singh was four days later, at about midday on Sunday 26 October, the day Joe died. Singh called Cammack on the phone and told her, in great agitation, that Joe Cinque had taken an overdose of heroin. Again the court heard the story: Cammack told her to ring the paramedics; they would give Joe an injection of Narcan, which would almost certainly revive him. But no, cried Singh: she couldn't call the paramedics, because if they did give Joe some Narcan and he came to, he would realise at once that *she* had given him the drug, and he would be furious. Singh became 'hysterical and manic'. She described Joe Cinque's state – breathing, then not breathing, then vomiting – and tried to get Cammack to come round to the house, but Cammack would not. She kept urging Singh to call an ambulance. She shouted at Singh that she had no right to take someone's life away, that she was a selfish bitch, that she *must* ring the ambulance. Singh finally said she would and hung up, but almost immediately rang Cammack again – she couldn't make the call, she just couldn't. Cammack at this point spat the dummy: 'Listen – if you ring the paramedics, you'll have an angry boyfriend. If you *don't* call them, you'll have a murder charge.'

This seemed to jolt Singh, who replied, 'Oh, shit – you're right', and hung up.

'Is that the last time you spoke to Anu Singh?' asked Mr Golding.

And Bronwyn Cammack said, 'Yep.'

❧

But now the focus of her story shifted to Madhavi Rao. At lunchtime the next day, Monday 27 October, Cammack phoned Rao and told her in detail about the weird phone calls she had received from Singh the day before. Madhavi Rao didn't want to talk about this on the phone. She suggested they meet in town, at Gus's Cafe in Civic, and at two o'clock that afternoon they did.

Once more, it seems, Madhavi Rao could not hold her tongue about the adventures of Anu Singh, this all-consuming so-called friend through whose extravagances she vicariously lived. She sat down at a table in Gus's with a junkie she hardly knew, and poured out again the whole gruesome story.

'First,' said Cammack to the court, 'she was hesitant – she said she didn't know if she should involve me. Then she told me that Anu had attempted to kill her boyfriend twice. On the Monday night she'd given him Valium, but he was tossing and turning too much. And she hadn't gone ahead with it on the Friday night either. Madhavi said that on the Friday night everyone else had gone home but her, and she was in the lounge room while Anu was upstairs.'

Cammack and Madhavi Rao spent two hours downtown together that Monday afternoon, while unbeknown to them Joe Cinque's body lay in the city mortuary. As they were leaving Gus's Cafe, Cammack spotted a dealer she knew, and asked Rao to lend her the money to buy some heroin. Rao waited nearby while she scored and hit up. The two women walked to Glebe Park and resumed their conversation under the trees: they spoke 'about other things', then Rao went off to the university library and Cammack called her mother, who came and picked her up and took her home.

So dully and faintly did Cammack tell this story that Mr Lasry was moved to challenge her blankness.

'After you left the park,' he said, 'am I right in saying that you then went to McDonald's? Where you bought something to eat?'

'I doubt it. I don't eat McDonald's.'

'I don't blame you for that,' said Mr Lasry sympathetically. 'I try not to either.'

The faintest shadow of a smile flickered across Bronwyn Cammack's face, and was gone.

That evening Cammack saw on the television news that there had been a murder in Downer. In the shot of the crime scene she recognised Anu Singh's car. At eight-thirty p.m. she called Madhavi Rao again and they spent another hour together, downtown at the Wig and Pen.

'Madhavi was worried that she'd be implicated,' said Cammack in her small, toneless voice. 'She was stressing about it. And she said maybe she shouldn't have told me everything that afternoon. She kept expressing sympathy for Anu. She said her life and her career were over. I told her she shouldn't be sorry for Anu. I said she deserved what she got – that it was disgusting, what she'd done.'

Home in Sydney for the weekend, I got a phone call from a young woman, now a journalist, who told me she had been a student at ANU with Madhavi Rao and Anu Singh. A lot of people who knew them, she said, and who had been distressed by the murder trial, were 'over it' now.

Over it? *But Joe Cinque is dead.*

She rattled on: 'All her friends are very defensive of Madhavi. They're scared that because Anu got a light sentence, Madhavi will bear the brunt, which would be the wrong way round.'

'People seem to feel warmly towards her,' I said.

'Oh, *I* do,' said the journalist. 'She was always ready to be in things – always smiling and friendly. How does she look?'

'I can tell you – she's not smiling now.'

On Monday, a fine fresh morning, I got to the Supreme Court ten minutes early and walked into the courtroom, expecting it to be empty. It was, except for Madhavi Rao. She was sitting quietly on her chair with her back to the side wall of the room, half-obscured by a trolley that overflowed with cartons of manila folders and envelopes. She looked very small and solitary, in her loose cream suit with a pale-green flowered shirt under it. She heard the big door open and looked up. Our eyes met. Neither of us made a sign or gesture of any kind, but a flood of significance passed between us – or so it seemed to me, as I sat down in the back row of the gallery. Of course I knew that there was no 'significance', that I was projecting it. But it unnerved me. I compared my response to Madhavi Rao with the feeling that the very sight of Anu Singh had provoked in me. Even without having met them, I was just like everybody else who had come in contact with these two women: one made my hackles go up, while the other aroused a puzzled, muted compassion, a curiously protective urge.

As Rao and I sat on opposite sides of the room that morning, waiting for the court to come back to life, it struck me that the world is full of these female doublings. I looked back and saw my own past, youthful and adult, sprinkled with them: symbiotic power arrangements that are called friendships because (outside of psychology, at least) we have no more accurate name for them.

Perhaps they are most flagrant in adolescence: one girl is wild, bossy, selfish, flaring with hormones, crackling with sexual thrill and careless of risk, but still dependent on the ballast provided by her companion, who is prim and cautious, not yet at the mercy of her body, one foot still planted in the self-containment of girl-hood. They need each other. The well-meaning 'supportive' one trails along in the wake of her narcissistic friend, half aware that she is being used – as a cover against parental suspicions, a second fiddle, a handmaid, a foil. But she also feeds off the wrecker's high-voltage energy.

The tendency to form such partnerships doesn't end with youth. Every woman I have asked about this knew immediately what I meant and could provide examples. Many a woman has shifted, as different stages of her life brought forth different needs, from one role to the other in the double act. We feel the depth of the pairing most poignantly when it inspires comedy: Dame Edna and her drab bridesmaid Madge; Kim and her browbeaten best friend Sharon Strzlecki in *Kath and Kim*. Even as we laugh, the spectacle disturbs us: we wait breathlessly for the worm to turn. And yet it is a relationship that benefits both partners. It would be hard to say, at its height, whose power is the greater.

Maria Cinque had told me one day, outside in the sunshine, how much she and her husband hated listening to the scientific evidence. I hated it too, partly in sympathy with them, but also because (as Maria had accidentally discovered when I sent her one of my books) I had once spent several days in a tile and steel mortuary, watching technicians perform post-mortem examinations –

or, to put it more bluntly, cutting up dead bodies to figure out why they had died. I could barely imagine how Joe Cinque's parents could tolerate hearing a long scientific discussion about the drugs that had been put into their son's body without his knowledge or consent, and what these drugs had done to his stomach, his bowel, his blood, his lungs, his brain – all those poisonous intimacies coursing through the body they had conceived in hope, nurtured, set free, and tenderly, proudly loved. But there they sat with the rest of us, listening, listening, and trying to understand.

Professor Olaf Drummer, a forensic pharmacologist and toxicologist from Melbourne, told the court that he was not able to state with any certainty whether Joe Cinque's death was the result of two injections or one. But the concentrations of total morphine found in Joe's body, he said, were consistent with the scenario that he had been injected first at about three a.m. on the Sunday, and again at some time between ten and eleven that same morning.

There was a great deal of discussion about absorption rates, plateaus, deep and shallow comas and so on, but Professor Drummer was questioned most closely on the matter of position.

If somebody injects heroin, said the pharmacologist, and collapses on the end of the needle, he can nod off to sleep in a position that obstructs his airways. If he's too out of it to change his posture spontaneously, his breathing can be dangerously compromised. It's even more serious if he's in a posture where he can inhale his own vomit. Heroin affects the cough reflex, the gag reflex. Such a person would have to be rolled on his side, and his mouth checked for objects or vomit – and then, if an ambulance were called and the paramedics suspected a heroin overdose, an injection of Narcan would rapidly reverse the effects of the drug.

'Was death inevitable,' asked Justice Crispin, 'or was it dependent on the vomiting?'

'We can never say death was inevitable,' said the pharmacologist. But on an opiate-naïve person like Joe Cinque, any fair-sized dose of heroin would have a powerful effect – and combined with Rohypnol, it would be even more likely to kill him.

At the morning break I went out into the fine air and sat gossiping under an elm tree with the spunky little dark-haired journalist who, with her blonde counterpart, was still on court rounds. She could not bear Anu Singh at any price, and expressed violent irritation against 'Mad Harvey', as she called her. She couldn't understand why Rao 'didn't *do* anything'. I didn't understand it either. It filled me with a sort of dizzy dread. But I had been thinking overnight about another murder trial I once covered for a magazine, the case of little Daniel Valerio, in which a man beat his girlfriend's two-year-old son to death. To many people the most appalling and frightening part of the story was that Daniel's mother seemed not to have noticed the slow torture her man was inflicting month after month on the toddler. With a selective blindness she had invented the most ingenious 'reasons' to explain his chronic injuries and bruises.

Now, under the tree outside the Supreme Court, I tried to explain to the journalist my sense that a sick and sinister relationship can exude a sort of hex, a glassy spell that none of the people involved can break. Only a complete outsider who stumbles fresh into the situation can see its weirdness – a stranger who is immune to the spell, who says bluntly, 'Something bad's going on here. I'm going to call the cops.' In the Valerio story this stranger was an electrician who visited the family's house to fix the wiring. His warning came too late. In Joe Cinque's story, Tanya Z— was the one who might have broken through, but her instinctive sense of danger was undermined by Anu's forceful pleading, Mancini's off-handedness, Rao's reassurances. It wasn't *real*, they told her. It was just how Anu talked. They'd worked it all out, they'd got it under control, nothing was going to happen, how could she *think* that such a thing would happen? If she spoke to Joe or went to the police she would wreck a love affair and blight people's personal and professional futures. Thus Tanya Z— was made to feel uncool, insensitive, literal-minded, a busybody, a panic merchant, a dobber. Her faith in her own instincts was damaged. Against her better judgement, she turned away. The journalist listened to my theorising with her eyebrows up and her lips pursed.

Maria and Nino Cinque came to sit with us on the shaded bench. I had not spoken with them for several days and I was glad to see them. We began to talk about gardening. Although his face was knotted with tension, Nino acted out in a self-mocking way his own tendency to be severe with errant plants. 'If tree I put not grow straight,' he said with a ruthless slicing gesture, 'I pull 'im out.' We all laughed. Then he said he had heard that the evidence would be finished before the end of the week.

'What on earth is Lasry going to say?' I said. 'How's he going to defend her?'

'Oh yes,' said Maria Cinque sarcastically. 'She's such an *innocent little girl* – so *innocent*. But if she's so innocent, why didn't she do something to stop my son being killed?'

For the first time I drew back from her harsh tone. I realised with a jolt that my allegiance had shifted: I was so shocked that I had to look at the ground and compose myself. I remembered how maliciously cranky I had been when the psychiatrist, Dr Lowden, had spoken at Anu Singh's sentencing hearing about her relationship with Singh: 'I think she trusts me.' At the time I had seen this as a professional's boast. Now I found a similar fantasy in myself – that for Madhavi Rao to turn her head and meet my eye with a long 'significant' look meant I must be special, not square or old or boring, but a cool, mature journalist who *with her little notebook* could go among killers and their cohorts and be accepted by them – slumming without compromising my virtue. I couldn't even look at Maria where she sat beside me with her bag on her knee, gazing out at the bright summer day.

'I hate Indians now,' she said, in a calmer voice. 'I know it's wrong – I'm not stupid. When I went back in Italy and we were watching TV, if we see an earthquake or something bad happen in India and a lot of people die, I say, "I wish the whole *lotta* them die." My family give me a dirty look. They say, "Don't talk like that." '

We sat with her in silence.

'Nino's best friend's son,' she went on quietly, 'is gonna marry an Indian. We can't go to the wedding.'

'If was just *her*,' said Nino. 'But it's her father, mother, sister, brother – thirty, forty people.'

'I don't trust myself,' said Maria, 'not to make a scene. And they don't want that.'

She didn't sound angry. She sounded unbearably weary and sad. I was ashamed of my private recoil. What she was expressing was not coarse racial hatred. She was telling two strangers, with a blistering candour, that her suffering had earned her the distaste of her siblings, exiled her from her social world, and estranged her from her beliefs, her intelligence, her generosity, her decency – from her own best self.

❧

The Crown's final witness in its case against Madhavi Rao was Lauren Taylor, a welfare officer at Belconnen Remand Centre. She was a friendly-looking person of forty or so, in heels and a silky teal-coloured outfit of trousers and shirt. Her fringe had grown so long that in order to look under it she had to hold her chin very high, in a pugnacious posture that was belied by her good-tempered manner of speech. She appeared to have an array of lively opinions on this whole matter, and a clear view of who was the rotten egg. She also played her own variation on the theme that runs right through the story: women's instinctive wariness of Singh, and protective sympathy for Rao. I remembered reading, in the transcript of the committal hearing, an exchange between Lauren Taylor and Mr Pappas. 'Was Anu Singh often tearful?' the barrister had asked, and the welfare officer replied tartly, 'She could turn her tears on and off as suited.'

Taylor first spoke to Madhavi Rao in D Yard of Belconnen Remand Centre on the morning of 30 October 1997, the Thursday after Joe Cinque died. Surprisingly – weren't co-accused people kept separate in custody? – Anu Singh was also in D Yard that day, and Lauren Taylor quickly picked up the dangerous vibe that she was emitting: Singh kept butting into Taylor's conversation with Rao, saying, 'We've got to get our story straight – we've got to put this together.' Taylor warned Rao to get her solicitor's advice before she had any further conversation with Singh.

Madhavi Rao was quite distressed and scared. Over the days she spent in Belconnen she began to confide in Taylor, who in her line of work did not wear any uniform or insignia, or carry anything, like keys or a radio, that would identify her as a correctional officer. 'I mainly just let her talk,' Taylor told the court. 'It was such a bizarre story.

'She talked about Anu, how she was very very intense, and

very over the top. Anu would ring her constantly. Madhavi had actually missed classes – missed *exams* – while she was trying to help Anu with her, *you* know, "debilitating disease", that Anu believed was caused by Joe giving her ipecac syrup. Madhavi said Anu wanted to kill herself, but that she was going to take Joe with her because he was responsible for her illness.

'Every time Ms Rao tried to do some study, or to have some time for herself, Anu Singh would be either on the phone or at her place wanting assistance. Ms Rao was taking her to doctors, looking at alternative therapies. She actually gave Anu money and bought her food. It was general all-round assistance. Ms Rao was there for whatever Ms Singh wanted.'

One of the reasons Rao had given Taylor for her continuing support of Anu Singh was that Rao herself had a sister with a disability. A lot of people had given up on Anu, and Rao's friends had urged her to follow suit – but if it turned out there *was* actually something wrong with Anu, Madhavi knew she wouldn't be able to forgive herself for abandoning her.

'One day,' Taylor told the court, 'when Anu was particularly stressed, they went for a drive. They had a script for Rohypnol, but Anu wouldn't get out of the car at the chemist, so Ms Rao got out and filled the script.'

When Rao mentioned heroin to her, Taylor commented that Rao and Singh certainly didn't look like the heroin-users *she* came across in her day-to-day role at the remand centre. Rao said she wasn't a user, but that she had got heroin from a man who had also taught her and Singh how to inject it.

The account that Rao gave to Lauren Taylor of the Saturday night before Joe died shed new light on this puzzling corner of the story. Rao had been at home, perhaps studying for her exams, when Anu rang up and told her that Joe was hungry. So Madhavi obediently trotted off to the supermarket, bought some apples and took them over to Antill Street. *Apples!* Surely these were the Granny Smiths I had seen in the crime scene photos, glowing innocently green on the kitchen bench?

Madhavi, said Taylor, thought this would be her chance to warn Joe about what Anu was planning to do to him. But when she arrived at Antill Street with the fruit, when they were all downstairs in the kitchen, Anu started talking about how she 'couldn't go on, the way she was'. At last, Madhavi thought, Anu was about to reveal to Joe how suicidal she was feeling – something she had apparently taken great pains, till then, to keep hidden from him.

While the three of them were sitting in the kitchen, however, Joe appeared to get 'very, very sleepy'. He went upstairs. At this, Anu suddenly turned 'really strange', and started to abuse Madhavi, accusing her of having spiked Joe's drink. Madhavi was upset and vigorously denied it, but the two women quarrelled, and Anu told Madhavi to leave. Madhavi tried to go upstairs and talk to Joe before she left, but Anu, she said, prevented her. Madhavi left the house, but came back, knocked on the door, and had another argument with Singh on the doorstep.

Then, she told Taylor, she went to the ball with her other friends.

Soon after Rao got home next morning, she was woken by Anu Singh knocking at her door, 'really really distressed, saying that Joe was not well, that she couldn't get him breathing, and that she needed money to buy some more heroin, so she could use it on herself – to kill herself.'

Rao told Taylor that she went with Singh to an ATM, withdrew a couple of hundred dollars, and gave her the money – to make her go away. 'She didn't go with Anu. Anu didn't drop her home. Anu went wherever she went. And Madhavi walked home because she didn't have the money for a taxi.

'Madhavi had had enough of Anu. She just wanted Anu to go away. She was very, very tired. She was distressed. She'd just *had enough*.

'I asked her, just out of curiosity, "Why didn't you call an ambulance?" She said it was because Anu had told her that Joe was all right.'

The day after she had this conversation with Taylor, Madhavi Rao was released from Belconnen on bail. Her father was on his way to pick her up. 'She was getting distressed,' said Taylor, 'about what she was going to tell him. I said, "Tell him the truth. Have you told *me* the truth?" And she said *Yes*.'

But Madhavi Rao had not told her the *whole* truth. She had left out the terrible part, the nub of the matter: the fact that she had gone to Antill Street with Anu that morning, and seen Joe lying unconscious on the bed. She walked up the stairs and into the bedroom. She looked at him lying there, and then she turned around and went away.

I have written 'terrible', but the word the Crown used was 'wicked'. *Wicked*. That awkward, helplessly old-fashioned, almost comical word, hung about with cobwebs, junking up the attic: how could such a bedraggled relic survive the modern light of day?

Madhavi Rao, argued the prosecutor Mr Golding that afternoon, had never completely withdrawn from the common purpose with Singh – the plan to kill Joe Cinque. Nor was she a mere innocent bystander who couldn't be held responsible. For several months before he died, she had played an active role in the welfare of both Anu Singh and Joe Cinque.

She was a close friend of Singh's who not only knew that she wanted to commit suicide, but actually helped her make plans to kill herself.

She knew what Singh's motive was for wanting to kill Joe Cinque; she knew that Singh intended to kill him.

She knew that Singh had in her possession the Rohypnol and the heroin that she planned to kill him with.

On the Saturday morning Rao tried to calm the concerns of people who might otherwise have interceded. By doing this, she was secluding Joe Cinque from people who might have come to his aid.

On the Sunday morning, when she saw Joe Cinque in distress, she knew how he had got into such a state; she knew this was not Singh's first attempt to kill him; and because she herself had contributed to the danger he was in, she had a positive duty to try to save him.

In other words, the Crown was arguing that Madhavi Rao had had a *duty of care* towards Joe Cinque – a duty that could be discerned from the very wickedness of its breach.

'The question of a *duty of care*. These are very difficult aspects of the law,' said Justice Crispin thoughtfully, and stood the matter over till Wednesday.

Difficult? I thought. Rao should have done something. She did nothing. What's difficult about that?

Court watchers seek drama. It is easier to understand than the law's intricacies. An extrovert like Jack Pappas, Anu Singh's counsel, knows how to gratify this craving with a pacy, adrenalin-producing performance. When Mr Lasry got to his feet and began to speak, on that bright Wednesday morning in November, I was so busy making unfavourable comparisons between my memory of Pappas's flashy style and the flat, conversational manner of Lasry that I failed at first to notice what he was doing. He wasn't defending Madhavi Rao. He was contending that he didn't need to. He was urging Justice Crispin to dismiss the charges straight away, without further ado. He was arguing that Madhavi Rao had no case to answer.

The spin Mr Lasry put on the events of Joe Cinque's last days was breathtaking in its gall.

The Crown case against Rao, he began, depended on *the doctrine of incomplete withdrawal from a common purpose*. But the common purpose she was supposed to have been part of – the plan to kill Joe Cinque – had come to an end on the Saturday.

Remember the conversation Rao had in her bedroom with Tanya Z—, early on the Saturday morning? Tanya Z— had asked Rao, 'Are you going to try and kill Joe, or is this all over with?' And Rao had replied, 'I'm not going to have anything more to do with it. Anu doesn't want me to. Anu said, "No offence, Madhavi, but I'm going to have to do this alone. It's just not working." '

This showed, said Lasry, that the original enterprise was at an end. Whatever else happened after that was not a continuation of the common purpose. It was a whole new enterprise by Anu Singh, and Madhavi Rao had nothing to do with it.

The hide of this, its cool, hair-splitting audacity, made my head spin. Could anyone really believe in such a mechanistic model of human behaviour? Can intention be flicked on and off like a switch?

But Lasry picked up two more familiar pieces of evidence, turned them upside down, and calmly juggled them into a new arrangement. First, the four-way phone call on the Saturday morning, when Tanya Z— had desperately asked Len Mancini for reassurance about Joe's safety. Anu had taken the phone out of Len's hand: she had screamed and wept and begged Tanya not to go to the police. After Tanya had abandoned her attempt to intervene and hung up in frustration, Mancini said to Singh, 'What are you going to do now?'

Singh replied, *in the presence of Madhavi Rao*, 'I'm going home to tell Joe.'

And she did. There was documentary evidence that she did. At ten-thirty that same night, Singh rang Len Mancini. Mancini's answering machine accidentally recorded the conversation. On the tape Singh can be heard telling Mancini she is worried about the sleeping pills she had given Joe the night before; then Joe himself comes on the line, assuring Mancini cheerfully, if rather fuzzily, that though he is tired and wants to sleep, his head is fine. Anu, says Joe, is worrying for no good reason.

This could only mean, said Lasry, that Anu *had* told Joe – at least about the Rohypnol she had given him the night before. In her anxiety about its effect on him, she was expressing 'at least overt remorse' for what she had done on the Friday night.

In other words, there was by then no common purpose from which Rao could withdraw or be dismissed. Whatever earlier purpose had existed was already terminated.

While I was reeling from the nerve of this, Justice Crispin unpropped his head from his hand and spoke. But hadn't Joe supposedly told Singh, in the middle of the Saturday night, that he was going to leave her? Let's imagine, said Crispin, that Singh *had* gone home and confessed to Joe that she'd given him Rohypnol the night before. Let's say that when the phone call was accidentally recorded, Joe was still too doped to grasp what she was telling him. What if he recovered fully, later that night, and the penny dropped? What if he said to her then, 'That's *it*. I'm fed up with you. That's the last straw – drugging me. I'm *leaving*.' And what if Singh made up her mind again, at that moment, to kill him? Would that be a fresh criminal enterprise? Or would it be a revival of the old one?

Oh, a fresh one, said Lasry. And anyway, since it would have taken place *in the mind of Anu Singh*, how could Madhavi Rao have been aware of it? Rao was entitled to conclude, on the Saturday, that the enterprise was ended.

Fresh? Revived? How could anyone know? My mind revved pointlessly, forced to acknowledge the pull of Lasry's logic, but resisting the direction it wanted to take me in.

Now, as he began to argue Madhavi Rao back into the status of an *innocent bystander*, his detachment became positively frigid. Early on the Sunday morning, he said, when she saw Joe Cinque lying on the bed, Madhavi Rao had no duty of care. She was part of no special relationship, *in a legal sense*, from which such a duty might have arisen. The history of her friendship with Singh and Cinque did not change this. Friendship of itself doesn't create a duty of care. For that to exist, the law requires a relationship of some *status* – marriage, or family, or a contract; or else one person has to have *assumed* the care of another. And anyway, even if Rao *had* adopted more than a casual role in the welfare of Anu Singh, how could that mean she had a duty of care for Joe Cinque?

Rao's knowledge of and participation in what had happened on the Friday night didn't make any difference either: even if Justice Crispin were to find her participation punishable as a criminal offence, she still had no duty of care when she went into the bedroom and saw Joe Cinque lying there, on Sunday 26 October.

The shiver that ran across my skin seemed also to lower the temperature in Justice Crispin's veins.

Wasn't it rather a chilling concept, he said, that one could take part in a plan to kill somebody, go out and buy the drugs for the job – and then say simply, 'I'm washing my hands of it now. I've got no responsibility. Let him die'?

It was a heart-stopping moment, but Lasry pressed the point: it still did not create a duty of care. Even though Joe Cinque is unconscious and in obvious distress – even though Singh tells her she has given him heroin – even though she has had previous knowledge and participation – Rao owes him no duty. At that moment, Rao is in the same position as anyone else who might have gone there and seen what she saw. She sees him *as an innocent bystander would see him.* She had not assumed any care of Joe Cinque. She had not gone to the house with the intention of helping him or taking care of him. The evidence was only that she went there with Anu Singh. She simply *went there.*

A wave of incredulity and revulsion washed through the gallery.

And why was it, Lasry continued, apparently unperturbed, why was it that Madhavi Rao was the one chosen to wear this so-called duty of care? Why wasn't it, for example, Bronwyn Cammack? If anyone assumed a duty of care for Joe Cinque, even temporarily, it was Cammack – but no one had charged *her* with any offence. She was an amateur expert where heroin was concerned, and Singh was aware of this. When Singh phoned her in a panic, Cammack assumed the role of adviser for some fourteen minutes. She might even have been giving advice while Joe Cinque was in his death throes. No matter how Singh pleaded, Cammack flatly refused to come to Antill Street – in fact, she hung up the phone, and tied up the line by making a call to her ex-boyfriend in Queensland.

But Cammack – I thought Cammack – I *admired* Cammack!

Because she was tough! Because she gave brutally pragmatic advice and tried to force Singh to act on it! Anyway how *could* she have gone to Anu's house? Anu refused to give her the address! Cammack didn't even know Anu's last name. And Cammack lived in Campbell! She had no car! A girl can hardly ask her mother to drive her to the scene of an overdose. And even if she could, by the time she'd got across town, Joe Cinque would have been dead.

How could this be happening? I sat sweating in my seat, completely thrown by Lasry's brazen manoeuvre.

He romped on down the list. Singh's 'suicidal tendencies' and Rao's assistance with them? Absurd. Sure, Singh had talked the talk *ad nauseam*, but had she ever walked the walk? Nobody who really knew her had ever taken a bit of notice of her histrionic declarations. (Again I recalled the Crown psychiatrist Dr Diamond: 'It was important *not* to commit suicide. The purpose was not death. It was to keep the drama going for as long as possible.')

And motive? The only one that kept recurring in conversation was the ipecac business – 'a ridiculous motive which no one believed'. Apart from Tanya Z—, who had met Singh only once, nobody ever believed that Singh was going to kill anyone – and for someone who was seriously contemplating murder and/or suicide, Singh spent an enormous amount of time telling a large number of people about it.

In his quiet way, Lasry was on a roll. He was almost rollicking along. The whole thing started to take on a kind of ludicrous aspect. One felt a fool for having been upset.

But Justice Crispin neatly thrust a pump between the spokes of Lasry's wheel. What if he were to find that there *had* been an attempt to kill Joe Cinque on the Friday night? It was all very well for Len Mancini to say, 'Singh was a histrionic person who went round making grandiose statements all the time – I didn't believe a word of it.' What if Mancini had actually been present, as Rao allegedly had, at an attempt to kill Joe Cinque the day before? That would rather change the picture, would it not?

Lasry wobbled, but stayed in the saddle. His Honour would find whatever he found about the events of the Friday night – but what effect would that have on the events of the Sunday morning? Right now Lasry was talking *only* about the Sunday morning. Justice Crispin sat back, and Lasry pedalled smoothly on.

Was Rao aware on the Sunday morning, as the Crown said she was, of 'both a previous and a current attempt to kill Joe Cinque'? This was getting dangerously close to the terrible part. How would Lasry get round it?

'I'm not clear,' he said, 'what "a previous and a current attempt to kill Joe Cinque" *is*.' The previous attempt, he presumed, was what was said to have occurred on the Friday night. As for the Sunday attempt, Madhavi Rao knows nothing about *that* until she gets to Antill Street at eight o'clock on the Sunday morning.

Hey – hang on – wait a minute! But Lasry had snatched the horrible accusation, blown it up like a party balloon, and tapped it into the air with the lightest of touches. It floated away over our heads.

When Madhavi Rao saw Joe Cinque on the bed, did she know, ought she to have known, that he was in peril of his life?

With the point of his blade Lasry peeled ethics away from the law. Whatever *moral* duty might have been on a person in her circumstances to act, no *legal* duty was created by those cirumstances – unless some responsibility had been *assumed* by Madhavi Rao. Anyway, said Lasry, 'Duty of care and duty to act are not the same thing.'

Aren't they? I had no idea. I had never thought about these things before.

This surgical slicing and drawing apart of concepts was almost Olympian in its remoteness. There was something frightful about it. The three grey-wigged men, counsel and judge, probed away together at the precedents in their quiet, well-mannered voices. They searched for guidance in the authorities – earlier judgements that had clarified or interpreted a law and shown how it may be applied, stretched, narrowed or pointed to take account of things that people do to each other – or fail to do. I hardly dared glance towards Mr and Mrs Cinque. How on earth were they able to tolerate it, this serene sailing through rarefied air, high, high above the bedroom in which their beloved son was drugged, and drugged, and drugged again, and in which he innocently died, choking on his own black vomit? What stamina they possessed, to sit straight-backed through hour after hour of abstruse legal arguments in a language not their own, according to a system foreign to them. They were doing it in honour of their murdered son. They were keeping vigil.

One strand of the Crown's case against Madhavi Rao was that, when she reassured Tanya Z— that Joe Cinque was not in danger, she had *secluded* him from possible help. By secluding him, she had taken upon herself a duty to help him when she knew his life was in danger. The authority Mr Golding had used to support this argument was a case known as *Taktak*: the pitiful tale of a fifteen-year-old Kings Cross prostitute who, having overdosed on heroin in the course of a private job, was taken by a certain Mr Taktak to a shop in Randwick, where he covered her with a blanket in the hope that she would sleep it off. Instead, she died, and the ineffectual Mr Taktak was convicted of manslaughter.

'So,' said Justice Crispin thoughtfully, 'a Samaritan may walk past the bound and injured person and leave them to their fate with impunity – but if he picks them up and attempts to look after them, he must do it properly or risk a conviction for manslaughter. That is not an altogether reassuring aspect of the law, is it?'

Be that as it may, said Lasry, the seclusion into which Mr Taktak had placed the comatose girl was quite different from the seclusion of Joe Cinque. In fact, Joe Cinque wasn't secluded at all. He had had a primary carer. That primary carer was Anu Singh.

My brain sizzled in my skull. Anu Singh as *primary carer*? The one who had knocked him out with a huge dose of Rohypnol? Who had tied off his two arms and hit him up with heroin? Wasn't this to strain the elastic of language till it snapped? Why wasn't the whole court on its feet, in a roar of protest?

But Mr Lasry, like a seamstress trying to alter the design of a garment that somebody else had created, went on unpicking the events of the Friday night from those of the weekend proper. There was no evidence, he said, that Madhavi Rao had had anything whatever to do with putting Joe Cinque in danger on the Saturday night and Sunday morning – beyond what the Crown would say were her 'involvements' in the getting of the heroin and the Rohypnol.

'Is there any evidence,' asked Justice Crispin, 'that Rohypnol and heroin was acquired by Ms Rao with the knowledge that it might be used in an attempt to kill Mr Cinque?'

By now I was completely flabbergasted. My mouth was hanging open.

All that was just an inference by the Crown, said Lasry airily. Anu Singh had certainly *said* she was going to use the heroin to kill Joe Cinque, but nobody – not Mr T, nor Mancini, nor anyone else who heard her – believed she was really going to do such a thing. And given the way Singh was in the habit of carrying on, there was no reason why anyone *should* have believed these utterances of hers.

At the break, nauseated from the shock of the arguments, I went outside for a breather. Mr Lasry swept past me in his big black gown. He took off his wig and was transformed from the steely tactician of the court into a large, heavy-headed, short-haired, middle-aged man, perhaps once a blond. I remembered reading in the transcript that when he had to ask witnesses to raise their voices it was because his hearing had been damaged by his pastime of playing drums; and once he had tossed off a line from an Easy-beats song, saying, '*I have Friday on my mind*, your Honour' – a joke which probably sailed straight over Justice Crispin's head.

Madhavi Rao also emerged into the lobby, and was met by a fresh-faced girl with a ponytail. They strolled away chatting quietly together, laughing and smiling. As they passed me I heard Madhavi Rao saying, in a conversational tone, '*My* advice would be to . . .' She still has friends who respect and love her, I thought. People ask her what she thinks, and she tells them. Her life goes on. Who was I to begrudge her this?

But Joe Cinque is dead.

I walked out and sat on the bench under the elm tree. The sky was seeded, as far as the horizon and beyond, with tiny, high, white puffs of cloud. I wasn't hungry. I felt sick, miserable, morally at sea. I wished I could stay out there forever, and heal myself by breathing the summer air. But I was in this story now, and I would have to stay in it till the end.

I had been assuming all along that the cause of Joe Cinque's death was pretty well agreed upon: that on the Saturday night he had drunk a cup of coffee (instant coffee, in a mug! after the tiny cups of perfect espresso that Mrs Cinque served at their house) which Anu Singh had laced with a violent dose of Rohypnol; and that while he was unconscious she had injected him with heroin. Apparently, though, where Madhavi Rao's involvement was concerned, my assumption was way too simple.

Was there anything in the evidence, asked Justice Crispin, to show that when Madhavi Rao went into the bedroom at eight o'clock on the Sunday morning and saw Joe Cinque lying on the bed, he was *at that stage* in peril of his life? To show that he had *already been given* a potentially lethal dose of heroin?

Again I sat gaping.

Let's suppose for a moment, Crispin went on in his musing voice, that an ambulance has been called. A couple of paramedics arrive. They have a look at Joe Cinque. They take the view that he's not in a state of *extremis*. They decide there's no need for him to be taken to hospital. So they tell Ms Singh to look after him, and they go away. Now – would that necessarily have prevented his death from a *later* dose of heroin?

No, said Lasry, it would not. The evidence showed that after Rao had quit the house early that morning, Anu Singh had gone round to Mr T's and bought another syringe full of heroin. *But what became of that heroin, nobody knew.* There was nothing to prove whether or not it was ever used. Not even the forensic scientists had been able to establish beyond doubt whether Joe Cinque had been killed by one injection or two. So nobody could be sure whether, when Rao went into the bedroom and saw him, he had already been given the fatal injection or not.

Logic forced me to acknowledge that it was so. Even if Rao *had* done the right thing and dialled 000 then and there, it was well within the bounds of possibility that Singh might have waited till the dust had settled, till the paramedics had given her a lecture and forged on to the next calamity, till Madhavi Rao had stamped home in a shit – and *then* she might have driven over to Mr T's and bought the second syringe, taken it home, and slid into Joe Cinque's arm the lethal hit.

Oh, it was all so fluid. Nothing ever settled, or became simple and stable. Everything could be flipped over and turned inside out – looked at afresh, upside down or backwards. Yes, it might logically have happened that way. And yet something in me rebelled against the deftness of the reasoning. It made sense intellectually, but on a gut level it went against instinct. It felt skew-whiff, all wrong. I wanted to cry out a protest – but in what words? Couldn't she – shouldn't she – wouldn't I – oh God, wouldn't I – have done *something*?

Again Justice Crispin articulated this mute disquiet. Couldn't one say that, when she found Joe Cinque unconscious, Madhavi Rao should have known he was at risk of being injected again? Wouldn't the Crown argue that she should have intervened, not just to get medical help, but to protect him from another attack?

Yes! I thought. Yes – surely she should have? Wouldn't *anybody*? But Lasry brushed this aside. It was 'completely inferential, and indeed, more than that – speculative'.

At lunchtime, heading along the colonnades of Civic, I saw a teenage girl bent over in a doorway. At first as I walked towards her I thought she was a shop assistant crouching to pick up a cardboard carton of books from the footpath beside her. Closer, I saw she had just hit up and was on the nod. She managed to stay on her feet, but then her eyelids slid shut, her jaw gaped, and her knees sagged in slow motion. She held that position, half up half down, for second after second, as if someone had pressed the pause button on a video. Other people too were glancing at her as they passed. Nobody paused. I thought about the hapless Mr Taktak, who had taken the dying fifteen-year-old prostitute to a squalid shop and inadequately covered her with a blanket. I remembered Justice Crispin worrying and worrying about the fate of the Good Samaritan: how disturbing it was to him that, in helping a stranger, a passer-by could put himself in the position of having a duty of care, which, if he failed to fulfil it, might leave him liable to criminal prosecution. But these were only vague thoughts. I left the girl to her fate and went looking for something to eat.

That afternoon, Mr Lasry turned his attention to the charge of attempted murder. This was a hard thing to prove: there has to be not just an intention to inflict serious or grievous bodily harm, but an intention to cause death. All right, he said – it was true that Rao had helped Singh to get hold of the Rohypnol tablets. But if she had known they were going to be used for a criminal enter-prise, to sedate the victim before he was murdered, why would she have signed her own name on the prescription form? Why would she have left the torn-up Rohypnol packet in her bedroom rubbish bin for the police to find?

Clickety-clack. Elementary. Like something out of a teenage mystery novel.

Next, Lasry turned to Tanya Z—. Along with Bronwyn Cammack, she was my favourite minor character in this tale. I clung to her desperate, bewildered decency, her almost-strong-enough desire 'to be moral'. Her testimony, for all its weaknesses, was dear to my heart. But like a man attacking a rickety chookpen, Lasry dismantled it with two well-aimed hatchet blows.

First, Tanya Z— had never actually stated, on the phone to Len Mancini on the Saturday morning, that Joe Cinque had been *injected* with heroin on the Friday night. If Rao had told her of an actual injection, the panicking Tanya would surely have men-tioned it to Mancini – and *he* would surely have raised it with Singh, during that complicated four-way call.

And secondly, there was simply no evidence to prove that Joe

Cinque *had* been injected on the Friday night. Two puncture marks were found on his arms at the morgue. One was estimated to be a bit older than the other, but there was nothing to show that it had been given to him as far back as the Friday night. And if no heroin had been given to him on the Friday night, then the attempted murder charge against Rao could not stand up – and neither could the charge of administering a stupefying drug.

Again, the gasp that follows a magician's dexterous flourish. That which was solid had melted into air.

And yet, I thought, yes – Joe Cinque may have been besotted with Anu Singh, but he certainly was not stupid. If he had come to, on the Saturday evening, and found a needle puncture in his own elbow crook, surely he would have grabbed his things and been out of that house in the twinkling of an eye.

But wait – how long was Joe's window of clear-headedness, between his waking from the Friday night Rohypnol, and his succumbing to the fresh dose of it that Singh slugged him with on the Saturday night? Rohypnol, a psychiatrist had told me, is a drug that you come out of as you would out of a general anaesthetic. You swim towards the surface but never get there; you are unable to recall what was real and what was only a dream. *Did* Joe Cinque have his wits about him long enough to grasp what was going on? Anu Singh must know, but she wasn't talking. Nobody else would ever be able to tell.

While I stewed over this, half stunned, Lasry polished off his submission. There was no direct evidence, he said, of what had occurred in the lead-up to Joe Cinque's death; and the evidence that did exist was so lacking in weight and reliability that no reasonable court could convict on it.

He sat down. The long Wednesday drew to a close. The court adjourned.

I set out towards my hotel along the cool, white, terracotta-paved galleries that lead to Garema Place. Sickened by the ugly divide between morals and the law, I wanted to put my head on a pillow and escape into sleep. But as I trudged along, I couldn't stop thinking about the authorities that the lawyers had been working through. There seemed to be an inexhaustible supply of these tales of human wretchedness. A pimp laid a coat over a dying junkie prostitute. A lone burglar, abandoned by his accomplice, dangled on a rope from a hole in a warehouse roof. A man climbed out a window and ran for help from a suicide pact gone wrong. Another stood by while his wife drowned their two children and then killed herself. A robber on his way with his mates to a break-and-enter threw up in the car and went home. Two sisters fled a house inside which their friends were finishing off a half-dead bikie with a base-ball bat. How soiled the stories were, how lacking in the glow of meaning, or even the high sheen of 'wickedness'. They oozed pathos and despair, a clumsy, sordid hopelessness. I couldn't understand how the summer afternoon could smell so grassy and good, so ordinary; how the world outside the court could continue its benevolent progress. Invisible magpies warbled in the plane trees. Softly, gently, never running out of melodic ideas, they perched among the leaves and spun out their endless tales.

It seemed to me, next morning, that Mr Golding, for the Crown, had the worst job in the world. He was wrestling with a cloud. To commit the crimes that she was charged with, Madhavi Rao would have needed to display energy, purpose, a certain *agency*. But this young woman, even when one looked across the court and saw her sitting there on her padded chrome chair, never seemed quite to inhabit the story. She did not fill out the template. It was impossible to get her alleged behaviour into focus and keep it there. Once again, Anu Singh took up all the available air. No matter what witnesses said – and apart from Tanya Z—, not one of them had a bad word to say about her – Rao remained elusive. She was always in the background. She flickered in the corner of one's eye: a phantom, the killer's faithful, passive, earnest little shadow. How could Mr Golding make this moral wraith concrete?

He did his level best, battling away with vigour in his husky, expressive voice. His arguments expanded my own confused ideas. On an emotional and psychological level they answered the seething disquiet I felt in the face of Rao's failure to act. He drew on ordinary human concepts of decency. He emphasised the morbid atmosphere of that final week, its saturation with talk of death. He deplored the chilly abstractions that Lasry had used to relieve Rao of legal responsibility.

Mrs Cinque sat in the front row with lowered face. Once she slapped her cheek with her open palm, and shook her head back and forth. Her husband in his good jacket sat beside her, occasionally coughing harshly.

Golding fought to resurrect Tanya Z— from the demolition job Lasry had done on her. He insisted that her evidence should be seen in the light of the horror, disbelief and confusion she must have felt when Rao woke her on the Saturday morning and told her she had been involved in an attempt to murder Joe Cinque. Golding pointed out – and the judge agreed with him – that if the evidence given by every emotional and distraught young woman were to be evaluated as harshly as Lasry thought Tanya Z—'s should be, then ninety-nine per cent of rape and child sex charges would wind up being dismissed.

But Lasry renewed his attack. Under his scalpel Tanya Z—'s testimony lost coherence and fell apart into many dubious strands. Its deepest weakness, he argued, showed in the long, long gaps between her bouts of memory. How come it had taken her eleven whole months after Joe Cinque's death to remember this exchange, on which the Crown relied so heavily?

Tanya Z—: 'Did you know that Joe was supposed to go as well?'
Rao: 'Yes – that's why I couldn't look him in the eye when he was talking about the conspiracy book I'd lent him.'

And if Tanya Z— had really believed Joe Cinque was going to be murdered, why didn't she go straight to the police?

Lasry had a high, clear, drastically simplifying approach that sliced through the entanglements of inaction and confusion. He made his points seem insultingly obvious, even while one's blood ran cold at their disdain for the complex mess of human behaviour. Madhavi Rao sat quietly on her chair, listening hard. Her usually smooth brow was crimped with concentration.

And as for Robin Mantoszko, the work-mate to whom Rao had made her weird, tantalising reports of the sinister dinner party – her evidence, too, Lasry swept loftily aside. Which night did Mantoszko think Rao was talking about? The Monday? How could it have been the Monday? Because, your Honour, nothing happened on the Monday night. *Nothing happened on the Monday night.*

At this, Maria Cinque, who had been silently weeping for some minutes, struggled to her feet and limped to the door. She turned to make a cursory bow, then shouldered her way out of the court, muttering audibly, 'Bullshit. *Bullshit.*' Several people glanced up. The door swung shut behind her with a soft clunk.

'Nobody was murdered,' Lasry persisted, 'and nobody was attempted to be murdered.'

'How do we know that?' asked Justice Crispin flatly. What about Cammack's evidence? Hadn't Rao told her that there had been an attempt to kill Joe Cinque on the Monday night?

Just for a second, the wind went out of Lasry's sails. 'There is no charge,' he said. 'I am really saying it on the basis of what the evidence shows. I do not know *what* happened on the Monday night.'

The submissions were completed by lunchtime. Justice Crispin adjourned the court till the following Friday. I went outside and stood helplessly in the lobby. One of the journalists came out behind me.

'What happens now?' I asked.

'Crispin goes off and decides whether or not she's got a case to answer. And if he does find there's a case, that's when the defence will launch itself.' With an ironic grin and a shrug she shouldered her bag and headed back to her office.

I called the airline. The earliest flight they could get me on left Canberra at nine p.m. Five hours to kill. I could either go to the movies or find a bar to drink in, by myself. The December day was hot, the dry, gusty wind was full of grit. I went wandering through Civic in search of a cool cinema.

The following Friday I got to the Supreme Court at eleven a.m. The lobby was almost empty. Mrs Cinque was sitting on a bench outside the closed door of the courtroom. She looked smaller and more densely made-up. She greeted me. Nino was outside having a smoke. Maria didn't know why nothing was happening. Neither of us could think of anything to say. We took it in turns to pace, to go outside, to pace again. The tension was awful. Towards twelve-thirty I went to the toilet. When I came out I found Maria Cinque gone and the court opened. I hurried down its shallow steps. There was hardly anyone in the public gallery: compared with Anu Singh's trial, this one, with its endlessly droning legal arguments and lack of high drama, had attracted little attention. Madhavi Rao in a jacket and long skirt was sitting with her back to the gallery. Her feet were crossed to one side. Her stiff new bag straps were drooping now. The rear legs of her metal chair were positioned on the trapdoor lid.

At twelve-thirty-four the tipstaff knocked and Justice Crispin hurried in. Without preamble, maintaining an impersonal distance, he read out his findings on the four counts: murder, felonious slaying, attempted murder, attempting to administer a stupefying drug.

Not guilty. Not guilty. Not guilty. Not guilty.

With each blow of the hammer the monstrous thing shrank. At the fourth stroke, it was gone. The case against the girl was not strong enough. The girl was free.

I sat there with my teeth clenched and my knees squeezed tightly together. The judge had barely swished behind his grey-green velvet curtain before Maria Cinque's voice broke out in a hoarse cry of pain.

'What's *happening* here? They kill my son!'

Nino Cinque was on his feet, yelling like a worker at a strike meeting, his head forward and his finger stabbing the air. In a frenzy, Maria Cinque dashed her handbag against the seatback. 'Corruption in the court! It's *wrong*!'

The bar table was a rigid tableau. Lasry and his junior, two tall men in wigs, sat half turned towards Nino Cinque where he raged behind them in the low gallery. Each barrister was twisted, one arm over the back of his chair and one long leg thrust out, frozen in the act of standing. The wild fury of Joe Cinque's parents pinned them to their seats. The air was thick with abuse. The lawyers could not get through it to their small client, who sat with clasped hands motionless on her metal chair.

Only after the Victim Liaison workers had once again helped the Cinques to limp from the court, trailing cries and curses, did Lasry's instructing solicitor get to her feet and go to Madhavi Rao. Standing in front of the seated girl, she took hold of her head and, like a mother, pressed it against her own belly. Madhavi Rao let her weight go, leaned on the woman, and burst into sobs. Mr Lasry drifted towards the two women and stood a few paces away from them, staring absently into the distance and murmuring the mantra of a worn-out father to a weeping child. 'It's aaaaall over now. You won't have to worry about it aaaaaaany more.'

A tiny, slender man with glasses and greying hair, correctly attired in a dark blue suit, walked shyly into the well of the court. He could only be Madhavi Rao's father – so self-effacing that until that instant I had not even noticed him. Trembling, he gripped the hands of the tall, fair-headed barrister in his robe and wig; then, wiping tears from under his glasses, he approached his daughter. She stood up and he enfolded her in a humble, almost timid hug, from the side, awkwardly, his head bowed lower than her shoulder.

At the outer door of the court a thin, blonde, tough-looking sheriff was handing out copies of Crispin's judgement. The stapled sheets she offered me from her folder were straight from the printer: I could feel their smooth mechanical heat. Did she hold my glance with a narrow look, or was I imagining it?

I carried the judgement to a cafe on the colonnade, took a window table, and tried to read it. My eyes wouldn't lock on to the print. All I could grasp was that the case the Crown had sought to make out against Madhavi Rao, though it was 'stark and brutal', had been circumstantial. Nothing could be proved beyond reasonable doubt. Justice Crispin had found hypotheses consistent with her innocence. There was a big, ragged hole between ethics and the law, a gap which only the legislature could close, and through it Lasry had masterfully steered the powerful vehicle of his defence.

I sat there at the big window, stupefied, hollow. Across the road, beyond the carpark, I could see the black-robed barristers in twos and threes striding down the steps of the building, heading for lunch. The Supreme Court had finished at last with Joe Cinque. The public drama that had surrounded his death was over. There was nothing left to say. His parents would have to drive home now, all the way to Newcastle, hauling behind them the fact of their son's murder, unsatisfied, unavenged. They would have to cram the huge foul beast into their house and cohabit with it for the rest of their lives.

Later I heard that, at the Italian club in Canberra that evening, while he and his wife were having a meal, Mr Cinque collapsed. He was rushed to hospital. A large quantity of fluid was drained from around his heart.

PART EIGHT

The following week, I sent a letter to Madhavi Rao in care of Mr Lasry, asking if she would agree to an interview. Then I phoned Dr Singh at his Sydney clinic. He couldn't speak to me right then, but took my number and promised to ring back. I waited for hours. He didn't call.

Weeks passed, Christmas, New Year. Now it was 2000. I called Dr Singh again.

'We don't want to open old wounds,' he said. 'Doesn't matter what *you* do, Helen, but there's nothing in it for us. It will only bring old traumas back – and for the other party too. I've heard the other party was very hurt when Madhavi went free.'

'What do you think about that?'

'I think they're crying wolf,' said Dr Singh. 'I think Crispin made a very good decision. I always thought her dumb. You see Helen a lot of professional people they're very clever but their lateral thinking is zero. Madhavi is one of these people. As far as I'm concerned she has no intelligence. I met her once or twice. I thought, "She wants to be a lawyer? She's bloody *dumb*!" There are even some doctors who know nothing but their profession! They are hopeless as a human being, a husband, a brother! Madhavi could have been given *something*, just to wake her up. If she'd had more human value she could have stopped it. Don't you think so, Helen?'

'I was amazed throughout,' I said, dodging his question, 'that virtually *nobody* tried to stop it.'

He pressed me. '*She* could have stopped it – more than any-one else – don't you think so?'

'There's some truth in that.'

'So,' he said. 'My daughter's getting used to it now. Time's a big healer. The other party's still very angry, though.'

'Maybe they'll always be angry.'

'I'd like to sit down,' said Dr Singh, 'and talk to them.' His speech sped up again to a rapid, slurring pace. I hung on by a thread as he galloped wildly forward. 'Perhaps *you* could help. I would speak rationally – tell them how we feel. "I feel so sad about your child." And of course they might say, "*Rrrrrreally?*" They might say, "Oh gee! *Do* you?" But there's nobody I know on their side. If you could convey that message: We are *sad*.'

I didn't know how to answer. He too fell silent.

After a while I asked, 'How did Anu go in her exams?'

'She passed. Yes – she may have been psychotic, but she has a brain. Now she's doing a Masters in criminology. She still doesn't remember it, you know. It just goes blank. Even the Monday only came back when she saw the video. She has lapsed memory. After such trauma, people don't remember what happened. Even normal people, when they've had such a hard trauma . . .'

He trailed off. Silence. He sighed. I sighed. I thanked him and we said goodbye.

Months later the postman delivered a letter. The writer identified herself on the back of the envelope, and at the top of the single tiny page it contained, as *Miss Madhavi Rao*. Her writing was small and unemphatic, young-looking, more like printing: an efficient student's hand. She apologised for her delay in replying to my letter. She had 'a plethora of excuses', none of which she would bore me with. Very courteously she declined my invitation to be interviewed. She hoped that I would understand the 'stance' she was taking in not wishing to put herself through the 'ordeal' again, and wished me all the best for the future.

I looked at the letter for a long time. This was as close as I would ever get to her. She had every right to say no. I folded the little page and put it in a drawer.

The women won't talk to me. Suddenly I felt very tired. Here I was, back at the same old roadblock. My fantasy of journalistic even-handedness, long buckling under the strain, gave way completely.

I wrote to Maria and Nino Cinque. I didn't tell them that I was scared to go on, to step round the barrier of the women's silence and face another public roasting. I told them that because Anu Singh and Madhavi Rao had declined to speak to me, there would be too many problems for me to go ahead with a book. Anything I wrote would be too unbalanced. I told them I was about to move back to my family in Melbourne, and gave them my new address. I thanked them for their kindness to me, in spite of their long suffering and terrible loss. I said that the privilege of having met them, and of witnessing their dignity and strength, had helped me to see that there was still a lot to value in life.

I must have actually imagined that they had not come to depend on me; that they would accept my mealy-mouthed abandonment of them without protest.

Four days later Maria Cinque called me. In a thick voice that shook, she said, 'Why. *Why* can't you do it.'

'I hope you don't think it's because I don't care,' I stammered.

'No – I understand that you care. But all I want – *all I want* is my son to be acknowledged.' She broke into hard sobs. 'Anthony's had a breakdown. He ran away from the psych hospital and tried to kill himself.'

Horrified, I too began to cry.

'*You* were in the court. *You* read the transcript. You *know* what happened. My son was murdered. For no reason. No motive. Without mercy. My family is destroyed and *I have to be silent.*'

For several minutes there was nothing on the line but the sound of her weeping. I was dumb with shame. How could I have thought that when I couldn't bend the story to my will I could just lay it down, apologise for inconvenience caused, and walk away? Her son's murder was not an opportunity for me to speculate on images of disharmony and disintegration. It was not a convenient screen on to which I could project sorrows of my own that I was too numb to feel. It was not even 'a story'. It was *real*. It was the brutal hand that fate had dealt her. It was the unendurable that she had to endure. Never in my life had I felt so weak, so vain, so stupid.

At last she became calm.

'Listen, Maria,' I said. 'I've got to move back to Melbourne. Let me think about it. Let me think what I can do.'

With her beautiful, unshakable courtesy, she wished me well for the move, and let me go.

So I gave up on Sydney, that summer of the new millennium, and went back to live in Melbourne. I had to rent a house. I had to find a money-making job. I had to organise my divorce. I had to help care for our ageing, demented mother. Months went by. A thousand distractions came between me and Joe Cinque's story. But it was always in my mind. It billowed like a dark curtain on every breeze that blew. It was standing by the bed when I turned over in my sleep. It was waiting for me when I woke up in the morning.

The world was a network of threads connecting me to it. I was invited, for example, to a formal lunch in Sydney. The delightful man seated on my left was a judge. He asked me what I was working on. I told him. It turned out he had sat on a solicitors' admissions board before which one of the law students who had given evidence in the Singh and Rao trials had appeared.

'Ah!' I said naïvely. 'Would that be – ?'

He cut me off. 'We'd better change the subject.'

'Oh – I'm sorry. That was indiscreet.'

He smiled and nodded. The conversation turned to other things. A lawyer's wife seated on my other side had overheard our exchange. 'He has to be careful,' she murmured to me, 'not to say anything that might compromise the witness's rehabilitation.'

'Of course,' I said; but I had to turn my face away, to conceal the bolt of blind rage that shot through me.

An email newsletter came to me from a refugee support group in Sydney. It bore the unusual name of one of the guests at the Monday night dinner party at Antill Street – the dinner after which 'nothing' was found to have happened. I called him at once. When I stated my name and business, he got off the line with a haste I am tempted to describe as unseemly, and never replied to any further communications.

In a second-hand bookshop, down the Victorian coast at Lorne, I came across a book written by Justice Crispin himself, and published in 1988 when he was plain Ken Crispin, still at the bar. It wasn't about criminal justice. It was a Christian treatise on divorce. But I snatched it off the shelf. I was struck by its straight-forward practical good sense. In a chapter entitled 'Law and Morality', he marvelled at the faith many lay people have in 'the ability of judges and magistrates to dispense justice'. To a lawyer, he said, such a faith is 'bewilderingly naïve'. A court of law is not necessarily a court of justice. 'A judge is merely a fallible human being like the rest of us. He has only the demeanour of the wit-nesses and the plausibility or otherwise of their evidence to assist him in determining who is telling the truth.' And I could not help noticing the relative unguardedness of his definition of *duty of care*: 'a person [has] a duty of care toward any other person whom he might reasonably expect to be affected by his actions.'

In April 2000, Maria Cinque called me. Guiltily I tensed myself for a question about the still non-existent book. But she spoke in a light voice, one I hadn't heard before – younger and fresher, less burdened. She told me that the week before Easter she and her husband had gone to Canberra to get the criminal injuries compensation that was due to them. They had received more than $88,000 – the maximum allowable being $100,000. They had already been awarded money to cover the cost of Joe's funeral.

But what she really wanted me to know was that she had been able to speak with Justice Crispin.

'In his chambers?' I asked, surprised.

'No – in the court. It was a hearing. We made an application. They said, "Crispin doesn't want to talk to you – we'll have to get another judge." But in the end it was Crispin. And they told us, "You can't say this – you can't say that." Nino got angry. He said, "If they tell me what I can say and what I can't say, what's the point? I'm not going." So I went in on my own. I wanted to tell Crispin everything he did that was wrong.

'I had to swear on a Bible. I told the barrister what I wanted to say to the judge, and then the barrister asked me questions. I had to be careful not to say "*You* did this, *you* did that." I had to say "The court this" and "The court that".

'I told him we couldn't accept the judgement and we never would. I said, "How can anyone think she try to save him, when she was on the phone for twenty minutes and she wouldn't give the address?" I wasn't allowed to name anyone. I had to say "The Italian from Griffith". I said, "He study law – maybe one day he's going to be a judge, like you." I talk about the psychiatrists – I apologise before I say this but I said, "These two bullshit artists –"

'I told him everything that happened to our family. I said, "How am I supposed, your Honour, to go on?"

'He nods his head. He says, "Yes, it's a terrible tragedy. But we have to go on. I pray you will be able to remember the good times." He was upset. He told us he lost a child, too, an infant child, I think. I didn't tell him that it's different, not the same as when your son is murdered – I didn't tell him that.

'We were there about half an hour. The money was nothing. The most important thing for me was to talk to him. I told him what I wanted to tell him. I got it off my chest.'

She asked after my family. Thinking that we were linked only by her sorrows, I gave a brief formal answer, but she pressed me: she really wanted to know how things were for me. I told her that my daughter was about to have a baby. Warmth flowered in her voice. I told her how crazed our mother was, how lost in her dementia. I told her that I couldn't think or write. She was quietly concerned. Later, when my grand-daughter was born and my mother died at last, Maria sent me cards inscribed with the good wishes of her whole family: 'Maria, Nino, Anthony and <Joe> Cinque': Joe's name was always there, enclosed in pointed European brackets. I felt the closeness of her sympathy. It touched me. For the first time I dared to hope that we might one day be friends.

Every morning for the next two years, I sat down to read the papers with the scissors in my hand. Nothing interested me but murder, trial, punishment. I hunted out accounts of psychiatric expert evidence. I compared different judges' styles of sentencing, trying to perceive the reasoning behind them, to make them scan. I read trashy tabloids that railed against the leniency of courts, screamed for harsher sentences, trumpeted about what it cost the taxpayer to keep murderers in custody. I collected horrors, pointlessly, fanatically, in a sort of secret grief. It was a long, grinding, obstinately interior process that had nothing to do with intelligence. My files bulged with cuttings that did not enlighten me.

I buttonholed lawyers in cafes and cocktail bars. I grabbed the sleeves of criminologists at literary festivals. I sat with judges at book launches and in their chambers, and saw the pack ice form on their faces as I babbled out my inarticulate questions. I forked out for psychoanalytic conferences and came home none the wiser.

One day I saw a notice on a lamp-post advertising a Victims of Crime rally on the steps of Parliament House. I got on my bike and rode down there.

The sun shone on a loose crowd that was forming at the top of Bourke Street. Many of the demonstrators had attached pictures of their murdered loved ones to their T-shirts. Some of these photos were miniatures fitted into the hearts of frilled rosettes. Others, life-size, had been screen-printed right on to the cotton garments. On their backs people wore the slogan MAKE THE PUNISHMENT FIT THE CRIME. A common poster read LET THE VICTIM HAVE THE LAST WORD IN THE SENTENCE.

I had never seen gathered in one place so many faces full of brute suffering. Yet even this group of tormented people was faction-riven. Their mode of argument was, for the most part, naked pain and rage. People Against Lenient Sentencing urged the return of the death penalty. The Homicide Victims' Support Group demanded the introduction of minimum sentences. Other groups saw their role as offering help and comfort to the unceasing flow of new wounded ones who staggered out of the courts. 'The laws are really there to protect the criminal,' declared a grey-haired man. '*We* are the ones serving the life sentence.'

A kindly-faced middle-aged woman took the microphone and said in the plain, modest accents of a housewife, 'I'm not a public speaker. I'm a mother. There are mothers here who want their children mentioned but they can't get up and speak. *We all have broken hearts.* Our daughter was murdered – *and* her unborn baby – and he got three years. I think they're worth more –' Her voice cracked and she broke into sobs. Another woman, her face working, stepped up beside the speaker and gripped her by the shoulders until she had composed herself. 'There are two ways you can react,' the speaker went on, wiping her eyes with a hanky. 'You can whine with self-pity, or you can help other victims.' Then she unfolded a sheet of paper and slowly read aloud from it a list of murdered women. For a moment the power of her simple rhetor-ical gesture – the naming of the dead – hushed the restless crowd.

The longer, more ambitious speeches consisted largely of blunt assertions. Victims are the battlers of our society. Judges –

these softies sittin' on the bench – don't seem to be able to get it right. Some of them don't bother to put in tax returns, and get away with it. Lawyers make too much money. Unless you are a member of the legal profession you cannot get justice. The money now being spent on frivolous appeals should be put towards building more prisons. Plea bargaining must be done away with. Victims are second-class citizens, a silent majority, fobbed off as ratbags and rednecks, sick and tired of these politicians, these judges, these cibble livertarians. And worst of all, it's the victims themselves, as tax-paying citizens, who foot the bill for the criminals' appeals.

A tall, rangy man with a weatherbeaten face, wearing a purple suit, cuban-heeled boots and an Akubra, seized the microphone in his work-hardened hand and launched into a speech of rough, skin-prickling eloquence. He shouted out a list of recent horrible murders and the 'pathetic sentences' their perpetrators had received. 'The blood and suffering of their victims would be sufficient to paint Melbourne in shame!' he cried. 'Bloody great stuff, isn't it! Did you know you can get ten years for smuggling a bloody *galah* outa this country?'

Whenever he paused for breath, hoarse male voices would rise from the back of the crowd in a chorus of protest against gun control. A red-faced old woman near me kept croaking, 'Bring back hangin'!'

Sprinkled through the crowd were certain anguished people, most of them women, who had come unaccompanied to the rally. They didn't seem to know anyone: they did not take part in the forming and melting of small groups whose members greeted each other with tears or smiling hugs. They stood singly in silent dignity. Their haunted faces seemed to show that they were being flayed again by the clumsy verbalising going on around them, and yet they still sought the company of fellow-sufferers. Throughout the whole event a young man and woman stood quietly side by side, high on the grey stone steps of the Parliament. They looked like brother and sister. Each of them held a burning candle, and between them they displayed a large colour photograph of a handsome young man. No one spoke to them. They were abstracted from the moment, facing out over Bourke Street.

When the rally broke up I approached several of the speakers and asked for copies of their addresses. The request puzzled them. They glanced down at the crushed sheets in their hands and looked at me helplessly. One, with a shaven head and thick moustache, asked warily, 'You're not from Fitzroy Legal Aid or anything, are you?' 'No,' I said, 'I'm trying to write a book about a murder.' The man in the Akubra, whose face close up was sun-creased, sparkly-eyed and intensely likeable, shook my hand warmly and said, 'Thanks for takin' an interest.'

As I was wheeling my bike back towards the road, I noticed a woman of my mother's age in a cotton sun hat, sitting alone, chin in hand, in a motorised wheelchair that she had parked against one of the huge pillars of Parliament House. I stopped beside her and said, 'Do you think it'll do any good?' She didn't turn her head. I thought she scorned to reply. I waited. Then she took her hand away from her mouth and said, 'No, dear, I don't. Nothing will do any good.'

She reached forward into the basket of her chair, and from under a crocheted shawl drew out a dull gilt frame. She turned and held it out to me. It contained a hand-tinted studio photo from the 1940s. A young man smiled broadly, showing large gappy teeth. His head was tilted protectively towards that of a soft-lipped, sweet-faced girl with permed hair.

'In a few days,' said the old woman, 'at eleven o'clock, it'll be fifty-six years since he was killed. My brother.'

'What happened?'

She told the story in a low, sardonic voice. 'He was waiting to be demobbed from the Navy. He'd been in Japan. He went down to the wharf to see a big troopship leave. A woman – someone he'd met in the city – ran out of the crowd. She called out "Watch this!" and put both her hands right in the middle of his back. Into the water he went. The ship was already moving, the propellors were – anyway, they didn't find him for a week.' She watched my reaction with the wry expression I had seen on Maria Cinque's face. 'No charges were ever laid. And you know – one of our neighbours had the temerity to say to my mother and me, "You've *changed*, since Brian died." '

I read miserably, wildly, at random. I bought personal memoirs by undistinguished, wounded people whose children had been murdered and who, like Maria Cinque, were asking the universe, 'How am I supposed to go on?' I ploughed through books on depression and mental illness and suicide. For the first time, awe-struck and angry, I read *Crime and Punishment*. I read true crime by writers who lacked the skill to portray decency, whose talent could not prevail against the leaping dark energy of badness and rage. I devoured everything I could find by Gitta Sereny. I read Hannah Arendt's *Eichmann in Jerusalem*. I wept over the quiet rea-soning of those who maintained that the purpose of criminal proceedings is not 'to still the desire for revenge in the victims' hearts', but 'to repair the rent in the social fabric'. I bowed before Primo Levi who had 'deliberately assumed the calm, sober lan-guage of the witness' rather than 'the lamenting tones of the victim' or 'the irate voice of someone who seeks revenge'.

I respected Levi's moral dignity, his restraint; but I was unable to emulate him. Where does this torment go, what can be done with it, the 'desire for revenge in the victims' hearts' that a four-year sentence and an acquittal could not still? Was the law the wrong place to look for an answer to this question? Would the Cinques have to carry the entire load, now, by themselves? I did not believe that the rent in the social fabric made by their son's murder had been repaired. I saw that there was no one to console them. I longed to write a lament for Joe Cinque. But what would be the use of one more victim story? What fresh understanding could it bring?

In 2001 I bypassed Anu Singh's parents and wrote to her direct at Emu Plains Correctional Centre. I drew a long bow: I told her I wanted to discuss with her 'the intersection of psychiatry and ethics, how they cross at points which continue to shift, and how the person in the street is often resistant to psychiatric concepts, preferring to think and speak in unmodulated terms of right and wrong.' A few months later, in July, I was surprised to receive a reply: a typed letter in an equally formal style, over a large, dashing signature. After initial doubts, she wrote, she had decided she would be interested to meet me. Her own personal experience, and what she had discovered in gaol, confirmed that ideas of *rationality* and of *right and wrong* did not necessarily apply to people, specially women, who had been suffering from an emotional/psychological disorder at the time they committed their offences. The thesis she was researching for her Masters in criminology would focus on precisely these matters. She hoped to be granted her parole in October, however, and would prefer to wait till after that for our conversation.

At first I was exhilarated by her reply. It shot a beam of light into the philosophical murk where I was struggling. A chance to balance the story! A hope for insight into its deepest causes! But experience had taught me that people in Anu Singh's position *vis-à-vis* a writer are apt to change their minds. So I considered several answers. At first I wrote grandly about 'psychological and philosophical questions of responsibility, justice, punishment, atonement, forgiveness and redemption'. Then I told her that Joe Cinque's parents had spoken to me at length on several occasions. Then I assured her that my aim was not to cause her further distress. But in the end I scribbled a couple of sentences, thanking her for her reply and saying I would be happy to wait till after her parole hearing.

On the last weekend of October 2001, the clocks were changed over to daylight saving. It was exactly four years since Joe Cinque had been killed. Two days later I called Maria.

'She's out,' she said drily. 'I went to the parole hearing. I paid a barrister. He said, "There's nothing you can do. It's gonna be a waste of time." But I didn't care. I went.

'It was at four-thirty in the afternoon. It was a different judge – older. He was understanding. There were women and men on the board. I wrote down what I wanted to say – what happened to our family, what happened to Anthony because of this. They listened. They retired, then they called us back in. They said they couldn't do anything – she did everything right in gaol.

'I challenge a lot. The barrister got cross with me. I interrupt the judge. I didn't wait for him to finish talking. I say, "I come to this country when I was seventeen. When I became an Australian I swear allegiance to the Queen, and to Australian law. But now I *despise* the law. If I don't do bad things from now on, it won't be because of the law. It's *because of my conscience.*"

'I say to them, "Four years for killing my son? What sort of punishment is *that*?" They say, "She has to report to the police several times a week." I say, "That's not so hard. *My son is dead*. My son die when he's twenty-six. She's twenty-nine. She's gonna have a life." They say, "Yes, but what *sort* of a life she gonna have?" I say, "Doesn't matter – she's gonna *have* a life." They say, "It's the law." I say, "Well the law is *wrong*." I thought, "What can they do to me? They can't do nothing to me – they can't put me in gaol." '

She gave a tired laugh. 'So – she's out. I think about her a lot. I don't know where she's living. She's not allowed to change her address. She's got conditions. She's not allowed to come near me – not to ring, not to write, not to come to Newcastle. If she comes near me I gotta tell them, and she's straight back in gaol.'

'Nino said to me, "I feel like a boat in the sea. I don't know which direction to go in. I can't see land. I can't see nothing." '

'He's in despair,' I said.

'Yes. Despair.'

'Is anybody helping you?'

'Nobody can't do nothing. Talking don't help. Nino don't want to talk about Joe. If I talk about him, he just walk away. He can't take any more.'

A long silence.

'It's a terrible story, Maria,' I said.

'When I first got married,' she said, 'I wanted all the things I got now – nice house, car, garden. I got everything I wanted. But now – I got nothing. It's . . .'

'It's empty?'

'It's empty.'

We said goodbye. I hung up the phone and put my head in my hands. I couldn't even shed a tear. I heard myself saying, dully, like somebody in a bad movie, 'Why. Why. Why.'

Not long after this I was offered a position for the first semester of 2002, teaching in the creative writing program at the University of Newcastle. I resisted the temptation to see this thundering coincidence, like the others, as a sign. But whatever it meant, something or nothing at all, I gladly accepted the offer.

I spent four months in Joe Cinque's home town. At first his parents and I tiptoed around each other. I called Maria and we talked politely on the phone about this and that. Anthony, she told me, had set up house with his new girlfriend. 'You know where we live,' she said. 'You can drop in any minute.' But I didn't want to lug my paralysis into their private lives. I waited for a more official invitation.

The first one – for a coffee – came a few weeks after I had started work at the university. I drove out to Charlestown on a scorching summer afternoon, and pulled up at their house five minutes early. Nobody answered the bell. I sat down on the springy buffalo grass outside the front door, and tried to squeeze myself into the patch of shade cast by the single cypress. Soon Maria sped up in her car, flushed and spouting apologies. Together we unloaded the supermarket shopping from the boot. She sat me at the kitchen table while she put the groceries away. From my chair I could see through an archway into the formal dining room. On its table, angled towards the kitchen, stood a large colour photo of Joe. He was seated on a sofa, leaning forward with clasped hands, looking up open-faced into the lens; he was not exactly smiling, but his expression was eager and pleasant. A rosary was draped over the corner of the frame. Each time I came to the house, in the months that followed, Maria would take from me whatever small guestly offering I had brought – a bunch of flowers, a bottle of wine – and place it quietly on the dining table beside Joe's portrait.

On this first brief afternoon visit, while Maria prepared the coffee and set out cakes, she launched in her low, rapid, husky voice on a great tale about their next-door neighbours, 'very nice people', whose tank, however, had a habit of overflowing and flooding the Cinques' side yard, and whom Nino (today he was out playing bowls) could not persuade to split two ways the cost of a wall. She went on at such enormous length and in such detail about these neighbours, and about another one, a woman who came into their garden without asking and took from their tree large quantities of figs before they were ripe, that I realised she was working to keep at bay the painful subject that I had presumably come to discuss; but the spontaneous images of her talk – an unstoppable flood, the theft of unripe fruit – seemed poetic in their aptness. Then, suddenly swerving, she asked me about my grand-daughter. Did I have a photo? While I was fumbling it out of my wallet she said, with a sweet look, 'Don't feel you can't talk about her. I'm all right about it. I love *all* children.'

A fortnight later Maria called and invited me over for tea. 'We eat at six o'clock.' I drove straight to their place after work. The heavy door again was closed. The fact that they called the evening meal

'tea' instead of 'dinner' reminded me comfortingly of my childhood in Geelong and places even more provincial, where only
strangers knocked at a front door; but I felt it would be a cheek to
go round the back. I rang the bell.

Maria came out looking *soignée* in a rose-pink silky top. She
took me inside to the lounge room, where Nino was smoking a
cigarette in front of the huge TV. They welcomed me with smiles
and formal kisses. Was this their ordinary way of being, this pleasant warmth? I forgot for a while that their son had been
murdered, that I knew them only through brutality and misfor-
tune. We sat in a curve like neighbours, drinking beer, laughing
and sighing over the Wayne Carey scandal. A great footballer! The
captain of his team! All the girls want 'im! And now he does this!
In the toilet! With his best friend's wife! *His* wife's in hospital,
under sedation! Look, there she is, poor girl! (as a bride, in a great
white dress and foaming veil) . . . People are very silly! Do stupid
things and wreck their lives! Ah well . . .

When it was time to eat, Nino took his place at the head of
the kitchen table with Maria on his left. I was put on his right, but
one seat further round. They didn't have to tell me to leave Joe's
place empty: I remembered with a cringe the *faux pas* of my first
visit to their house.

On this quiet summer evening, though, in the kitchen with its
cool tiles, we talked and laughed as people do who have nothing
horrible hanging over them. Maria served a sublime and simple
meal: spaghetti marinara, then some squid, a dish of small whiting
done in light batter, and a salad from Nino's garden. The wine was
in a knobbly glass bottle with a little handle on the neck. We talked
about prosciutto and melon in Italy, about the comparative merits
of certain makes of car we had owned, about how a timber house
can be loaded on to the back of a truck and moved hundreds of

miles without falling apart. Nino gave a thrilling description, with many precise and eloquent gestures, of having once seen a huge aluminium chimney being transported in just such a way.

When we had finished eating and drinking, Maria cleared away the plates and brought out two photo albums. We clumped our chairs closer together and worked our way through them at a leisurely pace: all the parties, the family trips, the Big Banana, the Dog on the Tuckerbox; a grandly ornate public building with a speck of a child standing in front of it.

'Is that . . . Rome?' I asked.

'Nah,' said Nino. 'Brisbane.'

There was Nino in Germany, lounging outside a cafe with his Italian workmates. Maria as a teenager, slim and long-legged, wearing the sash of Miss Azzurri. Nino with a beard, on a Trans- field site where he worked as a fitter. 'See? That's the chimney I talk about.' Two small boys in white shoes and tightly buttoned shirts sat on a floral carpet, looking up into the camera from behind the infinity symbol of a toy railway track. Maria and a woman friend grinned chirpily in student desks: 'We take a lot of courses.' A half-built two-storey brick house stood all bare and gawky on a block of land – the very house we were sitting in. 'We were so excited. But I don't care about any of it any more.' A tiny green sapling poked out of the dirt beside a cement path. 'That's the tree, see?' said Maria. 'In front of the door?' It was the cypress in whose dense shade I had sat, the afternoon when I arrived early. In the picture it was barely a foot high, a thin plume of green.

When it was time to go home, Maria opened the front door and we stepped out into a clear, grassy summer night. The sky was thick with stars. She gave me a hug. She seemed smaller these days, less grand, not so massive in grief. I asked her if she had lost weight. She pulled a face and shook her head. She told me she was going away for the weekend, without Nino, on a sort of outing to the country with other mothers and wives of murder victims.

'I ask what to bring. They say, "Just bring yourself. Your beautiful –"'

'Your beautiful self.'

She laughed. I drove away.

⚬

I wrote a note to Anu Singh at her parents' address, reminding her of our brief correspondence and asking if she was still inclined to speak to me.

I imagined her telling her parents, her psychiatrist – surely she still had one? – that I had made contact with her. I pictured their anger. I could hear their warnings. Don't answer. Who does she think *she* is? *You're* clever, Anu! *You* write the story!

What would I ask her, if we should meet? I was not interested in hearing the details of her psychiatric condition. Plainly it had been resolved to the satisfaction of the parole board – and what sense could *I* make, when the chips were down, of concepts from the *Diagnostic and Statistical Manual of Mental Disorders* like *delusion* or *depressive illness* or *Cluster B personality disorder*? I certainly didn't want to hear her academic views on the patriarchal nature of sentencing and its unfairness. What I wanted to know was more intimate than that, more philosophical. Perhaps I had no right at all to inquire into it. And yet if, as we are told and must accept, the chief aim of sentencing in a decent society is not retribution but rehabilitation, it was surely the crux of the matter. I wanted to ask her about her soul.

I remembered Dr Singh telling the court that she was 'too young to have any beliefs'. I wondered if she had any now. To what extent did she consider herself responsible – leaving aside what her defence had argued in court – for what she had done to Joe Cinque? Did words like *remorse, repentance, redemption* have any value for her, or were the categories and processes of psychiatry sufficient? Did she feel that by spending four years in gaol she had made amends?

And to whom did she believe she owed atonement, if she agreed that atonement was due? To the Cinques? To her own parents? Or was it broader, less personal than that – a matter of repairing the rent in the social fabric?

For all we know, she might have spent the years of her prison sentence in a moral agony. The trouble was that her soul, like everyone's, is invisible. Repent as a criminal might, the people she has caused to suffer have no access to her repentance. The brute fact of incarceration is all there is. Beyond it, there exist for us as a community no gestures, no emblems of contrition, no agreed-upon behaviours or signs that could carry such deep meaning.

In all the time I spent searching through newspapers, before I started to write about Joe Cinque, I found only one story that came anywhere near this longing for the symbolic. In Samoa, a cabinet minister was assassinated. One night his grieving widow heard voices under her window, and looked out. There, on their knees with ceremonial woven mats laid across their shoulders, was the entire extended family of the man who had murdered her husband, with forty of his fellow-villagers. They had come to bear witness to their collective responsibility, to express their grief and shame, and to offer reparation.

Samoa is tiny. Australia is big. There are too many of us. The possibility of soul-gestures that we would all understand died here long ago.

But I posted my letter to Anu Singh, just in case.

At the end of March 2002, two of Joe's old friends, and their wives, drove over to the Cinques' one evening after tea, to talk to me about Joe. Maria served coffee and cake at the kitchen table.

Dario was a wide, jovial fellow in shorts, T-shirt and good leather sandals. He worked as a salesman for a big company; he said he drove 70,000 kilometres a year. His wife Antonia was tiny, rather earnest, bluntly direct. They already had two small boys. Joe Cinque had been MC at their wedding.

John was slighter and shyer than Dario, smooth-faced, dressed in black, with round spectacles that magnified his eyes. His wife Tina sat on his right, a fragile, composed girl with a very gentle presence; she hardly spoke.

Nobody is going to say anything but good about their friend who has been murdered, specially not at his parents' kitchen table, with his mother sitting right there – and his father alone in the next room, smoking, with the TV turned up loud because he can't bear to hear a conversation about his dead son. But what bad is there to say, about a firmly brought up Italian boy who respects his parents, whom all his friends' parents adore, who works nights in a pizza shop while he's studying for his engineering degree? The sort of bloke everyone wants to MC their wedding because he's so funny and so kind? Who comes over to see you, when you're slaving away in your father's fruit and vegetable shop, and gives you a hand to *carry boxes*? Who lends you one of his flippers when you're both being pounded by a heavy surf? Who never once forgets to bring a birthday and Christmas and Easter present for your kid sister? Who takes your new baby son in his arms and calls him 'my little *paesan*'?

The first time Dario saw Joe was on a bus stop, when they were still at school. 'I looked at him and I thought, Now *he's* a wog. You know how ethnics take a lot of care of their appearance? Their haircut, and that? We just stared at each other on the bus stop for six weeks, then one of us broke the ice and said, "My oldies know your oldies." '

'Joe wasn't like the other guys,' said Antonia. 'They were all either shy or smart-arse. But he was always polite. At my doe show, down at the Brewery, when the guys were dancing in one part of the room and the girls in another, Joe came and danced with the girls. At the end, when everyone was leaving, a drunk guy we didn't know tried to force his way into the girls' hire car. Joe was looking after us – all the other blokes had had too much to drink. He threw the drunk out of the hire car, but then he said to him, *Come on, mate – let's talk about it.*'

'Yes,' said Dario. 'That's what Joe was like. He was the sort of guy who always said, *Come on – let's talk about it.*'

When they all started university, Dario and John still hung out, they said, 'with other wogs' at a service station in Tudor Street, whereas Joe would meet uni guys at Tattersalls Club. But a couple of times he did go out with Dario and John and the others. 'One time,' said Dario, 'we hired a bus to go to the drag racing in western Sydney. I convinced Joe to come. He always liked cars. We left Newcastle at six in the morning and got back at seven p.m. It was a great day – a really good and different day. Coming back we told Joe that Screaming Jets were on at the Palais, and to come with us. First he said he couldn't, but we convinced him. And on the way home later that night he said he'd thoroughly enjoyed it.'

There was a piercing pathos in everything they said, not just because Joe was dead, but because they were talking about someone they loved who, when alive, had already started to move away from them, and from their shared youth, into a different world. The stories they rehearsed were old ones, treasured scraps of history that made them burst out laughing; then they would fall silent, glancing at Maria Cinque with an apprehensive respect; but she laughed too, leaning into their group, enlivened by their affection.

'Tell her about your job in Canberra,' said Dario.

'After I graduated,' said John, 'I got a Defence job in Canberra.' The work was all right but Canberra itself he didn't like much. He found it empty and sterile. He was so lonely down there, without his girlfriend and his family, that all he did after work was cook. 'In eight months,' he said sheepishly, 'I put on three stone.'

By the time Joe Cinque had moved down to Canberra to live with − *her*, John was so homesick that he decided to find a job in Sydney; within four years he had gone home to the Hunter, married Tina and devoted himself to the family greengrocery business. But after he gave notice to Defence, there was a brief cross-over period when both he and Joe were living in Canberra. John used to drive back to Newcastle every Friday, as soon as he knocked off − a five-hour drive. One day Joe rang him and said, 'I'm going home too. Come and pick me up − we'll go together.' So John went over to Joe and − *that's* place. They got the car packed but just when they were ready to leave, Joe and − *her* had words. She threw a tantrum. She got her way. Joe didn't go.

'Another time,' said Antonia, 'Joe was going to come home to

Newcastle for our son's christening. Up to the last minute he was going to come – and then he had to take her to Melbourne, to see a doctor.'

There was a long pause. Nobody knew where to look. We sat studying the table surface. Someone reached out and took a slice of cake. Then in a rush Antonia launched a fresh topic, shocking in its brusqueness. 'Mrs Cinque,' she said, 'when you got Joe's stuff back, did you ever find a card in his wallet from Vivienne's the jeweller?'

Maria nodded warily.

'Because the last time he was up at our place,' said Antonia, 'a few months before he passed away, he asked me to show him my engagement ring. I showed it to him. And I thought maybe he was going to, uhm, get engaged.'

Maria said nothing. Her mouth set in a straight line. There was a flinching feeling in the room. Antonia soldiered on, hastily, but in a softer voice.

'He asked me, "What's the amount you should spend on a ring? Is it a month's wage?" I said, "You don't have to. You spend whatever you want." And that's when I gave him my Vivienne's card.'

The strained silence went on and on. Then, heroically, Dario waded into it. 'If *he* spent that much,' he said, pointing at John, 'the woman'd be –' He made a comical gesture, as if his left hand suddenly weighed so much that it dropped floorwards, yanking his shoulder out of line.

Everyone laughed, even Maria. The moment was saved. The conversation swerved to the superiority of eighteen-carat Italian jewellery over nine-carat Australian. Then Maria told us about the weekend retreat she had gone on, with other mothers of murder victims, up at Mangrove Mountain. She passed round a brochure from the hotel the women had stayed in: large modern rooms with a view of a pool, foliage outside the windows. She spoke of the pleasantness of the weekend, the relief it brought her to be with people who really understood her feelings and what she was going through. 'They give a journal,' she said. 'You cut out and stick pictures.' She flustered open an exercise book full of pasted cuttings from colour magazines. She laughed, a bit bashful, as if it were childish, but at the sight of the book Dario lit up.

'*I* went to a conference,' he said, 'and they made *us* do that, too! They can tell things about you from what you cut out.'

He and Maria glanced at each other tenderly.

'Those people there,' she went on, 'they don't laugh when I say Joe's around me. When I tell my friends this, they pretend to believe me, but really they probably think I'm crazy. I go to the cemetery but I don't feel him there. I feel him *here*. Not in his bedroom, but here in the kitchen, 'cause this is where he used to be – talking, cook, have something to eat.'

We sat with her in silence, listening. She wiped away tears. Then in a rush she told us that Anthony had met a girl, that he had fallen in love and wanted to get married.

'I'd like to think positive,' she said, 'but I –'

Dario cut across her with great vehemence: 'No but Mrs Cinque you *got* to. You *got* to.'

At ten the two young couples set off to drive home. Nino emerged briefly to say goodbye. I got up to follow them out, but Maria seemed eager to keep talking, not to be left alone with the thoughts that the evening had aroused. 'I don't go to bed before eleven o'clock, twelve – stay!' We sat down again at the kitchen table.

'When Joe was here,' she said, 'we always had full house. They don't come to see us so much now. We understand – they don't know what to say. I didn't even know John and Tina got married. It's too hard for us, to go to a wedding.'

In a little while Nino came into the kitchen, just in time to hear something I was saying to Maria about friends of mine whose son had committed suicide: how they longed for people to keep talking about him, not to let him disappear from memory. Nino listened, standing at the door. His face went dark and his mouth turned down in a harsh curve. I trailed off. He came forward and stood opposite me. He put both hands on the table, standing them upright on their outer edges like two fences facing each other. They were trembling. He held my gaze. With many deliberate pauses, breathing hard and controlling himself with difficulty, he said to me, 'Some people. Their son. Kill himself. Very sad. He choose to die. *He* decide. But *my* son. Somebody *take his life*. For *no reason*. Somebody kill him. That's different. *My* son got – no – choice.'

I lowered my eyes. 'Yes,' I said. 'That is different, Nino. It's terrible.'

I was afraid to say what I was thinking, which was – or would have been, had I dared to free my thoughts from the area he was delineating for them on the table between us – 'At least your son *wanted* to live. You brought up a son who *wanted to live*.'

But what difference does that make, now? Because Joe Cinque is dead.

A month, six weeks went by. Autumn came. I received no reply from Anu Singh. I made no further approaches. Silence, as it had been in court, was her prerogative. As a writer, of course, I had my own prerogatives, but I knew from painful experience that pestering people who are determined not to talk to you is always counterproductive. All right. I would content myself with the public record, with the things I had observed in court, and with whatever I could glean from other people's accounts.

And besides, the longer I stayed in Newcastle, the more my attention turned away from Joe Cinque's killer. Shadowy Madhavi Rao, of course, was long, long gone. It was Joe himself who seemed vital to me now. At last I was free to go looking for him.

When the Cinques flew down to Canberra to identify Joe's body on 27 October 1997, they were met at the airport by a young man called Robert Terrone. He was their godson; and *his* parents, in an interlocking Italian relationship, stood godparents to Joe.

Now, in 2002, the three Terrones were coming to Newcastle, to stay with the Cinques for Mothers' Day weekend. Maria asked me over for tea on the Friday evening. When I got there, Robert was still on the road: he had set out from Seven Hills straight after work. Nino and Leo Terrone were settled in the lounge room watching the football on TV. I was ushered straight through to the kitchen, where Maria was putting the finishing touches to one of her virtuoso meals. While she and Assunta Terrone were explaining to me how to make gnocchi, a powerful motor sounded outside. The women looked up eagerly. Doors slammed, there was a tap at the back, and into the room, pocketing his keys, strolled a slender young man in a leather jacket.

I was rocked by his appearance. His hair was shorn right back to the skull, and his beard trimmed till it was no more than a pencil line along his upper lip and jaw. His wrists were decorated with silver bangles, his fingers with ornate silver rings. He was the sort of man I might have dismissed, had I glimpsed him through the tinted windows of his car, as some sort of spiv; but close up his face was of a startling and austere beauty: dark-eyed, unsmiling and private. Gravely he accepted the affectionate greetings of his mother and godmother.

When the six of us gathered in the kitchen to eat, Robert's father Leo asked me, 'What's the English word for the father of your godson?' I racked my brains. I had to say I didn't think there was one. For all its warmth, it seemed a deeply formal relationship. Robert addressed Nino as 'Compà' and Maria as 'Commà'. They called him 'Compà.' He behaved towards them with grace and quiet respect. He knew where he fitted in here, how loved he was: without hesitation he took his place on Nino's right, in Joe's chair. The food – pasta with ragù, rabbit, polpette, a salad, a platter of fresh fruit, and heart-shaped Abruzzese waffles filled with creamy chocolate and vanilla – repaid in full the severe concentration that the young man brought to its ingestion. If I hadn't been there, the four parents would have been able to relax into Italian, but they battled on in English, teasing and joking with a generous sociability, working hard but making it look easy.

When the meal was over, Maria said to Robert and me, 'You want to go in the other room and talk?' We got up and went through the archway into the dining room where Joe's photo was enthroned on the polished table. We sat down awkwardly and I got out my notebook. The fathers sloped off back to the TV. Maria and Assunta Terrone washed the dishes together, talking quietly in Italian. They were only five metres away from us, well within earshot. It wasn't until they disappeared into the lounge room that Robert relaxed, opened up and began to talk.

'I can't remember my childhood,' he said, 'without Joe being there. My family moved to Wollongong when I was two, but we looked forward so much to seeing each other in the holidays – I used to sleep on the floor of his room and we'd talk till three in the morning. We used to cry when we said goodbye.'

At the age of nineteen, Robert got into a serious relationship with a girl. Over the next few years, during which they saved money and bought property, he felt he lost touch with his youth, and with Joe. 'I watched him become closer friends with my brother. I couldn't go with them – I had to stay home with my girlfriend. It saddened me.' At twenty-six, Robert broke out of the relationship and went overseas. When he came back he found a job that occasionally took him to Canberra. By that time Joe was living there with Anu Singh.

'The first time I saw them together was after the Italian Car Show. Joe met us there with Anu and we went back to their place for coffee.

'She was someone you felt wanted to make a good impression. She wanted people to walk away saying, "God, she's intelligent! God, she's beautiful!" She liked to start philosophical conversations, as if she was trying to prove something. She was articulate and well-spoken, but she had odd thought-trains. I never gave it much thought at the time, but she had very extreme views on the afterlife and reincarnation. She asked me, "Do you believe in an afterlife?" She said she did. I said I didn't know. I said, "I'm a Catholic. I believe there's a being greater than us. I believe we'll be judged."

'She'd hijack the conversation. She'd dominate, and Joe would sit passively, or offer an occasional opinion. I thought it was quite ball-breaking – she'd go on and *on*.

'One night we all had dinner at Rydges, and she spoke about the guy she was with before Joe. She talked in detail about their sexual relationship – about what it was like when they made love. I was very embarrassed. Joe was ill at ease. She hardly knew me. To share something like that with a stranger – it showed disrespect for Joe.

'She was much more experienced than he was. He was very much in love with her. There must have been some sexual attraction that over-rode his moral sense – something about her that captured him. Joe was an extrovert – a sociable, highly interactive person. He was a great guy to be around. He was funny. He had this *laugh*. But you didn't *see* Joe when he was with her. His character didn't show through. She wasn't the sort of partner who brought out the best in him. She needed to control and preside over everything. She stifled him.

'After the car show, when we went back to their place, he was nervous, as if he was scared he'd do something wrong. I noticed his hands were trembling. He was serving the coffee and he spilt some – as if she'd looked at him with distaste.

'The last time I saw him, about a month before he died, I went to their place for dinner. Joe said, "Anu's cooked an Indian dinner for you." I had chewy in my mouth, and I went into the kitchen to throw it away. When I opened the rubbish bin, I saw it was full of take-away containers. The kitchen was totally clean. It wasn't a kitchen that had been cooked in. It was all so nice, it felt unreal, as if they were shielding me from something.'

He clasped his hands tightly on the shiny table. It was causing him pain to talk about this.

'Joe went along with a lot of things he shouldn't have. He was a very intelligent person. He reasoned well. He had sound logic. But she infiltrated him on such a deep level that his logic went out the window. He took her to Melbourne to see a specialist because she believed she had some muscle-stripping disease – and yet she was the picture of health. When he described her sickness, how he had to care for her, he never said it to be derogatory. He never spoke badly of her, or had a bad word to say about her.

'I had the impression, though, that he was looking to end the relationship. He was becoming happier with things that were happening for him at work – positive things outside of Anu. I always felt Joe was going to make something bigger of himself than just an ordinary life in a town like Newcastle. The night we had dinner at Rydges he'd just bought a brand-new Mazda MX5 two-door coupé. He was really happy about it, and talked about it a lot, but Anu didn't share his enthusiasm.

'In Newcastle he had a lot of friends – whenever I was here with him the phone would be ringing every five minutes. But he didn't have any of his genuine friends in Canberra – only Anu's friends. His life there was Anu and that was *it*. It got to the stage where that wasn't enough. She'd taken and taken and he just couldn't give any more. He was sick of being her emotional crutch. If he was leaving, it wasn't because he resented her – it was because he was *tired*.'

The room with its tiled floor was chilly and the light hanging above him was harsh. He hunched in his chair.

'A week,' he said. 'It took a *week*. Why wasn't a phone call made to someone who was *sane*? The magnitude of what happened here is mind-blowing. And she's walking free. People get more time for killing a dog.

'I've prayed – I've asked myself, *Why didn't he call me?*

'When I went into their bedroom, the day after he died, the mattress was on the floor. The bed had no base. I know it was dishevelled because of the commotion with the paramedics and everything – but it looked like the room of a junkie out the back of the Cross. When I was gathering up his things I found tabs of Prozac all over the house. I didn't even know what Prozac *was*. There was a *dildo* in the bedroom. Joe wasn't *like* that. That wasn't what he wanted from life. Joe never even took a *Disprin*. She'd had an impact on him – she'd changed him. She'd violated the way he'd previously lived.'

He was shivering with misery and sorrow, rocking, with his arms folded across his chest.

'Please forgive me if this upsets you,' I said, 'but I read something in the trial transcript, that Anu told a university counsellor. She said Joe had been violent to her – that he had laid into her.'

He froze, staring at me with his mouth open. He took two slow breaths. Then he replied in a voice faint with shock, 'I don't believe it. I'd be willing to bet my life he'd never even have raised his hand to her. He wasn't into confrontation, or aggression, or anger, or trying to overpower. That's not what he was *like*. Even in a drugged state – oh no. No. No. I wouldn't be surprised if Anu had made it up – if she'd orchestrated it as part of what she was about to do.'

'It sounds like a pretty damaging relationship,' I said. 'You don't think she might have goaded him till he snapped? I know that can happen, because I once did it myself to a bloke, when I was a student. I treated him so cruelly and hurtfully that he hit me across the face. It was only an open hand but it knocked me to the ground. I never felt badly towards him for it, though. I was ashamed. Because I knew he wasn't that sort of guy. I knew I'd driven him to it. I pushed him past his limit.'

Robert listened carefully, thought carefully, his eyes quite still. He began again to shake his head. 'No. No. I can't *imagine* him hitting her. I think I'd have sensed any resentment he had towards her, even towards the end – and I never did.'

We sat there dumbly. Joe's portrait stood on the dark table with its back to us.

'My godparents feel abandoned by justice,' he said. 'They feel abandoned by all that's right in the world. You'd think it was worse for Commà, because she talks so much about it and she's so angry – she's a tormented soul. Compà's quieter, but he suffers at least as much as she does. It's affecting his heart. My godmother probably seems a very bitter person, but it's a superficial bitterness. Underneath it there's a huge warmth.'

His voice trembled. He huddled on his chair, holding himself in his arms as if he were chilled to a level that could never be reached or comforted. 'What I pray for is that Anthony will be all right – that he can be happy again. And that in the end they'll have a grandchild. If they could just –' He made a helpless cradling gesture with his two arms.

The room seemed to have grown colder. We were both shivering. I put my notebook away.

'Come on,' he said. 'Let's go in there.'

In the lounge room the Terrones and the Cinques were companionably absorbed in Italian cable TV: a cooking competition with a time limit. One contestant was frantically making pasta, rolling the dough flat-handed on a board and producing primitive worm-like shapes that were fatter in the middle than at the ends. The host of the show kept up a high-pitched running commentary. It was very funny. Nino turned to me and with a cheeky grin uttered a stream of jabbering nonsense syllables: how he thought the Italian must sound to me. We all burst out laughing. When the winner was declared I noticed it was after midnight, and took my leave. Everyone shook my hand and kissed me on both cheeks. Robert Terrone leaned against the door frame. His face had reverted to its cool impassivity. As I turned away, our eyes met. I smiled and nodded. His eyebrows intensified, infinitesimally.

'I like having boys around,' said Maria to me at the front door. 'They not picky, they eat everything, you can tell 'em off and they come back again.'

⤸

Joe's friends Steve Bernardi and Matthew Harris came back again to the Cinques' house on the Saturday morning of that Mothers' Day weekend, and so did I. Maria settled us at the dining room table and went out into the yard.

The two young men sat smiling warily at me. They were an appealing pair, the sort who radiate a familiarity with laughter and fun. Steve Bernardi had a narrow clever face with a glint of sharpness in it, and a voice that was surprisingly deep and resonant. His shirt-sleeves, rolled back to the elbow, showed powerful, smooth-haired forearms. He had trained as a nurse, he said, but was now the director of clinical services at a private psychiatric clinic in Sydney. His friend Matthew Harris looked like a straight-ahead Aussie bloke from some earlier era: fair-haired, square-faced and square-headed, with excellent teeth and an open manner. Harris had been, according to Maria, a very talented and respected young Newcastle footballer – 'he could get any girl he wants', as she put it – but he was injured too many times and had to get out. He worked as the assistant manager of a Leagues Club.

The robust conversation I had with Bernardi and Harris could hardly have been more different from the raw intimacy of my encounter with Robert Terrone the night before. Of course, it was daylight. There were two of them. They were on their way to play a game of football. They were not going to bare their wounds in front of a stranger. But their affection for Joe was just as obvious, as was their loyalty.

Joe never had much success with girls, they said, when he was young. His looks didn't mature till he was in his early twenties, and physically he was flowering towards the time of his death. He was something of an innocent. 'In the school of Machiavelli,' said Steve, 'he didn't rate.'

'Machiavelli?' I asked. 'Or Casanova?'

'Both, actually. I meant not only that he wasn't a classic charmer, but also that he wasn't deceitful.'

'His approach to a girl,' said Matt, 'would be to tell her a joke, something completely wrong, like a fart joke' – he gripped his temples and bared his teeth – 'and we'd be going, "Oh, *Joe*!!!" '

'My parents adored him,' said Steve.

'*Everyone's* parents did,' said Matt.

It so happened that both Harris and Bernardi were down at the Brewery with Joe on the night he first met Anu Singh. She was studying in Canberra and living there with her boyfriend, Simon, but she had come back to Newcastle over Christmas and New Year. Her friend Rachel Fortunaso was going out at the time with Matt Harris. Newcastle is a small city and Singh was a girl with a reputation. But that night Joe, who had just got back from Europe and started his new job, left the bar with her. 'We said to him afterwards, "Have fun! She's an attractive girl. Have fun – but don't get serious." '

There was quite a long and turbulent period of overlap before Simon left Anu. She then took up officially with Joe. His old friends in Newcastle noticed how quickly he seemed to become infatuated with her: they were troubled by the grip she was already getting on him. They felt she was restricting him. When he was out with them, he would be on the mobile to her for twenty minutes at a time. They were wary of her, and she didn't take to them, either.

'We were sorry for Joe,' said Matt, 'that he couldn't integrate her with his friends. That's what you always want – for your girl-friend to get on with your friends.'

Steve Bernardi worked with people who had personality disorders. Things Joe told him about Anu rang his alarm bells. 'Doctors and nurses will tell you,' he said, 'that people with personality disorders are the hardest patients to treat. Because they're people who are just all over the shop. They lack impulse control. And it's lethal, the combination of a gross personality disorder and being very attractive. They lie and lie and lie. You can feel them undermining you – but they seem so attractive and sincere that you start to doubt yourself and your own take on the situation. You start thinking, "Maybe . . ." and suddenly you pull back – you think, "Look out! They're doing it to *me*!" '

Early on he confronted Joe about Anu Singh. But Joe didn't want to hear.

'He only bit back once,' said Steve. 'We were at the pub. I made some comment about her, and Joe said, "This is coming from someone who Anu thinks is the most unattractive guy she's ever met." I thought, She's got *you* hooked.'

'After that,' said Matt, 'we never said much to him about her. We knew he'd tell her everything we said. So we bit our lip.'

'Sometimes,' said Steve, 'before he moved down to Canberra to live with her, he'd ring her up from Newcastle and her other boyfriend, Simon, would be there. She'd tell Joe they were still together. All those times, when we thought Joe had broken up with her, we *couldn't* have been *more supportive*.' He gave a sly grin.

'He must have known she wasn't right,' said Matt. 'He told us stuff that happened.'

'He'd talk to us about her drug use, for example,' said Steve. 'He'd say' – he imitated a light, earnest, naïve voice – ' "She's doing really well. She's off speed. She only gets a *natural* high now, like *guarana*." '

They laughed, with twisted lips.

'See what I mean?' said Steve. 'He was likeable. He was *innocently* likeable. He'd never hold a grudge. He was the butt of lots of jokes. Remember the swimming pool, Harry?'

They lowered their faces to hide their laughter.

'A bunch of us were going along one night in a car,' said Steve, 'and we passed a pool. Let's go for a swim! So Joe, ever enthusiastic, jumps out, strips off, leaves his clothes in the car, runs to the pool and dives in. We waited in the car till he got out of the water and came back on to the road, then we drove off and left him there. We went round the block and there was Joe, crouching behind a buxus bush in his undies. He got up and ran towards the car. We slowed down, then just as he was about to get in we sped off. We did it three or four times. Finally we let him get in.'

'And he wasn't even annoyed,' said Matt. 'He was still laughing.'

'His funeral was one of the worst days of our lives,' said Steve. 'The church flowed out on to the street. Joe had no idea how many people loved and respected him. I cried so much that I haven't cried since. I loathe the thought of going through those emotions again.

'And now, whenever there's an election, I always vote for the Law Reform Party.'

Maria came into the room and asked them about girlfriends – anything happening there? They shook their heads, smiling awkwardly, indulgently, with a sort of gentle defiance. Now, as planned, they had to go and play football. They stood up to leave, but Maria, talking in a rapid stream, started urging them to stay, stay, eat, eat, have something to eat. Gently, sweetly, they declined and edged towards the door, but she put heavy pressure on them: she thought they were staying, she thought they were coming for lunch, she made a lot of food for them, she bought some really good prosciutto for them, the best one, the one they like, she knew they liked it. They said they couldn't eat before they played, they'd get sick, their stomachs couldn't stand it, they'd throw up; they were sidling towards the door, smiling, smiling, but she pressed them, she must feed them, she must give them something to eat, she couldn't let them go, she couldn't let them go without putting some *food* into them, they were not to go out the door empty-handed, with empty stomachs, they needed to keep their strength up for playing football, have some prosciutto, here, have some of this bread, look, I got this special bread for you. She seized off the bench a clear plastic packet of sliced bread and held it open to them, she nodded at the table on which lay a platter of delicate pink prosciutto sliced into almost invisible feathers. Matt Harris kept up a steady sideways movement towards the door, he would not be swayed or turned aside, no, he wouldn't eat, thank you Mrs Cinque, no he wouldn't have anything, no, he couldn't because it would make him sick; and just as he was dragging Steve Bernardi through the archway and out towards the hall, Bernardi cracked. He peeled away at an angle, made a swerve past the head of the kitchen table, plunged one hand into the packet of bread and pulled out two slices: swinging the other hand over the platter of meat he swiped a couple of the translucent shavings, and dashed after Matt across the living room, roughly shoving the prosciutto between the slices of bread and wolfing down his first bite. Maria burst into a laugh of triumph. The front door closed behind them.

'Beautiful boys,' said Maria.

'Gorgeous. *Lovely* boys. But why aren't they married?'

'Joe scared them. What happened to Joe.'

I was silent with surprise.

'Yeah,' she said. 'I think so. They were *shocked*. They see what can happen. They scared.'

PART NINE

It is a very strange thing to go back, years later, to a court build-ing within whose walls you once sat gripped and disturbed by a murder trial. The ACT Supreme Court, on the fine Canberra day in February 2003 when I visited Justice Crispin in his cham-bers, had lost the mystique that had hummed around it while it dealt with the killing of Joe Cinque. Now I saw it as a shrunken edifice, bled of meaning, pale and two-dimensional.

Justice Ken Crispin himself, though, was more vivid than he had ever seemed on the bench. Without his wig he looked ten years younger: a small, densely sprung man in his late fifties, with clenched shoulders, brown eyes, and wavy hair that had gone sil-ver. He wore a grey and white striped shirt, dark trousers and a tie decorated with tiny human figures. He greeted me so cordially, jumping to his feet with his hand out, that he knocked his cup of coffee on to the carpet. Carrying as I was the Cinques' hatred of him for the two decisions he had handed down and for Anu Singh's sentence, I tried to examine him with reserve. I don't know what I thought I would learn from meeting him that wasn't already in the Singh and Rao judgements. Perhaps I wanted to know if judges, too, suffered from the icy chill, the moral fail-ure of the law. Maybe I just wanted to see him at close quarters: to get a sense of his nature, the tone of his being.

He struck me at once as a man of unusual directness and warmth. He seemed devoid of self-importance. Rather than keep his huge desk between us, he came out from behind it, and we sat together at a low coffee table in the centre of the room. His assistant brought in a tray of tea and biscuits. Perching on the very edge of the sofa, he gave me his full attention.

I didn't know if there was some protocol I was supposed to observe, so I asked him if he thought there was such a thing as 'simple wickedness'. His reply was an exemplary short lecture on the theories and principles of sentencing. He segued seamlessly to the legalisation of addictive drugs, and outlined in a crystalline manner the mechanisms by which the pressures of addiction can turn a user into a dealer. He had the lawyer's skill of keeping the conversation general. It took me several tries to steer him on to the specific topic of Anu Singh and Madhavi Rao. He seemed to find *my* speculations interesting, even at times amusing; but for quite some time his discretion was iron-clad. Eventually, though, he relaxed his vigilance and began to speak about the two trials.

I asked him how it was that the Crown psychiatrists had no access to Anu Singh:'Doesn't that render their opinions a bit hollow? A bit meaningless? If they've only got half the picture?'

He paused, as if to order his thoughts.'In most cases,' he said, 'where somebody kills someone and raises a defence of diminished responsibility, they've never seen a doctor before the incident. Everyone has to try to look backwards at the state this person would have been in, six months ago, when they committed the murder. That's difficult to determine. You're dependent on objective evidence – like the video of the way they behaved when the police interviewed them.

'But in the case of Singh, both her parents were doctors. They were terrified about the way she was behaving. They lugged her to doctors and psychiatrists. And they'd twice tried to have her locked up as an involuntary patient – imagine how frightened you'd have to be about your own child, to want to do *that*.

'So there was a wealth of evidence available to all four of the experts, that wouldn't normally be available to either side. They had medical records, they had nursing notes, they had psychiatrists' reports. To be frank, I'd never *seen* a case of diminished responsibility that was as easy to prove as that one. You couldn't have convicted on the evidence of either of the Crown expert witnesses. I'm not sure why they bothered calling them. I thought in fact that Dr Diamond proved diminished responsibility more clearly than the two defence experts.'

Did he? Surprised, I missed the moment to follow that train of thought.

'Also,' the judge went on, 'Anu Singh was part of this *university* group. They were law students, who were able to make observations about her behaviour. It had been so bizarre that it had stuck in their minds. And they were able to recount it with a degree of recall and accuracy that one wouldn't normally get.'

'You mean it was a middle-class story,' I said.

'It's not that she got a better deal,' he said quickly, 'by being middle-class.'

'But the milieu of the story was an articulate one.'

'It was. Here was a woman,' he said, 'who on *all* versions was pretty ill psychiatrically. And the interesting thing about it was that even that degree of mental illness did not evoke any sympathy – whereas it normally would, you see. If somebody has brain damage, if they're shuffling their feet when they come into court and slurring their words, they'll get a lot of sympathy. But if somebody has a personality disorder that makes them obnoxious, people tend to say, "She's just an awful person, and we'll discount the fact that it may be due to a mental illness."'

'I was very upset,' I said, 'about Professor Mullen's saying that

Anu Singh was "utterly terrified" of Joe. He seemed to have taken it at face value when she claimed he'd been violent to her. This went totally against my gut feeling of what sort of a person he was. I thought, Not only has she killed him – she's blackening his character as well.'

'But that full report wasn't run in the trial,' said Crispin sharply, lowering his formidable brow. '*Not – in – the – trial.*'

I backed off. He was right: I remembered Mr Golding vigorously filleting the report before it was admitted into evidence, and Professor Mullen's rueful joke: 'All my best lines are going!' We sat in silence for a moment.

Then he went on, 'I thought the case against Rao was pretty bodgie all round, frankly.

'The Crown case was that it was essentially a conspiracy between the two of them to kill Joe Cinque. Singh was deluded – that's why *she* wanted to kill him. But why would a person who was *not* deluded want to kill her friend's boyfriend? She had no grudge against him. The Crown wanted to draw great inferences from the fact that she'd been present when Singh had threatened to kill him. So had half the witnesses, and they weren't accusing *them* of being complicit in the murder.'

He was leaning forward, holding my eye, arguing earnestly.

'I think Rao was very concerned as to what to do. She was paralysed with indecision. Her friend was saying things that were off the planet. Nobody else was taking it seriously – should *she* take it seriously? What if she blew the whistle and rang the police and then it all turned out to be a hoax?

'She was a close friend, yes, and she bought the Rohypnol tablets. But that had to be considered in the context of what *all* the witnesses said about her personality and character – that she was a kindly, nurturing, dithering person who couldn't say no to anybody.

'When you considered all that, it seemed to me that the case against Rao was threadbare. The Crown just didn't prove that she knew or should have known Singh was going to kill him.'

But what about the Sunday morning visit to Antill Street? What about seeing him there on the bed, turning blue?

The miserable refrain ran through my head. But I didn't sing it. Justice Crispin had teased out these questions in his judgement, a document I had slogged through, in my ignorance of the law, a dozen times. From its painstakingly reasoned pages I understood the bases for his decision.

I knew he was deeply disturbed by *the failure of the criminal law to recognise a general duty of care to intervene, in order to save the life of a person in grave peril.* 'On the present state of the authorities,' he had written, 'it would appear that a person could watch a small child drowning in a shallow wading pool and walk away with legal impunity. However morally reprehensible such behaviour may be, it would seem that the law does not presently require anyone to be a Good Samaritan.' I knew he deplored this, but that he believed it was the job of the legislature, not the judiciary, to change such difficult aspects of the law. I knew too that, even if the Crown had been able to establish that Rao did have a duty of care, he would have had to acquit her on that charge, simply because it had not been proven that when she saw Joe Cinque on the bed, he had already been given the injection that killed him.

Sitting there at the coffee table with this tired, serious, decent man, I felt the self-righteous anger seeping out of me. There was nowhere for me to go with it. All that remained was sorrow, and loss.

'Is sentencing the hardest thing you have to do?'

'It's the most emotionally draining,' he said. 'Whatever you do is going to hurt innocent people as well as the guilty. It's a natural human reaction, when something terrible happens, to say "Someone must pay for this." The victims expect that the sentence is going to be a big thing for them – that they'll get justice. But even if the guy goes away for as long as they think he should, it doesn't make anything better. It's a false hope.'

So we don't punish, then? Punishment is primitive?

'The real aim of sentencing,' said Justice Crispin, 'is not retribution. The real aim is to try to protect the community by imposing sentences that are heavy enough to deter, but not so heavy that someone becomes institutionalised. And there's also the simple justice of it all. What *would* be a fair response under the circumstances? You've got to take some sort of hard line, but you can't throw humanity out the window.

'I've been involved either as prosecutor or defence counsel in two or three murders by people who've been completely coldhearted, probably psychotic. You look at them and your blood runs cold. You think, this bloke should be locked up for the rest of his life. He's always going to be a danger to people. But the vast majority of people who commit a murder are people you can feel sorry for. They've usually given way at a time of acute stress and in extraordinary circumstances. They're weak people who couldn't manage in life, who couldn't cope with the stresses, and suddenly they just snapped.'

Everything he said was calm and persuasive. It was reason, reason all the way, and I could not see a gap in it. I listened to him without arguing. But I was thinking, Where does all the woundedness, the hatred *go*? What becomes of the desire for vengeance, for a settling of the score?

Do we just pretend that this anguish doesn't exist? Is it a load that can only be shouldered by the sufferer? Is this what tragedy means – that you have to carry it inside you, weighing you down, poisoning you, for the rest of your life? I remembered what Maria Cinque had said to the judge: 'How am I supposed, your Honour, to go on?'

I knew that Justice Crispin was a practising Christian. I guessed what he would say if I voiced these thoughts. He would say, This is not the province of the law. This is the province of the Almighty. But I had seen those fundamentalists on TV and in the pages of magazines: the ones who had 'forgiven' the psychopath rampaging through the high school with a handgun, who 'felt no bitterness' against the drunken driver who had mown down their child in the street. Their protestations did not convince me, though I longed to believe that what they were claiming was possible, that transformation and healing might be within reach of the wounded. Just the same, I would have liked to ask him. I would have liked to say, 'Is forgiveness all there is, then? How is it done?' But we weren't in a church. We were in the Supreme Court, the temple of reason. So I said nothing. I sat at the little table, trying to swallow my sugared biscuit.

Then Justice Crispin said, in a low, difficult voice, 'I really felt for the Cinques.'

At the thought of Joe's family – bent double, the heart gouged out of them – I didn't trust myself to speak.

'We lost our first child,' he went on, 'when she was not quite two. We were . . . devastated. It's a long time ago. Thirty years. But you never forget it. And that made me acutely conscious of what Mr and Mrs Cinque must have been going through. The grief, of course, is very different. We lost a two – a not quite two –' He paused, and put one hand to his face. 'And they lost a grown man, nearly thirty. But you never forget. The Cinques made a speech on the front steps of the court. They said they hoped somebody would kill one of *my* children, so I'd understand.'

He sighed, staring at the carpet.

'I do realise that they were speaking purely out of their grief. When they came back, I let Mrs Cinque go into the witness box and talk about how they felt. By that time I think their barrister had told them that I had lost a child – that I had some idea of what they were suffering. But I'm obviously still not their favourite person.'

He looked up at me and raised his eyebrows, with a weary smile.

What would be the point of my telling him how they hated him still? Of course he must know it, and it couldn't have been the first time. How did he bear it? How *could* one bear it, without growing numb? A judge's detachment, I thought, must be a skill that came and went. It might desert you without warning. How hard-won it must be, and how dearly paid for.

Rebecca was the name of the lovely girl with the dark curly hair and the red dress whom I had glimpsed in the video of Dario and Antonia's wedding, the girl who had brought a big bunch of roses to the Cinques' house, after Joe died, and laid them on his bed.

In November 1993, when Joe got his engineering degree and went overseas, he broke off his three-year relationship with her: he knew he was too young to marry, and he didn't want to leave her hanging. While he was in Europe, Rebecca married someone else. Joe got home to Newcastle in November 1994 – only a few weeks before he met Anu Singh – and heard about it from Maria. He rang Rebecca's mother to ask her if it was true. Yes, she said, it was. And Joe cried.

This was enough to turn Rebecca, in some people's retrospective fantasies, into an emblem of Joe Cinque's alternative fate – a figure from a parallel universe. The actual Rebecca, when I tracked her down by phone in the vineyards near Cessnock, was sensibly reluctant to adopt this role, though she spoke lovingly of Joe's family, and told me that she called them every year on his birthday.

Her voice, which echoed off the walls and floors of the unfurnished house she had just that day rented, was very light and soft, almost girlish; and in her account of her time with Joe she stressed again and again how young they had been. She was seventeen and

Joe eighteen when they first met. They waited on tables in Emilio's pizza restaurant, an Italian family concern on Newcastle's famous Darby Street.

'Joe had good morals,' she said, 'and values that I always respected. He was *so* anti-drugs. He came from a solid background. There was a strength about him. He was an adorable guy. He had dreams, and plans – he made you feel excited. He was passionate about his car. He wanted to be sophisticated. He loved the idea of life in the fast lane. Even when Dario was getting married, Joe was making ball-and-chain jokes.

'I'm half Spanish, but there was no Spanish community in Newcastle, so I loved the Italian community. I wanted that multicultural thing. I went to Italian weddings and parties with Joe. We used to have fun dancing. I liked his friends. And I used to love going to the Azzurri Club. He'd look at me as if I was crazy. He'd say, "But that's where my *parents* go!"

'He'd stand behind me and teach me how to eat pasta. Once he cooked dinner for me at his parents' home when they were out. He was a pretty masculine guy, but sometimes I thought he was a spoilt brat. I remember one time his mother served him his meal, and he looked at it and said, "Is this pasta with oil or is it oil with pasta?" He was late for work at Emilio's one night, and when he walked in – he was never in trouble for being late because everybody loved him – the boss says, "Where have you been?" and he says, "I had to cook my dinner because Mum's out. Well, I had to put it in the microwave." He was . . . *well looked after*.' She laughed. 'There's no other side to Joe that I know. I never saw a dark side. He did have a bit of a temper – he could be fiery.'

'Were you ever scared of him?'

She let fall a pause exactly like the one that had occurred when I asked Terrone, Harris and Bernardi if they thought Joe would ever have hit Anu: a short silence of stunned incredulity. Then she replied, with a quiet dignity that made me feel embarrassed to have asked the question, 'No. I was never scared of Joe.'

'Would you have liked to marry him?'

'When it all happened,' she said, 'everyone suddenly thought, "What about Rebecca?" But I don't think it was meant to be. We had a lot of very warm feelings for each other. But it was a case of wrong timing. We were too young.

'I was so naïve back then, he didn't know what to do with me. I was like a shy little girl. I didn't even vote, when I was eighteen. Joe teased me – he said, "You'll vote for Fred Hollows, won't you!" I was scared of nightclubs – which is funny because I've ended up as a professional dancer – flamenco and Latin. But I don't drink and I wasn't into that scene. One time he wanted to meet some friends at Tatts or the Brewery. I didn't want to go.' She laughed, and said, in the voice of her younger, more timid self: '*I'll wait here at home and you come back when you're finished.*' Joe and I used to do things more like going for a swim in the middle of the night, and running along the beach. We'd drive to Catherine Hill Bay and jump off the cliffs into the water.

'He thought I was "too regimented". Those were his exact words. Because I didn't believe in casual sex. My beliefs are old-fashioned. I think nightclubs are really sleazy. I go to church every day. It scared me off, the nightclub thing. I shied away from Joe. People used to say to me, "What's the matter with you? He's so nice, he's so good-looking, he really likes you." But I wanted to wait.'

'What exactly are you telling me?' I asked.

She was silent for a moment, then answered carefully, with a delicacy I had never heard a modern young woman use. 'It's not that I thought sex was wrong,' she said, in her light, rather gentle voice. 'I was just too young. If I'd felt sure Joe and I would end up together, that would have been a whole different thing. But I wanted to save myself for marriage.'

I was thunderstruck. I didn't know such people still existed. I thought about myself at that age, straining at the leash, dying to get out there and get into it, no matter what the cost or who would have to pay. And contemplating the wreckage that was strewn behind me now, the selfish cruelties, the terrible waste, I was flooded with respect for her clarity and her self-command.

'Did you ever meet Anu Singh?'

'No,' she said, 'but I had a phone call from her once. I'd been working away from Newcastle, and I wrote Joe a letter. He answered it. And then one night she rang me up. She told me he was hers now and I should stay away. She sounded very forceful, very confident. She said, "Joe and I are unofficially engaged, so you shouldn't be in contact with him." I was shocked. I was speechless. I didn't expect that. Joe and I had had a relationship. I didn't feel good about her calling me like that. And I remember thinking, too, "That's *weird*."

'She had to be a very sick person to do what she did, but I think at the start she probably came across as confident and strong. He would have been attracted to that. She must have seemed stable, and warm. Loving. And when she showed her true colours, he wouldn't abandon her.

'I carried guilt around for a long time after Joe passed away. I feel guilt about Maria, because I moved on in my life, but Joe couldn't. It's different for me. His family and his friends still had real, ongoing relationships with him, but my memories of him are what *could* have been. For me, it's like a sad story from the past.'

⚘

The next morning she called me back. She had thought of something else she wanted to tell me.

'I know this will probably seem really trivial,' she said, 'and maybe it is – but Joe always used to eat a lot of apples.' She laughed. 'He really believed that if you ate an apple a day you'd always be healthy.'

'You wanna watch the whole thing again?' said Maria, as we settled on the couch in front of the TV. 'All the stuff in the church?'

'Whatever,' I said. 'I really just want to see Joe.'

She flashed me a small, conspiratorial smile, raised the remote and pressed the button.

The video opened on an extraordinary scene: among petrol bowsers on oil-stained concrete, a bridal party of young Italians was assembled, the men in dark suits, the bride in a froth of stiff white tulle, the bridesmaids with big hair and wearing cobalt-blue dropped-waist cocktail-length dresses with puff sleeves and low necks. Every single member of the party wore heavy, black-rimmed sunglasses. The camera panned across a strange industrial landscape in which the groomsmen leaned against lamp-posts and glanced moodily over their shoulders. A line of be-ribboned Chevrolets cruised in a sinister motorcade along King Street, Newcastle. Then a series of magisterial cuts shifted the action to the upper floor of the Azzurri Club. The tables were set, the balloons inflated and the streamers rigged for a big celebration.

With a joyful racket of laughter and shouting, the guests streamed up the stairs and took their places at the tables. Right across the top of the stairs, under a home-made arch all twined about with pale ribbons, someone had parked a large, empty pram. Nobody minded. They stepped around it, or gently pushed it an inch or two aside so they could squeeze past. Near the head of the staircase, microphone in hand, stood a nervous young man in a grey double-breasted suit, waiting for the commotion to resolve itself. It was the master of ceremonies, Joe Cinque.

Somebody wheeled the pram out of the way and stationed it against a side wall. Music broke out in a flourish, and up the stairs surged the official party: the bride's parents, the groom's, the bridesmaids and groomsmen in their shy or brazen pairs, and last of all the newly-weds, Dario and Antonia. They paraded towards the camera, beaming and shining. In a cheerful, unforced voice, rolling the Italian names euphoniously off his tongue, Joe Cinque identified each attendant's role and relationship to the bridal couple, and made the whole company welcome.

Maria and I leaned forward, rapt.

'Look how he moves,' I said. 'He's graceful.'

We heard Nino's key in the front door and he came in, smiling and wind-swept. He greeted me with a handshake and kisses, but when he saw what we were watching his face fell. 'I don't wanna see it,' he said, and walked on into the kitchen. For the rest of the video's duration I was sorely aware of him out there, moving restlessly, pushing his chair across the tiles, occasionally giving vent to his shattering smoker's cough.

But Nino too appeared in the video. Once or twice I glimpsed him at one of the long tables, elegant in a dark suit, standing behind Maria's chair while she, fresh and cool in a mermaid green dress, turned her face to smile at the camera as it glided past.

As MC, Joe knew how to play his part – how many such extravaganzas had he sat through, in the acceptance of social duty that to a lost bohemian like me is so awe-inspiring in its faithfulness? – and he played it with a light touch, hovering behind the bridal table to introduce each speaker, reading out the telegrams, smiling and gesturing and paying the ritual compliments; but he looked somehow different from his companions at the wedding, with his rather harsh haircut that swept away any hint of a mullet, bared his long slender neck, and stripped his cheeks of sideburns. How much of this was I projecting, with the knowledge I had of his horrible fate? It was magic thinking, sentimental. I tried to pull myself into line.

But I wasn't the only person to be struck by Joe. At a casual moment of the proceedings, while the guests were contentedly attacking their dessert and nothing formal was in progress, when children were tearing about the dance floor among the drifting balloons, and Joe was just standing there alone behind the long bridal table, smiling benignly and looking around him with a calm, bright curiosity, the camera zoomed in discreetly and framed him front-on, head and shoulders, against the dark curtain.

It had no reason to single him out at that moment, let alone to focus on his agreeable face. But it found him, and it dwelt on him. It lingered, intimately and without his ever realising, for a good seven or eight seconds. His face was fine and sensitive, still faintly blurred with youth, not yet set in the hard lines of manhood. He looked like a man who was lightly poised on the very rim of the world he came from. I sat on his parents' couch and watched him with my heart in my mouth. Maria too ceased her murmured commentary. We gazed in silence on her undefended son.